Art
in Small-Scale
Societies

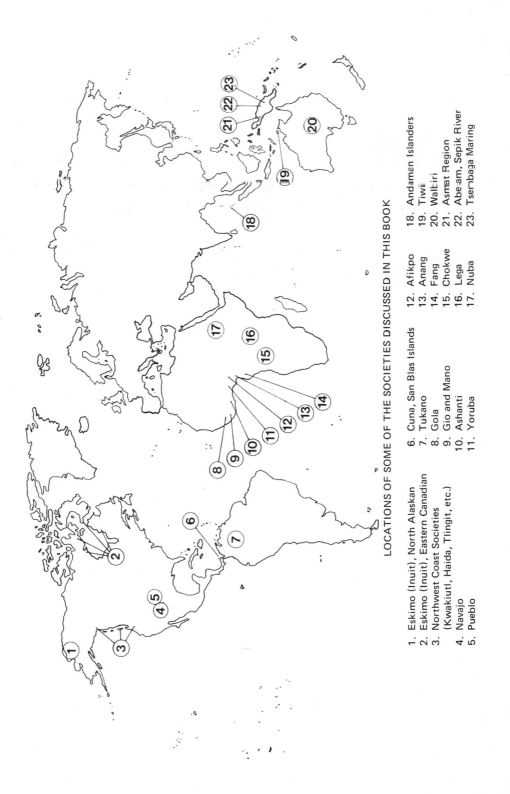

LOCATIONS OF SOME OF THE SOCIETIES DISCUSSED IN THIS BOOK

1. Eskimo (Inuit), North Alaskan
2. Eskimo (Inuit), Eastern Canadian
3. Northwest Coast Societies
   (Kwakiutl, Haida, Tlingit, etc.)
4. Navajo
5. Pueblo

6. Cuna, San Blas Islands
7. Tukano
8. Gola
9. Gio and Mano
10. Ashanti
11. Yoruba

12. Afikpo
13. Anang
14. Fang
15. Chokwe
16. Lega
17. Nuba

18. Andaman Islanders
19. Tiwi
20. Waltiri
21. Asmat Region
22. Abeam, Sepik River
23. Tsembaga Maring

SECOND EDITION

Art in Small-Scale Societies

Richard L. Anderson
Kansas City Art Institute

PRENTICE HALL
ENGLEWOOD CLIFFS, NEW JERSEY 07632

Library of Congress Cataloging-in-Publication Data

Anderson, Richard L.
    Art in small-scale societies.

    Rev. ed. of: Art in primitive societies. c1979.
    Bibliography: p. 203
    Includes index.
    1. Art, Primitive.   I. Anderson, Richard L.
Art in primitive societies.   II. Title.
N5311.A52   1989   709'.01'1   88-23179
ISBN 0-13-047762-1

Editorial/production supervision
and interior design: Virginia L. McCarthy
Cover design: George Cornell
Cover photo: courtesy Field Museum
of Natural History, Chicago
Manufacturing buyer: Peter Havens
Page layout: Charles Pelletreau

Previously published under the title of *Art in Primitive Societies.*

 ©1989, 1979 by Prentice-Hall, Inc.
A Division of Simon & Schuster
Englewood Cliffs, New Jersey 07632

Printed in the United States of America

10   9   8   7   6   5   4   3   2

ISBN 0-13-047762-1

Prentice-Hall International (UK) Limited, *London*
Prentice-Hall of Australia Pty. Limited, *Sydney*
Prentice-Hall Canada Inc., *Toronto*
Prentice-Hall Hispanoamericana, S.A., *Mexico*
Prentice-Hall of India Private Limited, *New Delhi*
Prentice-Hall of Japan, Inc., *Tokyo*
Simon & Schuster Asia Pte. Ltd., *Singapore*
Editora Prentice-Hall do Brasil, Ltda., *Rio de Janeiro*

Contents

CHAPTER 3   *53*
Iconography and Symbolism

CHAPTER 4   *84*
The Artist's Life and Work

Illustrations

Preface

A book on art in small-scale societies may adopt any one of several approaches, each valid for its own purposes. There are, first, the "picture books"—books with little text but many photographs or drawings of art works from non-Western societies. Such books, and the museum exhibits that often prompt their creation, are valuable in familiarizing people with the appearance of art in small-scale societies. Similar to such books are those, usually written by art historians, that give extensive verbal descriptions of regional art styles. These too serve a worthwhile service.

But "What does it look like?" is only one of several interesting questions regarding art from distant lands. Other questions are: Why were these art works created? Who were their makers? What do they mean? Queries such as these are typically the concern of cultural anthropologists who have pursued them ever since the time of Franz Boas. But with the notable exception of Boas's book *Primitive Art,* first published in 1927, there have been few attempts to bring together the many insights that have resulted from the systematic study of art in small-scale societies. The first edition of the present text was an attempt to begin such a synthesis.

In writing this book my thinking has been based on the conviction that *art is only partially mysterious.* Some aspects of art *are* "mysterious." For example, even the most sanguine of social scientists are at a loss to explain the exact means whereby art produces a thrill of excitement in those who appreciate it. But to concede that there are serious gaps in our understanding of art is not to belittle the amount of insight we do have into the phenomenon: Art is *only partially* mysterious, and the major portion of this book deals with those topics that are less refractory to systematic study.

Chapter 1 deals with problems of definition. What exactly is a "small-scale" society, and what do we intend to refer to when we use the word "art"? Neither of these terms is easy to define satisfactorily, and the opening chapter discusses some of the difficulties involved. Chapter 2 takes up the functions of art in small-scale societies. The question "What does this piece of art do?" seldom has a single answer. What, for example, did Chartres Cathedral do in thirteenth-century France? It provided a safe, dry location for church ceremonies; it was a powerful symbol of religious devotion for the people of the town and surrounding countryside; it gave symbolic legitimacy to the sociopolitical elite of France; its porches provided shelter for markets; its construction and maintenance gave employment to untold numbers of workers—all this in addition to the aesthetic pleasure that the cathedral engendered in all who saw it. Although they are typically smaller in scale than Chartres Cathedral, works of art from non-Western societies also serve economic, social, political, and symbolic functions for the people who create them.

Chapter 3 deals with symbolism; it asks how prevalent and important symbolism is in the art of small-scale societies. It also asks, Are there universal symbols? Chapter 4 discusses the makers of art in small-scale societies. Some general patterns will emerge as we compare the training, lives, and techniques of individual artists from various places in the world. Although they are not full-time specialists in their crafts, they nevertheless demonstrate impressive skill in the conception and execution of their works.

Chapter 5 discusses various psychological topics related to art, such as the sources of the artist's ideas for art works and the creative process itself. Chapter 6 deals with the topic of change, both in traditional settings and in response to contact with the Western world. The concluding chapter summarizes the cross-cultural patterns that may be discerned in art and aesthetics, and it also discusses the similarities and differences between the art produced in the Western world and that from small-scale societies.

The preparation of a second edition of this book reminds me of a nice morsel of gypsy lore recounted by Jan Yoors. A sage gypsy elder told the teenage Yoors that every individual has two mortal lives, one after the other: The purpose of the second life is to learn from the mistakes of the first. But Yoors, the older man went on to say, was already in his second life, so this was his last chance to get it right! Likewise, a second edition is a blessing both in proving that the first edition must not have been *too* bad, and in giving the author another opportunity to "get it right."

This edition's most obvious change is seen in its title, which has changed from *Art in Primitive Societies* to *Art in Small-Scale Societies*. In the first edition I decried the pejorative connotations often associated with the word "primitive." Then, after explicitly rejecting those connotations I reluctantly proceeded to use it, arguing that no satisfactory word exists to replace it. Now, however, I realize that connotations cannot be dispelled by fiat, and I have decided in this edition to use the somewhat cumbersome "small-scale" to refer to those societies that I previously denoted as "primitive."

Another quite visible change in this edition is the inclusion of "portfolios" that describe, in words and pictures, the art styles that occur in six of the most famous art-producing regions of the non-Western world. As a cultural anthropologist, my chief concern is the role of art in its cultural context, but I have come to realize that analytic thinking about anything is much easier when one has an image of that thing in the mind's eye. Considerations of space obviously preclude an exhaustive description of the art styles found in all of the societies discussed in this book; but I hope that the portfolios provide enough information to make their subjects transcend their identities as mere cultural artifacts and come alive as genuine—and often quite powerful—works of art.

A third change in this edition is less apparent but perhaps of greater significance. Since completing the first edition of this book, my own research has focused on the philosophies that underlie art production in 10 non-Western societies. The results of this research are being published separately, but they have necessarily influenced the rewriting of this textbook as well, especially its first and last chapters. In a word, they have deepened my appreciation of a statement by Robert Redfield that I quoted in the Preface to the first edition: "Whether we come to see the artifact as a creative mastery of form, or see it as a sign or symbol of a traditional way of life, we are discovering, for ourselves, new territory of our humanity" (Redfield 1971 [orig. 1959]:64).

Finally, this edition reflects the progress that has taken place in the discipline during the last 10 years. From the more than 1,500 books, monographs, journal articles, and unpublished dissertations and papers on non-Western art that have come to my attention since the first edition went to press, I have added mention here of those that have successfully explored formerly uncharted waters in addition to those that provide significantly more detailed maps of previously known territory.

For their assistance on the first edition of this book I repeat my thanks: To the Kansas City Art Institute and the Center for Professional Development of the Kansas City Regional Council for Higher Education for financially supporting some parts of the library research upon which this book is based; to Elizabeth Scholer Anderson, William J. Crowley, Warren L. d'Azevedo, and Paul D. Schaefer for their careful reading of the original manuscript and their numerous and thoughtful suggestions; and to many others who helped in various ways with the first edition—Katherine Arredondo, Janis Cram, Kenneth Cram, Anne Devaney, Georgeann Marsh, Susan McGreevey, John McGuire, Gayle Nelson,

Rosann Rahn, and Hal E. Wert; to Penelope Linsky and Stan Wakefield of Prentice Hall; and to David Gray, Kurt Eckhard, and Pasternak, Kizer, and Associates for their help with the illustrations and cover design.

This second edition has benefited from support from the Mellon Fund; from continuous feedback from students at the Kansas City Art Institute; from the many reviewers of the first edition; and from an ongoing dialogue with Kim Anderson about the nature of art and the artistic process. Zdenek Salzmann, University of Massachusetts; Zdenka Pospisil, Southern Connecticut State University; Joann W. Kealiinohomoku, Northern Arizona University; and Barbara M. Harkness, Kent State University, reviewed the manuscript for this second edition and made many helpful suggestions. To all these I tender my most sincere thanks.

Finally, grateful acknowledgment is also made to the following for permission to quote from copyrighted material:

George W. Harley, *Masks as Agents of Social Control in Northeast Liberia,* portions reprinted by permission of the President and Fellows of Harvard College.

Mary Jane Schneider, "But Is it Art? A Critical Look at Anthropolotical Studies of Non-European Art," 1976, portions reprinted by permission of the author.

Nelson H. H. Graburn, editor, *Ethnic and Tourist Arts of the Fourth World,* copyright 1977 by The Regents of the University of California; reprinted by permission of the University of California Press.

Simon Ottenberg, *Masked Rituals of the Afikpo: The Context of an African Art,* copyright © 1976 by the University of Washington Press, portions reprinted by permission of the publisher.

Photographs of two Liberian masks, Peabody Museum, Harvard University, copyright © by the President and fellows of Harvard College, 1977. Used by permission.

R. L. A.

CHAPTER 1

Introduction: The Meanings of "Small-Scale" and of "Art"

When the American folk song "Rock Island Line" is sung, it's often accompanied by the following story: At a certain time in the history of the Rock Island Railroad there were state-operated toll booths along the line, and only trains carrying agricultural products such as livestock were allowed to pass through the gates without paying a sizable toll. The engineer on one train outsmarted the system by telling the toll collector,

> I've got pigs,
> I've got pigs.

When he was given permission to pass through the toll gate without paying any toll, the engineer gave his machine full throttle, and as the train accelerated he shouted back to the toll collector,

> I've got pig iron,
> I've got pig iron,
> I've got all pig iron,
> I've got all pig iron!

The moral of the story is clear: If two people are to communicate in any depth about a particular subject they must come to some minimal agreement about the meanings of crucial words. Or, if they cannot *agree* about definitions, each must at least know what definition the other is using. If this basic requirement is not met, the individuals are at best

1

frustrated and at worst (as in the above story) deceived. If this is the case in discussions about tangible items like pig iron, it's an even greater hindrance to exchanges concerning abstract ideas.

This book is about art in small-scale societies, and although the terms "small-scale" and "art" may seem harmless enough, we must examine both with some care to avoid the kind of unjustified assumptions that led to problems for the Rock Island Line toll collector. The goal is not to proclaim final definitions of the terms, but rather to clarify what they mean in the present context. It is, for the moment, less of a philosophical problem and more of a practical one.

THE STUDY OF SMALL-SCALE SOCIETIES

Only a little more than a hundred years have passed since scholars in Europe and America began systematically studying the thousands of other cultures with which we Westerners share the globe.[1] And, inauspiciously enough, some of the most valuable lessons learned from the work of the first generation of cultural anthropologists was how *not* to proceed.

As beneficiaries of the "age of exploration," nineteenth-century thinkers were the first people in the history of the world to possess extensive accounts of the societies of sub-Saharan Africa, the native tribes of North and South America, and the panoply of cultures in the ocean Pacific. In reading the reports of explorers, traders, missionaries, and the like, these scholars were most aware of the dramatic differences between Western customs and the lifeways of other peoples. If monogamous marriage was the rule in Victorian England, for instance, then reports from other corners of the globe told of polygynous societies in which one man could have many wives, of polyandrous cultures where a woman could have many husbands, and, most shockingly of all, of places where the total absence of marriage rules left people no alternative but to practice "primitive promiscuity." So the reports claimed, at any rate.

When confronted by institutions unlike one's own it is perhaps only human to assume that our ways are superior and altogether more advanced than the crude, undeveloped, and generally disagreeable practices of others. This attitude, known as *ethnocentrism,* appears in many societies, and it certainly colored the thinking of the "armchair anthropologists" of nineteenth-century Europe and America. They had set out to answer an extremely interesting question, namely: What was the origin and history of human institutions? In the aforementioned case of marriage, for example, the cultural evolutionists assumed that monogamy was the highest form,

---

[1]As in most anthropological writing, "West" here means the general culture of Europe and America, not the western region of the United States.

sitting, as it were, atop a ladder of evolutionary development. Most theorists believed that the marriage customs found elsewhere in the modern world represented historical stages of marriage through which the more "advanced" cultures had previously passed. If this were the case, then the history of marriage came down to this: In some distant, primordial past, all societies had practiced "primitive promiscuity." Some societies progressed up the ladder through the successive stages of polyandry and polygyny until the most highly evolved societies (such as, conveniently enough, our own) ultimately achieved monogamy.

Early Evolutionary Theories of Art

Eventually the cultural evolutionists turned their attention to art. The late nineteenth century, after all, had witnessed several dramatic artistic developments. In European fine art, the quest for representational accuracy, which had motivated artists from the Renaissance to the Enlightenment, now competed with more stylized approaches ranging from impressionism to Art Nouveau. Moreover, the same world travelers who sent back tales of exotic marriage practices from abroad also told of alien artists whose methods seemed as distant from those of classical, Western painting and sculpture as polyandry was from Western monogamy. Indeed, the products of these artists were put on display for all to see in the world expositions that were so popular from the mid-eighteen hundreds onward. The situation became still more intriguing as evidence mounted for the great antiquity of highly naturalistic paintings that were being discovered on the walls of certain Spanish and French caves.

Thus, by the turn of the century a pitched battle was raging between the advocates of representational art and the defenders of more stylized art styles, with each camp laying claim to the true essence of art. Into this battle came anthropologists, armed with their recently developed paradigm of cultural evolution. Perhaps their methods could reveal whether the earliest human art was naturalistic, with abstractionism representing a later (and presumably higher) evolutionary stage, or vice versa.

The geometric designs that characterized art in some of the world's regions prompted one line of reasoning. Baskets, it was pointed out, necessarily have geometric figures as a result of the weaving process that produces them. The American W.H. Holmes speculated that the earliest ceramic pots may have carried similar designs because they were first molded inside of baskets. Many pottery traditions of the American Southwest were indeed decorated with geometric figures (albeit curvilinear styles now often supplanted the angular designs that supposedly reflected the seminal influence of basketry). Frank Cushing found that sometimes these seemingly abstract figures were named; Zunis, for example, said the scroll design was a symbol for the wind. Otis Mason extended the theory by surmising that named designs would become increasingly realistic, looking more and more like what they stood for. And in the final stage of evolution, such ideograms might become the letters for a written language. So the evolutionary picture might have been this: The first decorations were meaningless outgrowths of technique (for example, basketlike designs on pottery); symbolic associations came to be attached to some such figures (the Zuni scroll/wind); some of these eventually began looking like what they stood for; and ultimately a few may have provided the material for alphabets.

But Hjalmar Stolpe, a Swedish anthropologist, thought the Americans had it all backwards. Using black wax and Japanese paper, Stolpe methodically made thousands of rubbings of the patterns carved on the utensils that were appearing in the new natural history museums that had started to spring up; and a sailing trip around the world afforded him still more rubbings. The designs from Polynesia particularly interested Stolpe. Besides the apparently meaningless geometric decorations formed by rows of zigzags, many were quite naturalistic, some depicting paired figures with breasts that reminded Stolpe of the women's dances he had seen in Tahiti. Some figures, however, lacked heads; and Stolpe noticed that their bodies, joined arm to arm and leg to leg, were only slightly different from the rows of zigzags. All this led Stolpe to believe that art began in a primordial realism and that this gradually "degraded" to mere geometric decoration.

But how was one to choose which of the two competing theories was valid? Did stylized, geometric design come first and gradually evolve into naturalism, as Otis Mason had claimed; or was Stolpe correct in believing that the reverse had happened? Each camp was able to name numerous contemporary societies that fit its theory of the history of art.

But if you reread the preceding sentence carefully you may see the core of the problem. Evolutionary theories are intended to reconstruct the *history* of institutions, that is, how past societies changed with the passage of time; but *contemporary* societies were being used to create and validate the theories. Who is to say that modern society X replicates today the institutions that prevailed among X's ancestors in some long lost time? Archaeologists, who take as their goal the reconstruction of past societies based on their material remains, can seldom be of much help in the matter because the ideas, intentions, and values that most early theories of cultural evolution attempted to explain can rarely be deduced from the stones, bones, and potsherds uncovered by the archaeologist's trowel. And in the rare instance in which archeology does provide relevant information, the data are usually quite equivocal.

In fact, soon after the turn of the twentieth century, Franz Boas, perennially hailed as the "father of American anthropology," made a devastating critique of evolutionary theories of art by showing that in some instances geometric styles had indeed evolved into representational art; in other cases, however, exactly the reverse had occurred. That is, the available historical data indicate that no single line of evolution suffices to account for the changes that we know to have taken place in art around the globe. Boas also noted that until recently Eskimos had carved extremely realistic animal figures in ivory, but they also used thoroughly stylized patterns in bone-carving and tattooing. How could Eskimos make art that was simultaneously at the top and the bottom of the hypothesized evolutionary ladder? The whole idea of arranging the institutions of contemporary societies on an evolutionary ladder was turning out to be far more problematic than earlier scholars had thought.

The Anthropologist's Method

Boas's enormously influential book *Primitive Art,* first published in 1927 but extant in the form of lecture notes from 1903, holds another reason for the downfall of the early evolutionary theories. Coming to anthropology from a background of geography, physics, and mathematics, Boas pointed out that cultural evolutionism was seriously flawed not only in its theory, but also because much of its data was suspect. This was a result of the often uncritical acceptance of reports from individuals who had traveled the globe but whose knowledge of individual cultures was often superficial. To correct the problem, Boas and his students left the sheltered setting of libraries filled with leather-bound memoirs of well-meaning but untrained travelers and went out to gather the information themselves.

The result was a methodology that sets cultural anthropology apart from the other social sciences, namely *fieldwork* based on *participant observation.* By picking a single society, learning the language of its members, living in it for a year or more, and taking part in the day-to-day activities of the people, the researcher establishes a rapport with the society's members and eventually comes to see the society in its own terms rather than solely in the terms of the researcher's culture. (Boas was able to cite the example of Eskimo carving to prove his point so convincingly because he himself had worked in the Arctic.)

The data that came from such careful fieldwork further weakened the standing of cultural evolutionism. For example, whereas evolutionary theories traced the origin of marriage to a hypothetical state of "primitive promiscuity," actual fieldwork failed to reveal any such condition. To the contrary, *all* contemporary societies have rules for marriage. Marriage systems themselves differ greatly from place to place, and there are always some individuals who break the rules; but the concept of societies that practiced total sexual freedom was chimerical, a figment of ethnocentric imaginations and superficial observation.

Despite these problems we must still thank the nineteenth-century cultural evolutionists for raising intrinsically interesting questions. Recon-

structing the historical development of human institutions remains a legitimate enterprise, but contemporary efforts tend to focus on issues, such as
subsistence and state formation, that lend themselves to quantification and
to steer clear of areas such as art.

The Diversity of Human Cultures

If the institutions of contemporary societies cannot justifiably be arranged on conceptual ladders, with the "least evolved" at the bottom and
the "most advanced" at the top, are we to ignore the manifold differences
that seem to exist from one society to another? By no means. The nineteenth-century evolutionists were rightly fascinated by the diversity of
human cultures. It was their ethnocentric interpretation of this diversity
that led them astray.

Learning from earlier mistakes, twentieth-century anthropologists
have generally adopted an attitude of *cultural relativism,* that is, the belief
that efforts at understanding other lifeways are most successful if we view
those customs in their own traditional context and avoid judging them
according to the values of Western culture. No matter how different they
are from our own ways of doing things, the institutions and values of other
societies have been handed down from generation to generation. They
have withstood the test of time, and on close examination they typically
prove to be subtle and effective designs for living.

But having defined cultural realtivism, two kinds of restrictions on
the principle should be noted immediately. In the first place, no one,
neither scholar nor layperson, exists solely to "understand other lifeways."
Some circumstances demand that the scientist remove the white lab coat of
objectivity and take a stand, proclaiming that "this is right and that is
wrong." For example, cultural genocide must surely prompt more than
mere dispassionate study; one must also oppose it. The particulars of what
to support, what to condemn, and how to act upon those convictions are,
needless to say, difficult personal questions. Although cultural relativism
helps one analyze the world, it does not provide a standard for evaluating
it.

But even outside the area of moral judgment, should the principle of
cultural relativism lead one to the nihilistic conclusion that there is absolutely no pattern to human existence, that institutions and beliefs are
thrown together willy-nilly, obeying no general principles? The answer is a
resounding no. Indeed, insofar as cultural anthropology is a social science,
this must be so.

The "scientific" principles that have been uncovered by cultural anthropologists to date tend to be general in nature. For example, societies
are inevitably found to be *functionally integrated,* with traditional institutions
operating in a coordinated fashion to maintain the society as a whole and

the individuals who comprise it. (The concept of functionalism is the central topic of Chapter 2.)

The term "small-scale" prompted this excursion into the history and methods of cultural anthropology, and the concept of *scale* represents another general principle that informs much contemporary anthropological thought—so much, in fact, that we tend to take it for granted. The best way to understand exactly what scale entails is to compare the cultures of contemporary Europe, America, China, and India with the lives of traditional Eskimos in the Arctic, the San people who live in the Kalahari Desert of southwestern Africa, and the aboriginal peoples of Australia. The principle of cultural relativism rules out the facile, ethnocentric conclusion that the ways of life of modern Western society are simply "better" than the ways of life of small-scale societies. Moreover, in some respects these distant societies are altogether comparable to Western society. Each provides a kinship structure in which infants are socialized and grow into successive generations of adults; each provides for the material welfare of its members; each gives reflective individuals answers to philosophical questions such as "Where did we come from" as well as with ethical principles that define proper behavior, and so on.

But if you imagine the complex cultures of the West, China, and India as being at one end of a continuum, and the small-scale, traditional cultures of the Eskimo, San, and Australian Aborigines at the other end, the small-scale societies all have three traits in common, characteristics that systematically, fundamentally, and dramatically set them apart from complex societies. These are:

1. Societies at the small-scale end of the continuum obtain the necessities of life by means of a relatively simple technology.

2. In small-scale societies the population is relatively low, both in numbers and in density.

3. Small-scale societies have a relatively limited amount of social, economic, and political specialization. Thus, for example, while one member of the group may be acknowledged as the best healer among them, this person does not totally specialize in the role of medical practitioner but rather hunts or gathers along with the other adult members of his or her sex.

Most of the world's societies lie somewhere between the ends of the continuum of scale. Indeed, many of the case studies discussed in the following chapters come from horticultural societies that, on the one hand, lack the elaborate state bureaucracy of the larger complex societies and, on the other, do not have the nomadic life-style of the smaller hunter-gatherer bands. Admittedly, the precise placement of a particular society along the continuum of scale is not always possible; and the three traits that define the continuum do vary somewhat independently. For example, although the Kwakiutl, Tlingit, and other tribes of the Northwest Coast of North America subsisted by means of the relatively simple technique of hunting and gathering, their populations were relatively large and they had fairly elaborate systems of social and political specialization.

These complications aside, however, one important fact remains: When one of us, as a native of a complex society, reflects on cultures that exist elsewhere on the continuum, the only difference between "them" and "us" that can be safely assumed to exist is that of *scale*. As noted previously, compared to complex cultures, small-scale societies have relatively simple technologies; small, scattered populations; and limited social, economic, and political specialization. To assume that members of small-scale societies live lives of anarchic barbarism, that their intellectual horizons are narrowly restricted, or that their aesthetic sensibilities are dull is empirically unjustified—and ultimately racist.

One final point may be made about the words we use to refer to the cultures that concern us here. Societies toward the small-scale end of the previously discussed continuum are sometimes called "primitive." This term, however, carries negative connotations; in many people's minds anything that is labeled primitive is often tacitly assumed to be crude, brutish, and generally undeveloped—traits that should not be attributed to small-scale societies under any circumstances. Apparently no amount of argument can rid "primitive" of its pejorative associations, so although the word was sometimes used in the past to refer explicitly to small-scale societies and not to imply any negative qualities, it now seems best to avoid the term altogether.

THE MEANINGS OF 'ART'

The question "What is art?" has historically implied two distinctly different queries. First, it may mean, "How can art be distinguished from non-art?" Alternatively, it may suggest, "Among those things that are classified as art, what distinguishes great art from mediocre art?" For our purposes, it is helpful to discuss these two issues separately.

Art Versus Non-Art

Consider the following two sets of behavioral artifacts: The first set consists of a canvas done by a person whose paintings are highly acclaimed, a dance of the polka, and a tune that one sings in the shower; the second set consists of a grocery list, a leisurely walk through the woods, and a sneeze. Now quickly, without puzzling over it, tell me which of the sets is "art" and which is not. Unless you're in a particularly contrary mood, my guess is that you chose the first set—the painting, the dance, and the song, relegating the second set—the grocery list, walk, and sneeze—to the category of non-art. Admittedly, the members of the first set differ vastly from each other in terms of type (visual versus performing art), refinement (fine art versus popular art), and quality (the work of the talented and practiced painter versus the untutored tune in the shower). But despite their diversity, if your intuitions parallel mine, the painting, dance, and song of the first set fall into the general category of art in a way that the grocery list, walk, and sneeze do not.

Let us try another one. Imagine standing in front of two grand, marble-columned buildings that look suspiciously like museums. Through a window of the one on the right you can see what appear to be carved wooden masks and a stone relief depicting a number of figures; in the building on the left, by contrast, you get a glimpse of a case displaying a series of human skulls and another case with several sorts of stone tools. You happen to be in a mood for looking at some "art." Which way do you turn—right or left? To the right, of course, to the museum with the masks and reliefs, leaving the collection of skulls and tools for another day.

Your responses to these two questions prove one thing quite conclusively, namely, that when confronted with real, tangible objects and activities, some part of your mind and consciousness knows very well the difference between art and non-art.

Now one final task: Find a pencil and paper and write down an infallible definition of art. That is, state exactly what quality or qualities are shared by the painting, the polka, the song in the shower, and the masks and reliefs in the museum. These qualities, of course, must be absent from the things you do not consider to be art.

Only a brief reflection should make you realize that this question is as maddeningly difficult as the first questions were easy. *Beauty* is ruled out as a common denominator of art because it may very well be absent from the song in the shower but present in the leisurely walk and in some of the stone tools. (No account of the Upper Paleolithic fails to note the elegant, willow-leaf shapes of Solutrean stone blades that were created in France nearly 20,000 years ago.) And if sheer *pleasure* were the criterion, the leisurely walk would again qualify as art, but Picasso's *Guernica* probably would not.

Is art distinguished by being *nonutilitarian?* The painting certainly serves some useful purposes; among other things, its sale allows the painter (and perhaps the painter's agent and others) to earn a living, and its possession brings prestige to the owner. On the other hand, does the perfect symmetry of the Solutrean stone tool really make it any more serviceable, or is its elegant design a nonutilitarian trait of the tool? Moreover, the simple presence or absence of *skill* does not always distinguish art from non-art. Individuals who try their hand at stone-knapping quickly appreciate the considerable amount of skill that virtually all stone tools represent;

and speaking for my own singing in the shower, I can attest that, although it unmistakably is music after a fashion, it is thoroughly innocent of skill.

Sometimes dictionaries can resolve disputes about popular meanings of words, but a trip to the *Oxford English Dictionary* merely compounds the current problem by listing 17 separate meanings for "Art," none of which infallibly distinguish between the first and the second sets of items, much less between the still more diverse objects housed in the two hypothetical museums.

And the annals of philosophy are, if anything, even worse than the dictionary. Reflective individuals have debated the true meaning of art for ages, dating in the West from at least Plato's time and continuing right down to the present day. Moreover, we are no closer to agreement on what constitutes the necessary and sufficient properties of art than we were two and a half millennia ago, a fact that Morris Weitz has pointed out (Weitz 1967[orig. 1957]:3).

Weitz made the observation in an article that has had a tremendous impact on subsequent speculation about art. He argued that efforts to enunciate a once-and-for-all definition of art had consistently failed not for lack of effort or intellectual talent but because art simply cannot be so defined. Weitz predicted that we will never find a single trait or set of traits that is present in all art and absent from all else, if for no other reason than that art is everchanging, so even if we were clever enough to make a perfect definition for today, it would become less and less perfect through successive tomorrows.

Following the reasoning of the philosopher Wittgenstein, Weitz suggested that the most we can ever hope to attain is an "open" definition of art, that is, one that lists the traits that are usually present in the things that are commonly called "art" at a given place and time. If we do this, the task of defining art changes from an interminable search for art's essence to the listing of "bundles of properties, none of which need be present but most of which are," in the things we conventionally call art (Weitz 1967:9). The task is parallel to describing a set of siblings. One might say that Mr. and Mrs. Smith's children are tall (except for little Johnny), dark (although Jane is rather fair), and so on. There can be no doubt that the Smith children do constitute a genuine set, but the fact of the matter is that there is no single trait that sets them apart. In defining them we must settle for a somewhat clumsy list such as was just given.

What traits are usually present in art? The objects and activities from around the globe that are typically considered to be art are enormously varied, but I believe that they generally have most of the following properties:[2]

---

[2]The following traits are discussed at length in Anderson (in press). They are based on a systematic survey of art and aesthetics in 10 diverse societies.

Culturally Significant Meaning   Many Westerners think of art as a luxury, as icing on the proverbial cake of custom. But although this is sometimes the case, most of the art produced in most of the world's societies is anything but an epiphenomenon. Art may serve as a conduit for communication with the supernatural realm, as a means of conveying crucial information that does not lend itself to explicit, didactic statement, or as an embodiment of metaphysical truth. In these ways and many more, art conveys culturally significant meaning.

Style   Information theorists tell us that a message can be conveyed from sender to receiver only through the use of a code, and just as the Morse Code carries messages for telegraphers, style is the code through which art conveys meaning. Styles are shared traditions within cultures, but they are ultimately distinctive to time and place. Scattered throughout this book are a half dozen special portfolios that describe the styles of art found in the major art regions of the world.

Sensuous, Affecting Medium   Art is often beautiful, but even when it does not prompt a pleasurable sensation it nevertheless engenders powerful feelings of one sort or another in individuals who are attuned to its style and meaning. Almost all the things we consider to be art have a marked ability to stimulate the senses and affect the emotions. Thus a viewing of *Guernica* may prompt a sensation of horror at the thought of a senseless massacre of innocent Spanish villagers or an aesthetic delight engendered by Picasso's consummate use of the formal elements of composition. But no one who considers the work to be art can look at it with indifference. The inventory of emotions that art can spawn is sizable—awe at the ineffable supernatural realm, repulsion at the grotesquely ugly, or a refined but deep appreciation of the artist's use of the medium. But whatever the response, the art work does typically excite the senses and stir the emotions.

Special Skill   The exceptional talents and training of artists, be they manual or cognitive, are recognized in every society, setting the art-maker apart from the rest of the populace. In more complex cultures, the artist's special abilities may be rewarded by commissions and by fees from young apprentices, but even in hunting and gathering groups, with their relatively homogeneous social structures, the artist's exceptional skill is recognized. The nature of the artist's mastery, of course, is a function of cultural context and of art medium. Edmund Leach, a British anthropologist, has commented thus on the differential acquisition of skills:

> At the age when a European infant starts to play with a pencil, a Borneo Dyak boy starts to play with a knife. By the time the European can express himself

> reasonably well by writing conventional symbols on paper, the Borneo Dyak
> can do the same by carving conventional shapes out of wood. In such societies
> nearly every adult male can carve after a fashion. *Master carvers, of course, are*
> *just as rare as are master calligraphers in our society.* (Leach 1961:29; emphasis
> added)

As this example shows, artists are not characterized as possessing specific
skills above a predetermined, absolute level, but are set apart by having
manual or cognitive skills that are demonstrably beyond those of non-
artists in their own society.

Thus, when we look at the enormous repertoire of things made and
done by humans, the ones that we consider to be art have most or all of the
following properties: They convey culturally significant meaning; they are
made within a style tradition that is characteristic of their provenience; they
use a medium in such a way as to have a strong impact on the senses and
feelings; and they are the product of individuals who are recognized by
their fellows for their exceptional skill. Things having the entire bundle of
traits are unequivocally considered to be art; those lacking most of them
are not; and between art and non-art are things that may or may not be
considered to be art, depending on the circumstances. (The aforementioned song in the shower is not as clearly in the art category as the painting, and one could reasonably argue that a Solutrean stone blade represents the craft of stone toolmaking raised to the level of an art.)

The above definition of art makes no reference to either the possible
nonutility of art items or the "aesthetic response." Because both of these
factors are frequently said to be definitive traits of art, their omission here
should be commented upon.

The Nonutility of Art

Often the claim is made that art, by its very nature, is nonutilitarian.
Thus, for example, all that is needed for a headrest is a block of wood. To
make the piece weigh less, the inner portion may be carved out, leaving a
platform with legs. All this has been done in the interest of utility. But if the
carver goes on to make a special design on the headrest, perhaps even
ornamenting its legs to the extent of weakening them, then this part of the
headrest's form may be considered its artistic component. The handsome
headrests made by Tikopians have been described as exemplars of Polynesian art (cf. Jones 1974:266; Firth 1974:32–47).

The idea that a definitive trait of art is its uselessness or impracticality
may seem reasonable to many Westerners, accustomed as we often are to
equating "art" with the "fine art" displayed in galleries and museums,
ostensibly doing nothing. (Even with regard to Western fine art, however,
we are in error: Clearly, such art not only provides a basis for artistic

satisfaction for some viewers but it also plays a role in the realm of economics, legitimizes current tastes and values, and so on.)

The issue becomes even more complicated when the art of non-Western societies is taken into account. For example, an attractive amulet, such as those made by an Eskimo carver, may seem nonutilitarian to us, but its maker would disagree, telling us (if we asked) that the amulet serves a very important and specific purpose—perhaps helping its owner find more caribou in the summer months (Balikci 1970:202). Of course, we could maintain that we, with our scientific knowledge, know that the amulet does not really help the hunter find caribou in the summer. But before we make this claim we should remember that our understanding of the psychology of autosuggestion is rudimentary at best, and that the amulet might very well help the hunter get additional caribou—not by giving him magical aid but by providing the extra measure of self-confidence that is necessary for successful hunting. Or, to give another example, a cedar box from the Northwest Coast of North America may not keep its contents dry any better by having elaborate designs painted and engraved on its sides, but as Chapter 3 points out, the family pride conveyed by the design may be more important than the dryness of the box's contents.[3]

Chapter 2 is devoted to a discussion of the functions of art in small-scale societies, showing that in very many (if not all) cases, art serves a variety of important uses in addition to the obvious aesthetic pleasure it gives. It may be true that the functions of a particular art work may not be apparent to us or to its maker and that its functions are often far removed from mundane matters such as subsistence activities. Nevertheless, art inevitably "does" something. Limiting the definition of art to items or features that seem to us to be nonutilitarian belittles the great importance of

---

[3]Two additional examples of our relative naivete regarding the functional aspects of art are of interest:

1. The West African Yoruba, as will be discussed later in this chapter, strongly prefer statuettes whose smooth finishes give them a shiny luminosity. One might assume that this preference arises not from practical considerations but rather from purely arbitrary tastes. Native art critics feel otherwise, however. A Yoruba critic, when given several statuettes for evaluation, "praised one statuette and damned another on the score of luminosity: 'One image is not beautiful and can quickly spoil. Its maker did not smooth the wood. Another image was carved so smoothly that one hundred years from now it will still be shining—if they take proper care of it—while the unpleasing image will rot regardless'" (R. Thompson 1971:378).

2. In an effort to illustrate the distinction between instrumental and noninstrumental features, Maquet (1971:8) states that the rounded edge of a wooden bowl is instrumental because it makes cleaning easier, but that the perfect circularity of the rim is noninstrumental because it is difficult to achieve by use of only hand tools, and that the roundness serves no purpose. However, as Bunzel (1971:3) noted with regard to coiled pottery, a medium in which perfect roundness is at least as difficult to attain as in wooden bowls, roundness is highly desirable because it maximizes the strength and capacity of a vessel while minimizing its weight.

art's role in most societies. It is, I believe, a move that hampers, more than helps, our understanding of art.

The Affective Response to Art

One trait that usually characterizes art is its ability to stimulate the senses and affect the emotions. As noted, art prompts a wide range of responses, from the wonder of the supernatural to the sensuality of the erotic. Indeed, the very fact that most art skillfully conveys culturally significant meanings is enough to guarantee its power to evoke a strong response in most people.

Western theorists have long been aware of the importance of sensuousness and emotion in art. Aristotle recognized drama's capacity to purge the pent-up feelings of audience members, and his theory of *katharsis* is still important today. In the late eighteenth century the leaders of the Romantic Rebellion pointed to the high passions that often reign in the artist's temperament, and they acclaimed art's ability to prompt feelings ranging from melancholy to bliss.

The twentieth-century fruition of this line of thought is found in the school of criticism known as *formalism*. Whereas earlier aesthetic theories had gloried in art's ability to engender a wide range of feelings in a person, formalists claimed that the only thing that mattered for artistic purposes was the "aesthetic response." This is a state far removed from the joy of comedy or the despair of tragedy. Rather, it is a unique and positive state of focused attention prompted by purely formal features of the art work—the sculptor's sense of visual composition, the composer's mastery of the sonata form, the poet's choice of words to fit a rhyme scheme, and so on. An art work's subject matter and style may prompt specific thoughts and feelings, but these, so the formalist argument goes, have little to do with its purely aesthetic impact—in fact, they may detract from it. In the aesthetic response, it is claimed, we see art *as* art and not as a handmaiden to anything else (hence the phrase, "art for art's sake").

The formalist tradition dominated Western writing on art theory and criticism during the first half of the twentieth century. Recent years have seen increasing challenges from many quarters to its favored position, but its continuing use by some anthropologists necessitates a brief examination of the formalist paradigm.

Is the 'Affective Response' Definitive?

Everyone agrees that art can often evoke powerful feelings in those who experience it, but formalists claim that art's essential core is its capacity to evoke the "aesthetic response," and that this quality sets art apart from all else. The aesthetic response, remember, is unlike (and, some would say, above) crass emotions such as the sympathy or repulsion that might be evoked by the art work's subject matter, nor is it the pleasure caused by experiencing the artist's use of sensuous media. Instead, it is a state of positive, focused, unitary, and disinterested engagement that is prompted by the art work's formal properties. Thus, Warren d'Azevedo has claimed that art always has "a feature of enhancement and present enjoyment of experience" (1958:707); and George Mills says, "Art is like the vision of Saul: there is a voice, a presence, an impact" (1971:82).

One can hardly deny that some art, some times, for some people evokes the powerful, affective response of which formalist writers speak. In such experiences, the criteria of art set down in the earlier open definition—cultural significance, stylistic conventions, generalized sensuousness, and exceptional skill of creation—surely fade into phenomenal irrelevance. We may feel we are under the sway of the true essence of the art work.

But does the aesthetic response infallibly distinguish art from non-art? I believe the answer is no, and for two reasons. First, we should not ignore Weitz's observation that much experience has shown that art is too varied and changing an entity to be infallibly defined by any one trait. Second, we must ask how likely it is that the things we commonly call art will, in actual practice, prompt the aesthetic response. All discussions of the aesthetic response note its transience and rarity. Even the aesthetically sophisticated individual will not experience it unless he or she is in the proper frame of mind. (If, for example, you are too concerned with the work's subject matter or the artist's style, you will probably not appreciate the art for its own sake.) And some people are *never* able to bring such a disinterested frame of mind to the appreciation of art. Moreover, even describing the aesthetic response to such a person may not be possible because, as critics of formalism have often pointed out, the whole idea of the aesthetic response ultimately rests on circular reasoning: An object is considered to be art if it evokes the aesthetic response. What is the aesthetic response? It's such a unique feeling that I can only say that it is the state I am sometimes in when I experience art.

If the aesthetic response is an unreliable touchstone for distinguishing art from non-art in Western contexts, the difficulties are all the more insurmountable when we turn to non-Western art. Jacques Maquet has recently gone to great lengths to apply formalist assumptions to non-Western art. Maquet focuses on the formal qualities of "aesthetic objects," that is, things that "stimulate and sustain the beholder's undivided, whole, and total visual attention" (Maquet 1986:36).

Maquet has argued that "many societies—all the known societies, I dare say—recognize and actualize the human potentiality for aesthetic perception and appreciation" (Maquet 1986:64). But I find Maquet's reasoning thoroughly unconvincing. First, he notes the resemblance between the aesthetic response and the meditative state of mind sought in some Eastern religious cults such as Hindu Yoga and Theravada Buddhism.[4] But although this proves that the state of mind that formalists call the "aesthetic response" is not limited to Western art aficionados, it also shows that, far from being definitive of art, it is significantly present in non-art experiences such as some religions.

Second, Maquet cites a secondary source (Leiris and Delange 1968) that claims that several African languages have words that can be translated as "beautiful," "handsome," or "pretty" (Maquet 1986:59). Maquet interprets this to mean that tribal Africans experience an aesthetic response that is qualitatively the same as that felt by Western art connoisseurs; and, what's more, they talk conveniently about it without contriving such technical phrases as "aesthetic response." But if Leiris and Delange are correct in translating the African words as "pretty," and so on, how are we to know that the words refer to feelings prompted by formal and compositional features of art works and not just the generalized sensuousness that "pretty" implies when we use the word in English?

Moreover, going directly to primary sources on African art leads one to suspect that, in native thought, an object's "prettiness" generally depends not upon its formal features per se but rather on its association with desirable social, cultural, or moral values.[5] We will soon take a close look at art and aesthetics among the Yoruba of West Africa, who systematically equate aesthetic beauty with cultural goodness, and similar patterns have been reported for other African groups as well. For example, Daniel Crowley's extensive fieldwork among the Chokwe of Central Africa revealed that, although the Chokwe have an extensive vocabulary for differentiating such things as degrees of kinship and types of musical instruments, their language lacks a lexical distinction between "good" and "beautiful" (Crowley 1971:322); and Harold Schneider found that among the Turu of Tanzania the word *majiha* means "beauty, a lovely thing," but "more precisely, it is a voluntary action which makes people happy" (H. Schneider 1966:158).

These considerations lead to the conclusion that the formalist "aesthetic response," although it may be important at certain times and places, is not universally associated with art. I view a definition as a tool for increasing our understanding of the world. To insist on a formalist definition of art tends to limit, rather than expand, our understanding. To paraphrase Shakespeare, I believe that there are more arts in heaven and earth than

---

[4]Maquet is not the first writer who has sought to validate his own preferred approach to art by citing precedents in classical Indian thought. In his widely read *The Dance of Śiva* (1924), Ananda Coomaraswamy argues in favor of art conveying spiritual and mystical (or "anagogic") significance by noting the parallels between medieval Western writers such as Meister Eckhart and the aesthetic principles found in classical Indian texts.

[5]Leiris and Delange state this idea themselves, observing that "the truth is that the African likens 'beauty' to 'goodness' and especially to 'efficacy.'" (Leiris and Delange 1968:40)

are dreamed of in the formalist paradigm. An in-depth look at theories of art in a specific non-Western society, namely, the Yoruba, should conclusively prove this point.

Good Art Versus Bad: A Yoruba Example   As previously noted, the question "What is art?" often really means "What is good art as opposed to not-so-good art?" This question is unavoidable in certain situations. For example, many museums own more artifacts from small-scale societies than their available space permits them to display. Decisions must therefore be made as to which of the items are "better" than others and thus are to be displayed in preference to the inferior items that will remain in storage.

Although practical considerations such as these may force one to make his or her own value judgments, the careful and sympathetic study of art from small-scale societies is often hindered by such an approach. The reason for this is that to understand the art of a given society it must be taken on its own terms—or, more exactly, on the terms of the people who produced it. Studies of the aesthetic systems of small-scale societies, although they are relatively few in number, convincingly show that *their* terms are often dissimilar to *our* terms. The aesthetic values of the Yoruba of West Africa illustrate this point.

About 10 million Yoruba individuals live in West Africa, mostly in Nigeria, but also in the People's Republic of Benin (formerly Dahomey) and the Republic of Togo.[6] Organized into over 50 kingdoms, they share a common language, dress, and (to a certain extent) culture. By comparison to the other societies of the world, the Yoruba have a relatively complex technology in that subsistence is derived from hoe-cultivated agriculture; and weaving and iron working are practiced. Their populations are highly nucleated (towns with 20,000 to 50,000 people probably existed before major European contact), and their economic and political systems are highly specialized. Thus on a continuum between small-scale and complex, Yoruba society is clearly far from the small-scale extreme. (For more ethnographic information on traditional Yoruba society see Bascom 1969; Forde 1951; Lloyd 1966.)

Yoruba art deserves consideration here because of the unique thoroughness with which Robert Farris Thompson has studied Yoruba aesthetic values (1971, 1973). Thompson collected information by visiting a number of Yoruba villages, taking with him various pieces of Yoruba sculpture that he owned. In each village he began by collecting background

---

[6]Unless otherwise indicated, cross-cultural examples are described in the "ethnographic present," that is, *as if* they continue to exist today unchanged from their state as described by an anthropologist at some time in the past. Also, I have used those ethnographic examples that I feel to be the best documented and most relevant to the issue in question. Additional examples are cited in the "Guide to Additional Reading" sections appearing at the end of each chapter.

information about local carvers, the age of individual carvings, and so on.
Thompson describes the rest of his technique:

> This art historical research served as a kind of lure. Potential [art] critics
> moved in the curious crowds of bystanders which always formed around the
> writer, his wife, and assistant. The crowd was then asked, while pieces of
> sculpture brought out for study were still in the sunlight, was someone willing
> to rank the carvings for a minimal fee and explain why he liked one piece
> over another? Owners sometimes immediately made clear that they did not
> want to participate—"put it to another person," a twin image owner protested
> once. Almost without fail someone would step forward and immediately be-
> gin to criticize the sculpture. The rare delays did not stem from lack of verbal
> skill. Rather some informants were simply afraid that their efforts would not
> really be compensated. Others wished to study the works with care in the
> light, turning them around and testing their profile and mass. (R. Thompson
> 1973:26)

In all, 88 native Yoruba art critics gave Thompson their opinions—ranking
items and, more importantly, telling him the basis for their preferences.

From this mass of data, Thompson isolated over a dozen generalized
aesthetic principles that are commonly used by Yoruba individuals in judging a given piece of sculpture. (Figure 1-1 shows a sculpture that Yoruba
critics feel to be a successful realization of these aesthetic principles.) Some
of these have parallels in our own aesthetic value system. For example, for
a statuette to be considered beautiful by Yoruba standards it must possess
ifarahòn, which Thompson translates as "visibility" and which requires that
the major masses of the work be clearly visible and that all decorations
(incised knifework, etc.) by clearly seen.

Other Yoruba aesthetic values are alien to Western connoisseurship.
Thompson claims that perhaps the single most important Yoruba criterion
of aesthetic excellence is *ephebism,* or the depiction of people in their prime.
When one informant was asked why he preferred one statue over three
others, he answered with his own question:

> "Between a beautiful young woman and an old woman which would you
> prefer for a wife?" The expected reply was given. The informant was amused
> for he had led his interrogator into corroborating his argument. "I like one
> image best," he then stated, "because it is carved as a young girl while the
> other three are like old women." (R. Thompson 1973:57)

The acuity of Yoruba critics for judging ephebism is considerable. One
female image was rejected because it had "breasts which sagged, with the
right breast longer than the left, a not infrequent phenomenon among
Yoruba mothers whose children have favored one nipple over the other
while nursing. . . . The most elegant [female statuettes] possessed breasts of
the same length and consequently resembled a young woman" (R.
Thompson 1973:57).

FIGURE 1-1   Yoruba wood carving, *The Image of the Thundergod as Crowned Lord of the Yoruba.* Made before 1837, 91 cm. high. *(Nigerian Museum, Lagos. Photo courtesy Robert Farris Thompson.)*

As this rationale suggests, the Yoruba canon of art criticism is neither arbitrary nor determined by purely visual or formalistic considerations. Instead, Yoruba art style reflects fundamental cultural values. For the Yoruba, beauty is a concrete embodiment of goodness; and goodness, for its part, involves two specific dimensions of moral and ethical thought. On the one hand, people are good who live in harmony with the traditions of the past and who have the requisite "cool" temperament to live peacefully with others. But good people also have energy—both in their vitality to be productive members of their families and communities and in the potential fertility that produces and nurtures another generation of good Yoruba people. Harmony and energy are potentially contradictory goals in that an excess of one could overwhelm the other. So a carved Yoruba statuette, with its feet symmetrically and firmly planted on the ground but with its strong and well-proportioned legs flexed at the knee as if to leap into the air, not only embodies Yoruba stylistic conventions but also conveys a complex moral message to the viewer: One must strive to be both "cool" and vital at the same time.

What conclusions can be drawn from this brief survey of Yoruba aesthetic values? First, it is clearly apparent that the Yoruba have a highly developed set of ideas about art: There are clear-cut native standards for judging art; these standards are widely shared among art cognoscenti among the Yoruba; and Yoruba art criticism is articulated by means of a specialized vocabulary. The notion that only Westerners are aesthetically sensitive is clearly a product of our own ethnocentrism.[7]

The second conclusion to be drawn from Thompson's study is that the Yoruba system of aesthetics is markedly different from our own, both in specifics (for example, they abhor carved figures with open mouths because a fly, one of the traditional messengers of evil, might enter) and in some general principles: Luminosity, symmetry, and roundness *may* be praiseworthy attributes in Western art, but their absence from a particular work would not necessarily decrease its merit.

The situation is parallel to a tale told by the Bété (also of West Africa), the "Story of the Chimpanzee and the Antelope":

> In a village party, two of the men's captives lament on their misfortunes, then get into an argument. The antelope, a male, sighs at the thought of his mistresses back in the forest crying in his absence. Then, in his turn, the chimpanzee, nostalgic, longs for his own sweethearts, and what sweethearts they are!
>
> "What?" says the antelope, "you mean you have lovers who adore you enough to miss you?"
>
> "And why not?" asks the chimpanzee, puzzled.
>
> "Why, your reputation of. . . ."
>
> "Of ugliness?" hints the chimpanzee.
>
> "Yes. Ugliness is so proverbial in the memory of animals that your story sounds like a joke or a lie," the antelope concludes.
>
> "Yes, I understand," says the chimpanzee. "But remember simply that there is no absolute ugliness of chimpanzees except in the village and in the minds of antelopes and other animals" (Memel-Fotê 1968:49).

---

[7]Westerners are not the only ones whose views reflect such an ethnocentric bias. R. Thompson notes that one difficulty in obtaining information on aesthetic values from some traditional Yoruba individuals is that they "seem to assume a White man's ability to perceive aesthetic import in art as weak or underdeveloped." (R. Thompson 1973:30)

We can learn a lesson from the chimpanzee of the Bété story: If the goal is to try to make sense of art from small-scale societies, we will gain more understanding by keeping our own inevitable aesthetic judgments to a minimum and by trying, insofar as possible, to take art from other societies on its own terms.

PORTFOLIO

The Arts of West and Central Africa

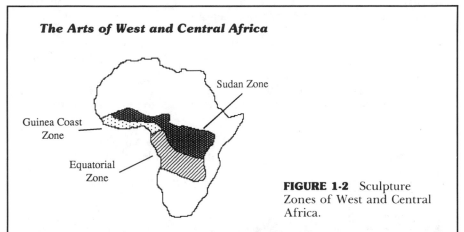

FIGURE 1-2 Sculpture Zones of West and Central Africa.

All regions of sub-Saharan Africa produce art, and virtually all media are utilized in one place or another, but the African art best known in Europe and America is the sculpture of West and Central Africa, where human and animal figures, masks, and decorated implements are made in great quantity and diversity.[8] So eclectic is this art that few generalizations can be made, but it is safe to say that in West and Central Africa art is not created as art for art's sake but as an integral part of religious, social, and political life. It usually serves this purpose by embodying moral or ethical power (often suggested by an emphasis on the face and head), rather than by conveying narrative themes. The best way to comprehend the enormous complexity of sculpture from this part of Africa is to divide it into three zones, each with component regions and subregions (see map, Figure 1-2).

The Sudan Zone presents a cosmopolitan blend of indigenous and Islamic traditions that often place art in a position of considerable importance. Stylization and geometric abstraction typify Sudanic art. Carved human and animal figures are blackened by scorching or through the application of ritual libations, often blood; masks, on the other hand, may be polychromed, a dichotomy found elsewhere in

[8]The following typology of West and Central African sculpture is based on that of Rubin 1976.

Africa. Western Sudan tribes such as the Dogon produce sculptures to honor recent ancestors; and masks are important for public ceremonies (see Figure 1-3). Marionettes and children's toys are also produced, and in the Eastern Sudan stylized figures are made for men's secret associations.

If the Sudan looks northward to the Sahara and Islam, the Guinea Coast Zone (Figure 1-2) is oriented to the sea, where difficult terrain impedes travel and leads to great stylistic diversity. Art from the northwestern end of the Guinea Coast Zone resembles that of the Sudan, but moving eastward from Sierra Leone one finds a distinctive art sponsored by a complex of voluntary associations known generically as *Poro* (for men) and *Sande* (for women). These associations are often graded into levels, and the elite members of the highest grades are custodians of masks and figures used both in initiations and in other activities that extend beyond the association proper, ranging from leadership in war, through dispute settlement, to entertain-

FIGURE 1-3 Dogon wooden figurine. Mali, West Africa. 46.7 cm. high. *(Courtesy Field Museum of Natural History, Chicago.)*

FIGURE 1-4 Yoruba diviner's staff. Iron; length of bird, 15 cm. *(Courtesy Parkersburg (West Virginia) Art Center, Marietta (Ohio) College Collection.)*

FIGURE 1-5 Ashanti fertility doll (*akua ba*) from Ghana. Black-stained wood with beads, 42 cm. high. (*Courtesy Saint Louis Art Museum. Gift of S. Thomas Alexander.*)

ment. Carved figures from this area are less elongated vertically than the carvings from the Sudan to the north, and they have little geometric ornamentation. Masks and portrayals of the face remain stylized, often with a smooth, black, lustrous finish, as in the Liberian masks shown in Chapter 2 (see Figure 2-1).

Moving further eastward we come to the central region of the Guinea Coast Zone, famous for several rich and complex kingdoms such as Ashanti and Dahomey, Benin and Yoruba, each with populations numbering in the hundreds of thousands or more. The centralized authority of the king's court is legitimized and displayed by its patronage of weavers, brass casters, wood carvers and, especially among the Ashanti, goldsmiths. In addition to the regalia of state, artists in the central Guinea Coast are also commissioned to produce great quantities of masks and other items (Figure 1-4) for use by cults that honor ancestral and other spirits, as in the carved figure of the Yoruba Thundergod, Figure 1-1. Stylistically, the smooth surfaces found in *Poro* art to the west is even more marked in the central Guinea Coast, with masses becoming increasingly circular, cylindrical, or spherical, as in the Ashanti fertility doll (Figure 1-5).

Moving further eastward, Guinea Coast sculpture remains largely religious but on a more abstract and personal level. Themes of opposition—male/female, violent/tranquil, and so on—become important, conveyed both theatrically as well as in the organic, curvilinearly ornamented sculptures that are produced. Finally, in the Cameroon Grassfields that constitute the eastern limit of the Guinea Coast Zone, large, expressionistic sculptures are produced for the masquerades of secret societies and for the courts of the kingdoms such as Bamum, Tikar, and Bamileke (Figure 1-6).

In the third major zone, Equatorial Africa, carved figures may be given magical power by attaching ancestral relics and other materials to them. Carvers in the northeast corner of the Equatorial Zone consistently paint masks a characteristic matte white, as in the Fang mask, Figure 1-7. In the Zaire River basin to the southeast, the huge Kongo Kingdom sponsors art that is distinctive for the presence of figures, often ancestral effigies, in rather naturalistic poses, atypical in a continent where most sculpture is relatively symmetrical in composition and cylindrical in overall outline. This region is also famous for the production of charm figures, which are residences for either benevolent or malevolent spirits, the latter riddled with nails or pieces of iron meant to activate the in-dwelling spirit to carry out a magical purpose such as causing one's enemy to fall ill (see Figure 1-8).

East of the Kongo Kingdom, the Kuba Kingdom also produces a rich courtly art, but masks for use in male initiation ceremonies are

FIGURE 1-6 Wooden dance mask from the Kingdom of Bamum, Cameroon Grassfields. *(Courtesy Saint Louis Art Museum. Gift of Sharon and Stuart Hollander.)*

FIGURE 1-7 Fang dance mask to be carried on a pole and danced over stuffed figure. Said to depict either Franco or DeGaulle. Made by Mvole Mo Ze in the early 1950's. *(Photo courtesy James Fernandez.)*

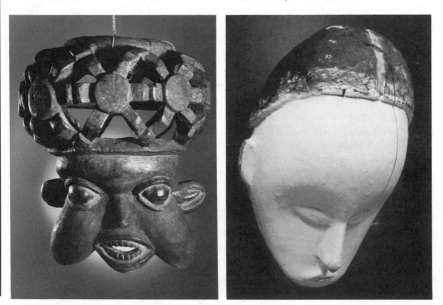

FIGURE 1-8 Large wooden idol studded with nails and pieces of iron, fiber paint, cowrie shell, and clay. Made in the late nineteenth century by the Yombe of Zaire. *(Courtesy Field Museum of Natural History, Chicago.)*

most important in the smaller surrounding groups. In some areas these are polychromed and have distinctive, turned-up noses, but elsewhere styles are so diverse as to defy categorization.

CONCLUSIONS

Discussions of definitions of fundamental terms can be frustrating; and when they are only disguised arguments about the *ultimate* meanings of words, they are little more than ends in themselves. If, however, polemics are avoided, a discussion of definitions can be doubly useful: It can serve as a basis for subsequent communication between people by providing an agreed-upon set of meanings for terms, and it points to possible problem areas that we should be careful about during the course of our discussion. I hope the preceding account of "scale" and "art" has provided these two benefits.

Other cultures are, in very fundamental ways, simultaneously like and unlike our own, and that situation inevitably makes it difficult to think and talk soundly about other peoples. When we exchange the inevitably distorted vision of facile ethnocentrism for a judicious cultural relativism we recognize that all traditional societies provide designs for living that are adequate, indeed often ingenious. In that sense, all cultures are alike. But when we, as objectively as possible, appraise the hard-won ethnographic reports of other societies we find important differences too. For while no society is intrinsically better than another, it may be significantly *bigger,* and a society with larger populations is also typically based on a more complicated technology and division of labor. Applying these considerations to art leads to the conclusion that although all societies make and appreciate art, other aspects of art (the uses to which it is put, the ways in which artists acquire their skills, and so on) do vary in important and interesting ways. These topics constitute the proper subjects for an anthropology of art.

Defining "art" presents a different sort of challenge. Most of us would doubtless prefer a definition that provides a simple, hard-and-fast test that distinguishes art from non-art. Unfortunately, the quest for such a "litmus-paper" definition seems doomed to failure. A persistent feature of art is that just when we think we have it pinned down and know exactly what it is—it changes! And just as artistic change is perennial, so too are borderline cases, troublesome instances of "almost-art" and "almost-not-art."

Probably the best we can hope for is a tentative list of traits, each of which is usually present in "art" as we currently use the word. I suggest the following features as members of such a list: The things we now generally consider to be art, both from our own society and from others, typically convey culturally significant meaning, are produced in accordance with a style that is characteristic of their time and place of origin, and are made in a sensuous, affecting medium by individuals whose skills markedly exceed those of others in the society.

One might well wish that the problems of defining "scale" and "art" could be solved more elegantly. But despite their messiness, the solutions I propose are serviceable, and to sweep persistent definitional problems under the carpet is seldom productive, if for no other reason than that such an approach creates a false and dangerous impression of the perfection and finality of our current state of knowledge.

GUIDE TO ADDITIONAL READINGS

General Reference Works   Those interested in locating more detailed information on particular societies or their arts might begin by consulting the Human Relations Area Files (HRAF), available in many academic libraries. Also, the 15 volumes of the *Encyclopedia of World Art* contain many articles describing the art of numerous non-Western societies. Ehresmann (1975) lists bibliographies of published literature on art from most of the world's culture areas.

Definitions of Terms   Use of the term "primitive" has been both decried (Gerbrands 1957:9–23) and supported (Diamond (1974); and W.T. Jones (1974) and P.J.C. Dark (1978) have discussed anthropologists' tacit definition of "primitive art." Several introductory works (for example, Osborne 1972) survey Western philosophies of art.

The Nonvisual Arts   The nonvisual arts have only recently begun to receive their fair share of cross-cultural study. Classics in the field of ethnomusicology are Nettl (1956), Merriam (1964), Blacking (1973), and N. McLeod (1974). These studies are updated in May (1980), McAllester (1971), and Nettl (1983).

Likewise, older treatments of dance by Sachs (1937) and Kurath (1960) have now been supplemented by Kaeppler, et al. (1977), Royce (1977), Hanna (1979), and P. Spencer (1985). Forbes (1986) provides a bibliography of works on non-Western dance published between 1965 and 1982.

The illusive territory between drama and ritual performance was first identified in Gregory Bateson's *Naven* (1958[orig. 1936]), and it has been further explored by Blacking and Keali'inohomoku (1979), Bauman (1984), Schechner (1985), and Turner (1986).

Highly sophisticated studies of oral and non-Western literature have appeared in recent years (see Tedlock 1972, 1985, D. Ben-Amos 1975, and Rothenberg and Rothenberg 1983). For Native American literature, a good sampling appears in both Swann (1983) and Swann and Krupat (1987).

Ethnoaesthetics   The study of non-Western philosophies of art remains in a formative stage. Robert Farris Thompson's Yoruba work (1973, 1974, 1976), Witherspoon's (1977) penetrating study of Navajo art and thought, and Miguel Léon-Portilla's account (1963) of Aztec cosmology stand out for their descriptive rigor. Comparative analyses are now starting to appear (Maquet 1986; Anderson, in press).

CHAPTER 2

The Functions of Art in Small-Scale Societies

To understand something is often a matter of grasping just what that something does. If you understand your car's carburetor, then you have (among other things) some knowledge of the job it performs in your car—that is, you comprehend its mechanical function. If you thoroughly understand Banquo's ghost in *Macbeth,* then you are aware (among other things) of the role's contribution to making the play work—you grasp its dramatic function. Certainly functional knowledge alone is incomplete: If you understand your car's carburetor, in addition to knowing its function you also know what it looks like and where it is located; and undoubtedly the chill that goes down your spine when Banquo's ghost appears on stage is a far different thing from the dispassionate analysis of the ghost's dramatic role in the plot of *Macbeth.*

But even though functionalist knowledge is not everything, anthropologists well appreciate its analytic value. The emergence of functionalism can best be understood by recalling the history of cultural anthropology itself. In Chapter 1 we saw that one reason for the failure of nineteenth-century evolutionary theories was their unwarranted assumption that all cultures pass through distinct stages and that the institutions of contemporary, small-scale societies are best understood as representing earlier, and simpler, stages that modern, complex societies transcended long ago.

THE FUNCTIONALIST APPROACH

Functionalism, as developed around the turn of the century by the French sociologist Emile Durkheim, provided a way out of this theoretical *cul de sac*. Instead of using ethnographic data in an ultimately futile attempt to reconstruct the early history of the human race, Durkheim used available field reports to study just how contemporary, small-scale societies operate today. His work, and that of subsequent generations of functionalists, analyzed the beliefs, institutions, and practices of individual societies, searching for the contribution they make toward the maintenance of human life and the cultural stability of the society in which they occur. When confronted with customs that initially seem strange and inexplicable, if one attempts to discover their function, the customs begin to make sense to us. Often that which had seemed purposeless, or even counterproductive, becomes thoroughly reasonable, perhaps ingenious.

The functionalism of Durkheim and his French colleagues was brought into the anthropological theory of the English-speaking world by Bronislaw Malinowski and A.R. Radcliffe-Brown. For his part Malinowski emphasized the individual and psychological functions of culture. The brand of functionalism that evolved from Radcliffe-Brown's writings has been even more fruitful with regard to art. Radcliffe-Brown, like Durkheim himself, conceived social systems to be composed of more than just the individuals who comprise them: They may be thought of as being organic entities, with existences and needs of their own. The social patterns that exist in a given society can be conceptualized as effective ways of meeting these needs. Thus, Radcliffe-Brown emphatically states, "The function of any recurrent activity is the part it plays in the social life as a whole and therefore the contribution it makes to the maintenance of the social continuity" (1935:396).

Although functionalism can be a valuable analytic tool, three of its limitations must be borne in mind:

First, there is seldom a neat, one-to-one correspondence between practice and function. A particular phenomenon in a specific society may fulfill numerous psychological, social, or cultural needs. Moreover, the same practice may serve quite different purposes in another society. As the examples in this chapter show, art is just such a multifunctional phenomenon.

Second, although in some cases the functions of art are fairly obvious, in others it serves more covert functions, ones that might not be immediately apparent to others or to the artists themselves.

This leads to the third point: Sometimes it will be difficult, if not impossible, to prove conclusively that art serves a particular function. All scientists generate theories to help them account for the things they find in the world around them, but unlike the physical scientists with their controlled experiments, social scientists usually can only support their theories with whatever cross-cultural data have been collected—that plus a strong dose of good judgment.

One might argue that for an aesthetic appreciation of a work of art it is irrelevant to know its function within the society it came from, just as knowledge of meteorology is unnecessary for the enjoyment of a beautiful sunset. Such information, so the argument could go, adds nothing to the viewer's experience and may even be an undesirable distraction.

This position cannot be refuted on logical grounds. If an individual's only goal is the immediate, sensuous response to a physical stimulus, then *any* reasoned discussion about the stimulus is pointless. But as the aphorism of the 1960s had it, there are "different strokes for different folks," and undoubtedly there are many people (I am one myself) who not only enjoy an immediate, sensuous response to an object but who derive additional pleasure from having extra background information about it. For people in this category, some of the most useful information about art in small-scale societies will be derived from an examination of art's functions in these societies.

ART AND THE ECONOMIC REALM

Economics, in the broadest sense of the word, is the study of those goods and services that are deemed valuable in a particular society, and of the exchanges of those goods and services between people. Since art is inevitably the result of personal skill, and since such skills are necessarily limited in supply and are valued by many people, art often has an economic aspect, despite the fact that we ourselves sometimes think of art and economics as being in complete contrast with each other. If it seems philistine to place beautiful art objects in the workaday arena of economics, a thorough consideration of the functions of art in primitive societies requires that this be done, at least for the moment.

Trade and Social Relations

When goods or services are exchanged between people, often more happens than meets the eye. The obvious transfer of tangible goods has certainly taken place, with individual *A* giving something to individual *B*, while *B* either gives something in return or promises to reciprocate at some later date. But in addition to this overt, material exchange there is also typically a *social* exchange, with *A* and *B* exchanging bits of local gossip, discussing past and future trades between themselves and others, and so on. Such conviviality between trading partners, far from being an unnecessary luxury, is often quite valuable in itself in that it furthers mutual trust between the traders, an important prerequisite for future trading between the two, and it may be the basis for other sorts of alliances. Trading partners, for example, may support each other during wars, or they may acquire spouses from each other's group.

These fringe benefits of the trading relationship may be valuable enough in themselves to justify such a relationship even when there are no goods of practical value to be exchanged between the partners. In such a situation an arbitrary value may be attached to some otherwise non-utilitarian objects, and these may be used as a basis for the trading partnership.[1] At this point, art may enter the picture, as art works are typically arbitrarily valued objects whose material contribution to subsistence is covert at best. An ethnographic example will serve to illustrate how such a mechanism can work.

Tsembaga Ornamentation and Trade The Tsembaga, a Maring-speaking group numbering only about 200 people, live on the south wall of the Simbai Valley in the east-central New Guinea highlands (Rappaport 1968). As slash-and-burn horticulturalists, they must have stone axes to clear land for garden plots in the dense secondary forest. Unfortunately for the Tsembaga, however, varieties of stone suitable for making ax heads occur only in a few scattered localities in the highlands, and the Tsembaga are separated by several other tribes' territories from the stone quarries closest to them. Thus, axes come into the hands of the Tsembaga only after having been traded from one person to another through several different groups. Fortunately, the Tsembaga produce salt, a vital commodity that the ax-producing groups can obtain only through trade.

One might expect that the trading arrangements would be relatively straightforward, with the two kinds of goods that are necessary for subsistence, axes and salt, being traded back and forth between their respective producers. But in fact, there are serious drawbacks to such a system, as has been noted by Roy Rappaport, who studied Tsembaga subsistence and ritual in considerable detail:

> It may be questioned whether a direct exchange apparatus that moves only two or three items critical to subsistence would be viable. . . . If all that the Simbai people [including the Tsembaga] could obtain for their salt were working axes they would be likely to suspend the manufacture of salt if they had a large supply of axes on hand, regardless of the state of the salt supply in the Jimi Valley. The converse might be the case if the ax manufacturers had large stockpiles of salt (Rappaport 1968:106).

[1]Malinowski's classic description (1922) of the Kula exchange in the Trobriand Islands, and the vast literature of economic anthropology that has grown up around his account, provide numerous examples of such trading.

Since salt producers are typically separated from stone ax producers by at least two intervening peoples, and in the absence of any supratribal authority, no direct pressures can be exerted to relieve possible inequities in the system: If "a man must put pressure on a trading partner to put pressure on a second, who will in turn put it on a third, who will attempt to get an ax from the manufacturer, success is less likely" (Rappaport 1968:107).

How do the Tsembaga and their neighbors overcome this problem? Their solution is to trade, in addition to the utilitarian goods of salt and working axes, several kinds of nonutilitarian items, including bird of paradise plumes, fur headbands, and shell ornaments. All of these things are used by Tsembaga men for decorating their bodies and their shields, thus providing an important means of aesthetic expression. For all these items there is a constant, unlimited demand by all groups. Therefore the producers of salt and working axes always have an incentive to produce these utilitarian goods and, by trading them for the primarily art-related goods, they provide their entire region with a steady supply of salt and axes.

In essence, then, Rappaport's argument goes thus: For a group to survive in the New Guinea highlands it must obtain stone axes and salt. However, given the scattered distribution of the sources of these goods and the lack of communication between nonneighboring groups, a trading system based only on the exchange of these two items alone is probably not feasible. In practice, however, there is also an exchange of bird of paradise plumes and the like—items that are valued for aesthetic rather than subsistence reasons and for which there is an unlimited demand. Trade in these items ensures the steady production and even distribution of the necessities of salt and stone axes.[2]

The Tsembaga case illustrates the unexpected ways in which the fields of art and economics can overlap. This example is typical in that the relationship between art and economics is neither simple nor obvious. Indeed, from the Tsembaga point of view, they exchange their salt for art-related items, not in order to make the trading system operate smoothly, but rather because "they consider fine plumes and shells, gold-lip or green sea snail, to be among the most beautiful of objects and men enjoy possessing them for their own sakes" (Rappaport 1968:106). Moreover, the decorations make a man more attractive to women when he dances; and the shells can be used, along with other items, in payments to the bride's family after marriage.

Although economic factors become increasingly important in more complex cultures such as the West, in small-scale societies economic considerations rarely dominate art production. (In the Tsembaga case, body decoration serves to communicate social standing, marital status, etc., and,

---

[2]Michael Harner's account of the Jívaro of eastern Equador provides another instance in which the trade of art-related items facilitates trade in goods that are directly necessary for survival (cf. Harner 1972:129).

presumably, it brings a greater measure of enjoyment into the lives of the wearers and those who see them.) However, the economic functions of art, if they are sought out, often shed valuable light on the cultural context of art in small-scale societies. And undoubtedly the subject's importance will increase in proportion to the exposure of traditional societies to international cash economies. There is a growing market in the West for art from the Third and Fourth Worlds, and there is no lack of entrepreneurs who are eager to promote such sales. Thus, the relations between economics and art from small-scale societies are becoming more overtly important.

ART AND CULTURAL HOMEOSTASIS

Small-scale societies, as a rule, change much more slowly than Western societies have during the last two centuries. Small-scale societies are not actually "changeless," as some of the more romantic writers on the subject have implied; it is nevertheless the case that in most such societies the amount of change that occurs during an individual's lifetime is relatively small. Further, those changes that do occur, such as shifts in the locations of hunting territories or the succession of one political leader by another, are usually superficial. The *structural* aspects of the society—for example, the very fact that the group has a hunting territory or that it has a particular sort of political system—are highly resistant to change.

With the passage of time all systems, social or otherwise, tend toward chaos unless there is an input of energy directed toward maintaining the system. How is it then that societies generally remain structurally stable for long periods of time? What is it that allows societies, especially those which have no written laws or constitutions, to remain so conservative?

The functionalism of Durkheim, Radcliffe-Brown, Talcott Parsons, and others offers an answer to these questions. These writers suggest that social solidarity is maintained chiefly in two ways. First, social life inevitably entails a modicum of uniformity of belief and action within the population: Through various institutionalized means, individuals come to accept, to a greater or lesser degree, the goals, value systems, and styles of living that are in harmony with those of others in the society. Second, insofar as differences do exist in a particular society, they tend to be complementary in nature: Specialization and independence create sectors of the population that are dependent upon each other's continued existence. (Inasmuch as change does indeed occur and as revolutions sometimes drastically alter individual societies, the effectiveness of these two centripetal forces is clearly limited.) These solidarity-maintaining principles operate through the established social institutions and cultural patterns of a society—its educational, political, and economic systems, its language, religion, and laws, and (as the following sections illustrate) through its art.

The notion that art may help maintain the status quo is a conclusion that goes contrary to many of our own preconceptions about art. For most of us in the twentieth-century Western world, artists are first and foremost innovators—bohemians and visionaries who would rather ignore or renovate their social milieu than produce works that support the status quo. But such a characterization of our own art community may be in error; and, more importantly, ours is only one of the thousands of societies that inhabit the earth.[3] Because *our* art often seems anti-establishmentarian we cannot safely assume that art is thus everywhere. The following examples illustrate several ways in which art can aid the stability of societies. They are case studies in the cultural homeostatic functions of art.

Art and Social Control

George W. Harley lived in northeast Liberia for 23 years working as a missionary, primarily with the Mano and Gio tribes. During that period he acquired a large collection of ceremonial masks and a wealth of ethnographic information concerning their use, which he recorded in *Masks as Agents of Social Control in Northeast Liberia* (1950). As the title suggests, Harley's thesis was that among the Mano and Gio, besides whatever "higher" needs their art might satisfy, it was also a major aid to the maintenance of law and order.

During Harley's stay, political authority in these tribes was vested principally in a group of chiefs and a council of elders. The authority of these individuals was public and known to all in matters of everyday management of towns and the enforcement of common laws. However, their control over more important matters, such as the handling of crises and emergencies of life, depended upon their being leading members of the Poro. This was a secret fraternity that all young men joined when they came of age. Poro leadership was in the hands of a hierarchy of individuals. The more important the issue, the smaller and more secretive was the circle of chiefs and elders who held ultimate authority:

> Chiefs had the custom of calling in the elders to help decide matters of complicated or obscure nature. They might sit in the town council and express their opinions openly and informally, but as a matter increased in importance, the meetings of the elders became more and more secret until they reached the final high council. This met at night in a secret part of the sacred Bush, presided over by a high priest with a simple but highly effective ritual (Harley 1950:viii).

[3]It is possible, of course, that art in the contemporary western world *does* aid cultural homeostasis, but that we are as oblivious to this function of our art as the Tsembaga are of the economic functions that Rappaport has attributed to their art. Tom Wolfe's controversial *The Painted Word* (1975) discusses some of the establishmentarian functions of art in the United States.

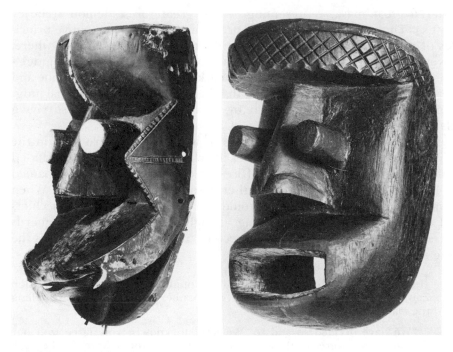

FIGURE 2-1   Two black wooden masks. Liberia. *(Courtesy Peabody Museum, Harvard University. Photographs by Hillel Burger.)*

Within the Poro there was a small, elite group, the *Ki La mi*, for which "there was a stiff initiation fee, and a limitation of membership to individuals of outstanding intelligence or high hereditary standing" (Harley 1950:viii). Within the *Ki La mi*,

> there was a still higher group called *Ki Gbuo La mi*, against whom personal insults or violence was considered no less than treason. When one of these men died it sometimes happened that his death was not only kept secret but was, in fact, minimized by making a death mask before his burial. This was carved in wood, as a rude portrait or characterization, and in it his spirit was supposed to find an abode at least reminiscent of its former fleshly habitation (Harley 1950:ix).

Thus, the death masks came to be worshiped in and of themselves, representing as they did individuals who were of the very highest importance during their lives and who, after their deaths, were believed to be free spirits capable of interceding between mortals and deceased ancestors.

These masks, with their supernatural power, were important tools for the administration of justice. For example, court cases involving issues of life and death were presided over by a judge "whose identity was hidden under a great mask, representing . . . the great forest demon" (Harley 1950:x). The case would be decided according to traditional native principles of right and wrong, as applied by the masked judge. As everywhere, however, disputes seldom ended without some ill feelings; and the judge's anonymity, protected by his wearing a mask and head-to-foot costume and speaking in a falsetto voice, ensured that he could make an impartial judgment without fear of retribution by a condemned person's surviving relatives.

Harley recounts another instance in which masks were used in the political process (1950:16). Zawolo was the chief of a territory that included some seven or eight towns. The office—and the mask that accompanied it—had been handed down from father to son for four generations. When an important issue arose Zawolo would call a meeting of the lesser chiefs and elders in his territory. Meeting at night in the forest, with guards placed on incoming roads to insure secrecy, the council would discuss the issue at length. Then,

> after the old men had talked the case through and reached their decision Zawolo would uncover the mask, call it by name, and review the case, telling the mask:
>
> "We have decided so and so. We want to know if you agree with our decision. If you agree let the cowrie shells fall up. If you disagree let them fall down."
>
> Then he would take the [four] shells and throw them like dice on the mat in front of the mask. The decision was supposed to be the decision of the ancestral spirits and was final. . . .
>
> I have never known a man more dignified and gentle [than Zawolo] and I was a little surprised to learn that in the old days he literally had the power of life and death over his people, for, as keeper of the great mask, he was a judge from whose decisions there was no appeal. The casting of lots before the masks was something of a formality. [Chiefs like Zawolo] were too sincere to decide everything by throw of dice upon pure chance. Old Zawolo knew how to throw them to get the answer he wanted. If he got an answer that did not suit him he could always invent an excuse for reopening the question and giving the cowries another throw (Harley 1950:16).

Note exactly how a decision was reached: A council of (presumably) the wisest men in the territory, led by the region's most influential individual, reviewed the matter and reached a tentative decision, based on the traditional values of the culture. This decision was then ratified and given supernatural warrant through approval by the mask. The decision became, in effect, the choice not of mortals but of the revered ancestors. If the decision was not purely traditional but involved a case for which no precedent existed, the decree would be announced by a town crier and become law (Harley 1950:11) Thus, law was interpreted and created in northeast

Liberia; and, significantly, works of art—masks—were the agents through which this was accomplished.

Harley remarks in summary that masks representing spirits (gε's),

> exercised all the functions necessary for control of society on the religious, the executive, and the judicial levels, reinforcing their authority by oracular responses. The human manipulation of these inanimate objects was so regulated by custom that abuse of power was kept at a minimum. The "owner" or high priest-judge could send gεs as his messengers, police, magistrates, extortioners, or entertainers; but he himself was subject to the will of the people through the council of elders.
>
> If the wearer of a mask died, his place was taken by another and the mask continued to function without interruption. Thus the equilibrium of the community suffered a minimum disturbance, being that occasioned by the loss of an individual not especially important as such, rather than the loss of an important official whose individual character could not be replaced, whose successor might be activated by policies divergent from those already established. The mask thus provided continuity of authority, regardless of the personal attributes of the current wearer (Harley 1950:42).

Art filled additional functions in the societies described by Harley, and the political system had several other dimensions in addition to the uses of masks described above. Nevertheless, this case shows how art works can be used as a means of social control.[4]

Authority, Legitimacy, and Art in the Andamans

As intellectual heirs of the thinkers of the Enlightenment we may sincerely believe that all people are created equal. The fact of the matter is, however, that in every known society social inequality exists—between the sexes, between adults and children, or between the politically influential and those with little influence. When one individual claims control (partial or total) over another, the claim may ultimately be based on the individual's having greater physical power at his or her command. But obviously all of a people's time cannot be spent in fighting to establish and maintain dominance patterns, and in fact such internecine fighting is usually the exception rather than the rule. Instead, dominance may be maintained on a day-to-day basis through cultural precedent: Everyone, including the "have-nots," knows that the "haves" possess relatively greater power, that this power differential has been in existence for some time, and, perhaps, that it is traditionally considered right and proper that such an inequality exists.

---

[4]Additional examples of art being used as a means of social control in West Africa can be found in Sieber 1962; Messenger 1962; and Cole 1972. In the West, too, masks are sometimes used to conceal the identity of individuals responsible for punishing aberrant behavior. Thus, for example, in some localities masked Halloweeners reek havoc with the property of people who are considered inordinately cranky, stingy, or malicious.

If those with relatively less power are reluctant to accept the rightness of their position, those with power can—and often do—use various techniques to display their power *symbolically*. Both the powerful and the powerless benefit from the fact that the display is symbolic: In an actual show of force, both the weaker and the stronger sides waste energy (and perhaps lose lives) that could be put to better use.

The accumulation of valuable items is often a most convincing means of displaying one's power. But what should an influential person collect? One could accumulate utilitarian items—usable stone axes, for example— but what purpose would they serve, since one's personal needs would quickly be met? Further, the society as a whole would suffer if the collection of stone axes deprived others of their use.

In some societies the problem is elegantly solved for the relatively more powerful by their collection of items that are valued, that are limited in supply, and that are not overtly utilitarian. Art works meet these criteria admirably and thus may conveniently serve as status symbols.

Social inequality exists in every known society, but it is much more extreme in some than in others. The society of the Andaman Islanders is one in which there is relatively little inequality. The Andaman Islands lie in the Bay of Bengal, about 300 miles south of Burma, and their inhabitants were described by one of the anthropological fathers of functionalism, A.R. Radcliffe-Brown. The Islanders live in local groups of 40 to 50 people each; local groups are loosely linked in tribes, with about 10 groups per tribe (Radcliffe-Brown 1964:28). There is no organized government within the local groups, but "the affairs of the community are regulated entirely by the older men and women. The younger members of the community are brought up to pay respect to their elders and to submit to them in many ways" (p. 44). The authority of the elders is not maintained by outright force, however.

> It must not be thought . . . that the older men are tyrannical or selfish. I only once heard a young man complain of the older men getting so much the best of everything. The respect for seniority is kept alive partly by tradition and partly by the fact that the older men have had a greater experience than the younger. It could probably not be maintained if it regularly gave rise to any tyrannical treatment of the younger by the older (Radcliffe-Brown 1964:44).

The only sort of political power in the local groups is a generalized sort of influence that accrues to men who possess "skill in hunting and in warfare, generosity and kindness, and freedom from bad temper" (Radcliffe-Brown 1964:45).

Alvin Wolfe (1969) has suggested that, in Africa at least, the amount of art produced by a society is roughly proportional to the extent to which the society is divided by social cleavages. The geographic generality of Wolfe's thesis is debatable (cf. Houlihan 1972, McGhee 1976, and A. Wolfe

1976), but Andaman society certainly fits the rule. The only visual "art" described by Radcliffe-Brown in this virtually cleavage-free society is the decoration of individuals' bodies by means of scarification, painting, and the wearing of ornaments, and the decoration of utilitarian items such as bows, canoes, and baskets (Radcliffe-Brown 1964: 315–23). Nevertheless, this scant amount of art is directed largely toward the end of stabilizing the social order.

Andaman Islanders' decoration (of either individuals' bodies or of utilitarian items) is always prompted by a desire to signify increased "social value" of the person or thing decorated. For example, a young person is scarified on the occasion of a ritual that marks his or her coming of age. The Islanders justify the scarification on grounds that "it improves the personal appearance and that it makes the boy or girl grow up strong." However, there can be little doubt that the scars serve also as social insignia, symbolizing to the wearer and to all others that the person is no longer a child but rather a legitimate adult, with all the authority and responsibilities that accompany adulthood.

Ashanti Art: Symbols of Power

The thesis that was presented in the preceding paragraphs—that art may provide status symbols for the more powerful members of a society—is difficult to document in a relatively egalitarian culture such as that of the Andaman Islanders. By contrast, evidence is often quite ample in highly stratified societies such as the traditional African states, of which the Ashanti (Asante) of southern Ghana is an excellent example.

The Ashanti Confederacy, a political union formed in about 1701 and now encompassing over a million people, stands in sharp contrast to the small-scale, politically simple society of the Andaman Islanders. The Confederacy maintains an elaborate political hierarchy, headed by a hereditary king called the Asantehene. The Asantehene is the keeper of a wide variety of ritual objects and regalia, symbolic of his supreme position in the Confederacy. The most important of these items is the Golden Stool.

The origin of the Stool deserves to be recounted here, illustrating as it does the Stool's importance for Ashanti unity and stability. The Confederacy was formed by the joining together of a number of previously independent city-states.

> To seal their union, Okomfo Anokye, chief priest, adviser, confidant, and paternal nephew of Osei Tutu [the first king of the Confederacy] promised the king and the nation that he would call down from the skies a supernatural stool of solid gold which would enshrine and protect the soul of the nation. As a precondition to fulfilling his promise, however, he demanded that the ancestral (blackened) stools, state shields, state swords, and other regalia of all the member states be surrendered to him. This was done, and he

buried them in the bed of the Bantama River in Kumasi. The purpose of this action was two fold: to ensure that no item of regalia in the new kingdom could have a longer history than the Golden Stool and hence take precedence over it, and, by depriving the formerly independent states of the relics of their respective pasts, to pave the way toward a new and broader union (Fraser 1972a:139–40).

These conditions were met by the new member-states of the Ashanti Confederacy, and a Golden Stool did indeed appear, falling (as tradition has it) from heaven onto the lap of the king. In case the message was missed by any present, the chief's priest publicly proclaimed that the King was "the Father and Supreme Ruler of the people. The Golden Stool, he stipulated, must be treated with the utmost respect and was to be fed at regular intervals, for if it should become hungry, it might sicken and die; with it would perish the soul of the Ashanti nation" (Fraser 1972a:140).

The beautiful Golden Stool of the Ashanti remains today the most important symbol of the unity of the Ashanti people and of the supreme power of their king. It is considered to be supernatural and to it are given honors that are, broadly speaking, "those rendered to an individual of the highest rank. The Stool must never touch the bare ground, and, when it is exhibited on state occasions, it rests on its own special throne, the silver-plated *Hwedomtea,* an elaborate chair" (Fraser 1972a:141).

In addition to stools, the Ashanti king's importance is also symbolized by his owning a great number of gold state swords (what could be more impractical for use as a weapon than a sword made of such a soft metal as gold?), decorated gold containers for holding gold dust, and state um-brellas. The latter, made of richly colored materials and sometimes topped with wood carvings and sheathed in gold leaf, again often carry political messages that are quite explicit. "On one belonging to the Asantehene, there appears a representation of a certain fruit called *prekese,* which has a very strong smell. This signifies that the Asantehene is omnipresent: like the *prekese,* he is to be sensed even where he is not seen; in other words, no gossip or plotting can evade his hearing" (Fraser 1972a:145–46). The king owns 23 umbrellas, each reserved for a special occasion.

The art works owned by Ashanti political leaders serve a variety of uses—aesthetic, history-recording, religious, and patriotic. But without doubt they also serve another purpose: They stand as constant, awe-inspiring proof that their owners are the most powerful people in the kingdom.

Lega Art and Ethical Education

Ashanti art is a publicly visible expression of the proper relationship between follower and leader. In other cultural contexts, art provides a model for proper behavior between all people in a given society. It can, for example, be used as an adjunct to moral or ethical education. The Lega of Central Africa provide an excellent example of such a didactic use of art.

The Lega number about 250,000; most adult males are members of an important voluntary association called *bwami* (Biebuyck 1968, 1972). The *bwami* is hierarchical in structure, composed of five grades (with three complementary grades for women), each grade being subdivided into a number of subgrades. All men aspire to an elevated position in the hierarchy, but advancement in the association comes only to the few who are most enterprising, who can marshal sufficient support from other members, and who can accumulate the large quantities of goods that are needed for gifts and payments. At the pinnacle of the hierarchy are those few men, always over the age of 50, who have attained the highest subgrade of the *kindi* grade. These men, whom Biebuyck calls aristocrats, "are looked upon as outstanding examples of virtue and morality. They have passed through all initiatory experiences, assimilated the teachings and values connected with them, and for that reason they are also considered the very wisest" (1972:12).

It is in the moral training of the initiates of the upper *bwami* grades that art enters the picture. Lega art includes figurines of humans and animals made of ivory, pottery, bone, wood, and wickerwork; most of it is owned by members of the highest grades of the *bwami* association. Initiation of new members into these grades of the association provides the most important occasion for use of Lega art. Each statue is associated with certain proverbs, and these proverbs provide moral training for the initiates, graphically illustrating a behavior that is either praiseworthy or, more often, reprehensible. For example, Biebuyck describes one figure as a carved stick

> whose top is slit so as to suggest an open mouth. . . . The object illustrates the saying, "He who does not put off his quarrelsomeness will quarrel with something that has the mouth widely distended." (In other rites this idea may be rendered by a crocodile figurine with widely distended jaws). The aphorism alludes to the disastrous effects of quarrelsomeness and meddlesomeness (Biebuyck 1973:217).

Biebuyck (1973:184–226) describes a vast number of other Lega items—both natural and manufactured art works—that are used in *bwami* ceremonies. Each is associated with from one to twenty or more aphorisms. Any one aphorism considered in isolation may seem trivial; but taken as a whole, the corpus represents an overwhelming compendium of Lega ethical ideals.

Art and the Social Order

In all the examples given thus far, the relationship between art and cultural stability has been overt, obvious, and relatively amenable to description and study. But what about the deeper relationships between art and the social order? Many writers (among them Adams 1973; Paul 1976;

L. Thompson 1945; Lévi-Strauss 1963, 1970; Fraser 1955; Hatcher 1974) have suggested that in a particular society the predominant art styles mirror the basic cultural values of the society—values so fundamental that they may not be explicitly verbalized by members of the society itself.

An example of such a subtle relationship between art and culture is given by James Fernandez in his account of the aesthetic values of the Fang of equatorial Africa:

> The data suggest that what are given in Fang life, what are basic, are two sets of opposition. One is spatial, right and left, northeast and southwest; the other is qualitative, male and female. Both the social structure and the aesthetic life elaborate on these basic oppositions and create vitality in so doing. . . .
>
> In both aesthetics and the social structure the aim of the Fang is not to resolve opposition and create identity but to preserve a balanced opposition. This is accomplished either through alternation as in the case of complementary filiation [i.e., kinship] or in the behavior of a full man; or it is done by skillful aesthetic composition in the same time and space as is the case with the ancestor statues of cult ritual (Fernandez 1971:373).

Nancy Munn's work among the Australian Walbiri, discussed at length in Chapter 3, provides another example of art functioning as a "cultural gyroscope," as Bellah (1965:173) has termed similar symbolic systems.

Claims such as these are quite intriguing. If they are valid, if a society's aesthetic values mirror its nonaesthetic values, then the ethnographic payoff for studies of art would be great indeed. The difficulty lies in the fact that such claims tend to be highly speculative. What may seem patently obvious to one observer may seem sheer fantasy to another. And the deeper the relationship that is hypothesized between art and culture for a given society, the more difficult it is to support the hypothesis empirically.

One way out of this dilemma has been suggested by John L. Fischer (1971). Fischer asked: Is there generally a relationship between a society's social structure and certain stylistic aspects of the society's art? To find an answer, he compared the results of two previously published cross-cultural surveys. In one of these, Berry had examined art from 30 different non-Western societies, ranking them according to 18 different criteria (Berry 1957:380). For example, he ranked the societies with respect to the *symmetry* of their art, ranging from the relatively symmetrical works of the Yakut, Teton, and Omaha, to the relatively asymmetric art of Bali, Dahomey, and Alor. For statistical simplicity, Berry contrasted two groups—the 15 societies with more symmetric art versus the 15 with more asymmetric art.

In the other cross-cultural study that Fischer utilized, George Peter Murdock had previously evaluated a large number of societies with respect to numerous sociological variables. For example, he considered the *degree of social stratification* of societies, specifying such things as whether or not a

society has numerous social castes or classes, whether there was a hereditary aristocracy, and so on (Murdock 1957:675).

Drawing on these two surveys Fischer was able to look for correlations
between numerous sociological variables and art style variables—for example, between stratification of society and symmetry of art. By performing
some relatively simple statistical manipulations, he found that these two
particular variables were indeed correlated: The odds are better than twenty to one that if a society is highly stratified socially, it will produce relatively
asymmetrical art, whereas a society with little social stratification will more
than likely have symmetrical art. As the probabilistic aspects of this statement indicate, there can be exceptions to the rule, but the great strength of
the statistical method adopted by Fischer is that these cases are shown to be
just that—exceptions. (The existence of numerous exceptions does, however, lead one to a conclusion that may be arrived at from several other
directions—namely, that the relationship between art and culture is seldom
obvious and straightforward. Thus, the use of a society's art alone as a basis
for deducing its fundamental cultural features or *Zeitgeist* is risky at best.)

As tedious as statistical studies such as Fischer's may seem, cross-
cultural surveys are invaluable for our understanding of the social and
cultural functions of art. If Fischer's findings are valid, one can conclude
that whatever else art does, it provides "a sort of map of the society in
which the artist—and his public—live" (Fischer 1971:159).[5] The relationship between the map and the terrain it represents may not be simple
or perfectly accurate, but insofar as there *is* a correspondence, art must be
seen as a conservative, rather than innovative, expression of culture. Art
gives legitimacy to the traditional way of doing (or thinking about) things,
providing a tangible support for the status quo.

Such a conclusion leads us to ask a further question: What features of
art make it widely useful as a means for aiding cultural stability? There are,
I think, several answers to this question.

First, art can be (and art in most small-scale societies is) representational. Thus, it has an unlimited potential for recording in a tangible and
(usually) lasting form information that would otherwise be lost to the past.
This history- and precedent-recording ability of art works is particularly
valuable in nonliterate societies. (Viewing art in this light, it is easy to see
how some writing systems evolved from pictograms, thus institutionalizing
the communicative capacity of art.)

Second, art can be (and typically is) public in nature, providing a
medium for communication between large numbers of people; and the

---

[5]Fischer's study, though seminal, has a number of serious methodological shortcomings. His conclusions should be validated and expanded by studies that (1) are based on a
larger number of societies with less geographic bias; (2) use better sampling techniques for
choosing the art to be considered from each society; (3) use more than one judge for the
evaluation of art styles; and (4) use more sophisticated tests for correlation. Works by Robbins
(1966) and Dressler and Robbins (1975) have been valuable additions to this line of inquiry.

message remains largely intact from place to place and from one time to another.

Third, the explicit message communicated by art can be made even more potent by the evocative, affective level of the medium. When art speaks, we listen—both with our heads and with our hearts.

Continuity and change are necessarily present in every society, but traditional societies typically exhibit more of the former than of the latter. Stability does not occur automatically, but must be constantly maintained in the face of individual needs that are contrary to traditional patterns. What is needed is a means of encoding traditional norms, disseminating them to the population at large, maintaining them for future generations and, if possible, doing all this in such a way that the population will "get the message." Art, in all the diverse ways discussed in this section, may be called upon to perform these duties, and often it does so in a highly effective way.

ART AND THE SUPERNATURAL

Judging from many museum collections of art from small-scale societies, where item after item is labeled "fertility god," "ancestral figure," "fetish," or "altar piece," one might conclude that art in small-scale societies is predominantly, if not wholly, used for religious purposes. Such is absolutely not the case. For example, the Chokwe of central Africa produce only insignificant religious artifacts—miniature charms and shrine figures that any Chokwe adult male is capable of producing. Chokwe secular art, by contrast, is very highly developed, produced by a small number of professional artists—predominantly carvers and blacksmiths, but also potters, tailors, matmakers, and basketmakers (Crowley 1972:25). Most of their produce is totally secular in its use, providing furnishings and decorations for chiefs' houses. In addition, some Chokwe art straddles the borderline between sacred and profane—masks made for stock characters (*mikishi*) in traditional dances, for example. But even for works in this genre, while

> it would be deceptively simple to describe the *mikishi* as the deities of the Chokwe . . . , actually the Creator god, Nzambi or Kalunga, is aloof from the affairs of men and never appears in inconography. In the contemporary Congo, where half the Chokwe are Christian, the religious aspect of the *mikishi* might be compared to that of Santa Claus in an American city—figures of ancient piety now reduced to generalized symbols of festivity (Crowley 1972:25).

Art is also predominantly—or wholly—secular among the West African Tiv (Bohannan 1971), Bush Negroes of Dutch Guiana, South America (Herskovits 1959), and in the traditional cultures of Madagascar (Linton 1941), to name just a few documented cases.

Rather than conceiving art to be universally the handmaiden of religion (or vice versa), it is more profitable to note the similarities between art and religion in regard to what they each do and how they do it. Religion, like art, serves various needs, but one of its more common functions is the contribution it makes to the maintenance of social stability and cultural homeostasis through its embodiment of both an ethos and a set of ethical principles that are more or less shared by all members of the society. As shown in the preceding section, art very often performs a similar homeostatic function. Furthermore, as Marvin Harris has noted, art, religion, and magic

> satisfy similar psychological needs in human beings. They are media for expressing sentiments and emotions not easily expressed in ordinary life. They impart a sense of mastery over or communion with unpredictable events and mysterious unseen powers. They impose human meanings and values upon an indifferent world—a world that has no humanly intelligible meanings and values of its own. They seek to penetrate behind the facade of ordinary appearance into the true, cosmic significance of things (Harris 1975:583).

Moreover, art, religion, and magic attain these goals in similar ways: Arbitrary distinctions are made—for art, between the beautiful and the ugly; for religion, between the sacred and the profane; for magic, between that which can and cannot be controlled by humans. And these distinctions become culturally encoded traditions, handed down from generation to generation by means of emotionally charged socialization of the young.

Thus, the realms of art and of the supernatural may be similar in many respects. In a given society the two phenomena may intersect, performing similar functions in parallel and mutually reinforcing ways. Alternatively, the two may operate independently of each other, drawing, perhaps, on related subject matter, but using it to different ends. Thus, for example, the art of the Pacific Northwest Coast, described in Chapter 3, uses mythic people and animals as subject matter, but the ends are by and large secular, namely the glorification of the aristocratic families that sponsor the art.

Future research may shed light on such questions as: What factors predispose a society to support secular, rather than sacred, art? When is art distinct from religion and magic? What is the interplay between the three institutions?[6]

[6]The notion that art evolved from religion is sheerly speculative, based on one possible interpretation of Paleolithic art, especially the extant cave paintings of Europe. Some of these paintings may indeed have been prompted by religious belief systems, although one might equally plausibly argue that in these cases art inspired religion, rather than the other way around. In any case, not all of the ancient cave art can be so simplistically explained. Ucko and Rosenfeld (1967) provide a critical survey of the various theories that have been proposed to account for Paleolithic art.

PORTFOLIO

The Arts of New Guinea

FIGURE 2-2 Map of New Guinea, with major art areas.

Lying near the equator, north of Australia and east of Indonesia, the large island of New Guinea is an important resource for students of non-Western cultures and their art. New Guinea was one of the last major regions of the world to be explored by Westerners, and most indigenous institutions there remained viable well into the twentieth century. Field workers in New Guinea's luxuriant coastal regions and mountainous interior have found thousands of tribes, each with its own unique culture. Subsistence is based on small-garden horticulture, sometimes supplemented by hunting, gathering, and fishing. Political integration rarely extends beyond the village, and intervillage hostility is common. Thus, New Guinea gives us a unique opportunity to study traditional, stone-tool-using people who live in a state little influenced by colonialism.

New Guinean cultures are rich in ceremonialism, a fact that leads to another reason for our interest in the island. New Guinean religions generally posit a world controlled by mythical and ancestral spirits. These must be propitiated, and the necessary rituals require many kinds of art production. Some idea of the extravagance of art production in New Guinea is seen in the testimony of Anthony Forge, who lived with the Abelam of the Sepik District for more than two years. Within a five-mile radius of his base village, Forge counted more than a hundred large ceremonial houses, each filled with carved and painted art work. During one six-month ceremonial season, Forge's Abelam neighbors built more than 15 cult houses, complete with paintings. Such an enormous production of art probably puts the Abelam ahead of the "art capitals" of the Western world in sheer quantity of artistic activity.

The ancestors of today's Pacific islanders originally came from Southeast Asia, and New Guinean art still resembles Indonesian art somewhat. But most of it has such a distinctive style that even the novice is soon able to recognize New Guinean art works in museum collections.

The traditional New Guinean artist works with stone tools, and although sand and sharkskin are sometimes used to smooth wood, the relative simplicity of available technology is apparent in the unrefined quality of most visual art from New Guinea. (Note, for example, the contrast between the works shown here and those of West and Central African art described in Chapter 1.)

But New Guinean art is most distinctive for its expressive quality: It is spectacular, dramatic, and vigorous. The robust power of cult spirits and ancestors is everywhere apparent in the art made in their honor. Moreover, the spirits typically transcend humans in their physical features. Therefore, although most subjects have human or animal features, individual traits may be fantastic in scale (with, for example, greatly oversized noses) and some figures combine the attributes of more than one species—for example, the head of a long-beaked bird atop the body of a human. (Again, the contrast with the relatively more naturalistic art of Africa is instructive.)

With a population of more than 3 million people, an area considerably larger than that of Texas, and with over 700 mutually unintelligible languages being spoken, one would hardly expect New Guinea to be culturally and artistically homogeneous, and a closer look at New Guinean art does indeed reveal various discrete style areas (cf. Linton and Wingert [1946], Wingert [1962], and Guiart [1963]). Starting in northwestern New Guinea and moving clockwise around its coast, several areas of particular importance should be noted. (See map, Figure 2-2).

Ancestor figures known as *korovars* are made in the Geelvinck Bay region. Their blocky, cubistic heads (which sometimes hold a human skull) are distinctive for their large size, the protrusion of the lower face, and their eyebrows that join with the nose at the middle and are pointed at their ends.

Standing ancestral figures are made to the east around Lake Sentani, too, where clan totems are also painted on bark cloth. These, as well as utilitarian items such as bowls, canoe prows and paddles, and lime spatulas and containers, are made in a style that is more softly molded than elsewhere (Figure 2-3).

The Sepik District lies midway along the northern coast of New Guinea, extending far inland along the Sepik and Ramu rivers. In addition to the dramatic architecture, carving (Figure 2-4), painting, basketry (Figure 2-5), clay modeling, and body decoration also proliferate in the Sepik. By any reckoning the Sepik is surely one of the most artistically fertile areas in the world; and, fortunately, sufficient fieldwork has been carried out to allow outsiders such as ourselves to get a rare glimpse of the philosophical ideas that underlie art production in this non-Western setting.

In the Sepik, men dominate religion and art, and a theme common to both is the display of male dominance over, and protection from, those forces that men feel threatened by, namely the dangerous sexuality of their own women and the aggressive competition of their male

FIGURE 2-3 Chisel from Lake
Sentani area of New Guinea. Wood,
iron, and rattan; 42 cm. long.
*(Courtesy The Saint Louis Art Museum.
Gift of Morton D. May.)*

FIGURE 2-4 Ceremonial plaque,
Sepik River Area, New Guinea.
*(Courtesy Field Museum of Natural
History, Chicago.)*

enemies. We can only speculate as to why Sepik men are so insecure
about these issues, but the theme of assertive masculinity is clearly
apparent in the visual style of Sepik art. For example, not only psy-
choanalytically inclined Westerners but also the Sepik men themselves
view the exaggerated noses found on most Sepik masks as having
phallic associations and as being expressive of male power and ag-
gressiveness (see Figures 2-4 and 2-5; cf. also Anderson, in press,
Chapter 5).

Moving east from the Sepik to the Huon Gulf a somewhat more
schematic style of art appears in geometric decorations painted on

ancestral masks, bowls, cups, and neckrests (see Figure 2-6). The designs are owned by individual clans and form a link between the clan's male members and their ancestors.

Rounding the eastern tip of New Guinea and moving into the Papuan Gulf, large masks and ceremonial boards appear, painted with both angular and curvilinear designs which are, again, clan-owned (Figure 2-7). The impressive scale of the Papuan Gulf continues as one moves westward into the Asmat area, famous for its 20-foot-high *bis*—poles carved with stylized humans and animals. Ceremonial shields displaying geometric designs also are made (see Figure 2-8).

In addition to these major art-producing areas around the perimeter of New Guinea, the interior highlands are rich in art. There the

FIGURE 2-5   Iatmul mask from New Guinea's Sepik District, made of basketry, with clay, wood, bamboo, paint, and feathers; 103 cm. high. *(Nelson Gallery-Atkins Museum, Kansas City, Missouri. Gift of Mr. and Mrs. Herbert Baker.)*

FIGURE 2-6 Carved wooden head rest. Huon Gulf, New Guinea. *(Courtesy Field Museum of Natural History, Chicago.)*

FIGURE 2-7 Ancestor tablet. Carved and painted wood. Maipua, Purari Delta, Gulf of Papua, New Guinea. *(Courtesy Field Museum of Natural History, Chicago.)*

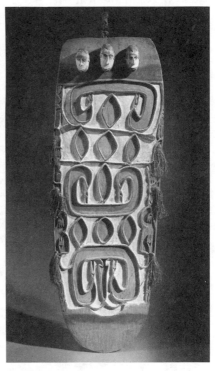

FIGURE 2-8 Asmat war shield. Wood and fiber, with red, black, and white paint; 169 cm. high. *(Courtesy The Saint Louis Art Museum. Gift of Morton D. May.)*

decoration of the human body replaces carving and painting as the primary medium of aesthetic expression.

The richness and diversity of the visual arts of New Guinea are remarkable. They provide students of non-Western art with samples of work that are at once affecting and alien to Western sensibilities. Fully appreciating their appearance and understanding their significance will be important challenges for years to come.

CONCLUSIONS

Even the most superficial acquaintance with art from small-scale societies should convince the Westerner that it is mostly "about" people. Walk through a gallery of art from small-scale societies and most of the pieces you see will depict people or animals with human qualities. As Firth noted some time ago, "The essentially social character of primitive art is reflected in [the] forms themselves. There is almost entire absence of landscape. What depiction of landscape does exist appears as subsidiary material in hunting scenes and the like" (1951:173).

Viewed in its social and cultural context, art in such societies is far from a useless luxury. It does give enjoyment, to be sure (if indeed this may be considered a luxury). But it also often plays an important role in the economic and political realms, as the examples in this chapter have illustrated. In addition, it probably serves other functions that have as yet been little studied. It may, for example, record history for a prehistoric people; or it might serve as a testing and practice ground for developing skills that are primarily useful for subsistence activities or defense. Throughout this chapter I have tried to emphasize the fact that art can—and typically does—do many things. An understanding of the functions of art in small-scale societies helps one avoid simplistic, naive misconceptions about the nature of art in general. When one becomes aware of the rich texture of the functional context of art in a particular society, he or she begins to view it in a way that approaches that of a native member of the society—that is, as a vital and necessary part of culture.

GUIDE TO ADDITIONAL READINGS

Functionalism A vast amount of twentieth-century British and American anthropological writing reflects the functionalist approach. Classic ethnographies are Radcliffe-Brown's *The Andaman Islanders* (1964 [orig. 1922]) and Malinowski's *Argonauts of the Western Pacific* (1922). Rappaport's *Pigs for the Ancestors* (1968, 1984) is a contemporary functionalist *tour de force.* Hempel (1959) discusses the shortcomings of the functionalist approach.

Art and Cultural Homeostasis   Sieber (1962) and the essays collected by Fraser and Cole in *African Art and Leadership* (1972a) provide a variety of case studies of art fulfilling political functions. Biebuyck's *Lega Culture* (1973) is an excellent study of the interaction of art, education, and ethical values. Witherspoon's *Language and Art in the Navajo Universe* (1977) is a masterful study of Navajo culture via art and language. Outside the visual arts, Chernoff's (1979) *African Rhythm and African Sensibility* provides an excellent account of the interplay of moral and ethical values in the education of Ghanaian drummers.

CHAPTER 3

Iconography and Symbolism

When we first look at a work of art from a small-scale society we are immediately struck by its appearance—the colors that are used, its shape, the materials from which it is made, and so on. But often there is more to a piece than first meets the eye: Its appearance may have some meaning behind it; its maker may have intended to remind the viewer of certain things or people, events or ideas that transcend the piece itself. It may, in short, be symbolic or iconographic.

Symbolism is a huge topic, permeating virtually all spheres of human society and culture. Some writers have even claimed that our ability to use symbols defines our very humanness (cf., for example, White 1959; Langer 1951). In any case, symbolism is a very important component of art in some small-scale societies. The present chapter discusses the most central subjects related to symbolism, using as illustrations the art of the Pacific Northwest and of the Walbiri of west-central Australia.

WHAT IS A SYMBOL?

The word "symbol" has had a long and interesting career in Western thought. More than 2,000 years ago the Greeks used the word *sumbolos* to refer to the rejoining of a thing that had been divided or broken in two. For example, two friends might break a token in half, each of them keeping one of the halves. The fact that the two parts—and only they—could be rejoined to form the whole was proof of the common bond of friendship between the two individuals. Already in this early usage of symbol there was a meaning that still often recurs: Some tangible item (the divided token) was being used to stand for an abstract idea (friendship).

Symbol was redefined and broadened in meaning by the early Christian writers, and since then other nuances have continued to accrue to the term so that today it has a whole range of meanings. Some indication of the breadth of this range is illustrated by the fact that while some items may be disparagingly referred to as "mere" symbols, to call other things "symbolic" is to elevate them in importance far above their mundane meaning.

The common denominator of many of the current usages of symbol derives from the work of the influential nineteenth-century writer Charles S. Peirce. Professionally, Peirce was a physicist and astronomer, working most of his life for the United States Coast and Geodetic Survey. But in addition to his activities as a scientist, Peirce was also a tough-minded philosopher who published essays in various scholarly journals and corresponded with other philosophers of his day. He developed many ideas that proved seminal to modern symbolic logic, information theory, and semiotics. (This last field was begun by Peirce himself—he called it "semeiotics"— and consists of the systematic study of signs and meanings. It has been useful in areas ranging from computer theory to animal communication.)

Peirce's work is relevant here because of his approach to the definition of symbol. He began by noting that in our everyday lives some things are commonly taken as indications of other things. Peirce called all such things *signs,* and went on to make a useful distinction between three types of signs—index, icon, and symbol. These terms are used throughout the rest of this chapter, so it is important that their exact meanings be made clear at this point.

An *index,* according to Peirce's definition, is a sign that emerges from some natural phenomenon rather than being an arbitrary convention of culture. For example, a person's pulse is an index that he or she is alive. It's an index rather than an icon or symbol because the relationship between pulse and being alive stems from natural features of the human body; clearly it is not something that humans have merely agreed upon by cultural convention.

Both icons and symbols, however, derive from human convention; they are products of culture rather than of nature. The difference between icons and symbols is that icons bear some resemblance to the thing for which they are a sign; symbols, by contrast, bear no resemblance to their referents. Consider, for example, two roadsigns that might be seen along a rural highway. One has on it only a silhouette picture of a running deer, the other simply says Deer Crossing. In Peirce's nomenclature the first sign is an *icon* in that the thing itself (the painted metal sign) bears some resemblance to the thing it signifies (a deer running across the highway). The second roadsign with its printed message is a *symbol* because there is absolutely no visible resemblance between its appearance and the deer the sign is warning motorists of. (Thus, the ancient Greek *sumbolos*—a token or coin that two friends break in half and divide between them—is still a symbol in the Peircean sense: The token is something that, by convention, stands for something else, namely, a bond of close friendship.)

Index, icon, and symbol—three types of signs. The categories are not clearly demarcated, of course. Signs that at first seem to be symbols, for example, often turn out to have some resemblance to the thing they represent. That is, they are slightly iconic. But despite this problem Peirce's approach can be accepted for what it is, namely a useful set of terms that help clarify discussions about art and other forms of human communication.

THE ICONOGRAPHY OF NORTHWEST COAST INDIAN SCULPTURE

The native tribes that lived along the Pacific Northwest Coast of North America, from what is now the state of Oregon in the south, to Yakutat Bay in Alaska in the north, are justly famous. The Tlingit, Tsimshian, Haida, Bellabella, Bella Coola, Kwakiutl, and Coast Salish produced art in such great quantities and of such striking appearance that its media, materials, and styles will be the topic of the Portfolio in Chapter 4.

Here, though, we are interested only in the symbolic conventions whereby Northwest Coast art uses iconography and symbolism to communicate meaning. To understand this topic one needs only to know that these prehorticultural peoples produced art based on religious themes for use in ceremony, personal decoration, and public display. The figures portrayed in Northwest Coast art were actually owned by individuals and were a mark of the social rank of their owners. Like European family crests, they were inherited or acquired through marriage, warfare, or other means. Most seem to have been associated with traditional stories or myths. Some represented a single creature; others portrayed several of the personae of a given myth. Into this last category fall many of the so-called totem poles—"so-called" because as anthropologists have come to use the word, a totem is a thing, often an animal or a plant, with which an individual (or a kin group such as a clan) has a special religious or ritualistic relationship such as mutual protection. Noble Northwest Coast families owned specific folk tales, and the characters in the stories were carved on poles to be used as burial or commemorative objects, but the families had no special supernatural relationship with the animals or people who played roles in the stories and were portrayed on the poles. Hence, the figures on the poles were not "totemic" in the strict sense of the word.

Northwest Coast Iconography

Northwest Coast art is, in Peirce's terms, iconographic. That is, people and animals are depicted in a conventionalized manner, and at least in some ways the designs bear a palpable resemblance to the person or animal depicted. The interesting aspect of the art, however, is the manner and extent of the resemblance. Some pieces strike us as being quite literal, as in the case of the Northwest Coast portrait mask shown in Figure 3–1. Not only is the Native American physiognomy very accurately rendered, but the grain of the wood has been used in such a way as to suggest a furrowed brow.

Much Northwest Coast art, however, is the result of varying degrees of stylization so that the resemblance between the work and the person or animal represented becomes increasingly tenuous, passing through several steps of conventionalization. To begin with, the artist could ignore or modify many details of a given animal, retaining only those traits that were considered definitive for the species. An example will make this technique clear. Figure 3–2 shows a Tlingit carving. Someone unfamiliar with Northwest Coast art would probably identify it as representing an animal of some sort, or perhaps a person with abnormally large front teeth. The maker of this piece, however, would tell us that he has depicted not just any animal; for him, it's obviously a beaver. Why? Because the position of the ears indicates it to be a nonhuman animal, and because it has two large front teeth, a scaly tail (indicated by the hatching on the roundish area at the bottom center), and its forepaws are raised as if the animal were holding a stick—as, indeed, the beaver does in some Northwest Coast sculptures. All of these, in the shorthand of Northwest Coast iconography, are characteristics specific to the beaver. The short nose with spiral nostrils is also often found in representations of beavers, but this may be omitted or changed at the discretion of the artist. Indeed, necessity may force the artist to modify or omit any of the details except the enlarged incisors and the scaly tail; the figure will still be recognized as a beaver (Boas 1955:186). Other species were similarly stylized: The hawk always had a large curved beak whose point curved back to touch its face; the frog, always a wide, toothless mouth, a flat nose, and no tail; and so on.

Some features were semidistinctive for each species as well. For example, beavers' eyes were usually (but not always) represented by Kwakiutl artists as being shorter and higher than the eyes of eagles (see Figure 3–3).

The next possible step in stylization that the Northwest Coast artist might take was to rearrange the component parts of a given animal in order to fill the area he wished to decorate. Often this was done by conceptually cutting the animal along a few lines and spreading out the resultant

FIGURE 3-2 Tlingit model housepost. Collected ca. 1900. Whalebone with abalone inlay, 51 cm. high. *(Courtesy Kansas City Museum of History and Science.)*

FIGURE 3-1 Northwest Coast portrait mask, probably Tlingit. Wood with paint, 20 cm. high. *(Courtesy Donald D. Jones.)*

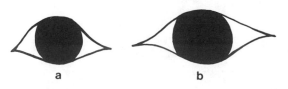

a   b

FIGURE 3-3 Stylized representations of animal eyes, Kwakiutl. (a) Beaver. (b) Eagle. *(After Boas, 1955.)*

parts so as to fill the design field. Another example will illustrate the technique: Figure 3–4 shows a Haida or Tsimshian dancing hat made of spruce roots. It is in the shape of a truncated cone; to its top would have been attached a series of rings, each ring symbolizing a step up the social ladder. In the first drawing the hat is viewed from above so that only the decorations on the wide conical brim of the hat are seen; the second drawing gives a side view of the front and back of the hat's conical top.

The decoration of such hats presented Northwest Coast artists with a difficult problem in that the design field was basically circular with an empty space in the middle. How could the decoration—in this case the beaver figure we met in the previous example—be distributed around such an oddly shaped field? The artist ingeniously solved the problem by imagining a three-dimensional beaver complete with its distinctively large incisors, hatched tail, erect ears, and forepaws in front of his body. This he conceptually split down the middle, leaving only the face and tail intact. The two resultant profile views were unfolded and stretched out to fill the design field. The final product might initially strike us as being totally abstract, but a closer look confirms that all the crucial parts are present: the two front teeth (d), the hatched tail (a), the erect ears (b), the forepaws held in front of the body (e). (The forepaws are not holding a stick in this instance.) To fit the face into its allotted space, the usually roundish beaver eyes (c) have been elongated to very narrow forms; and in this case the hind legs are shown folded under the beaver as if it were sitting up on them.

The parts of the beaver shown in Figure 3–4, though split and unfolded, are still more or less in proper relation to each other. The manipulative process can be carried one step further, however, so that the disassembled parts are distributed around the design field with only the most tenuous resemblance between their placement on the field and their ana-

FIGURE 3-4   Conical hat decorated with beaver design, Haida or Tsimshian. Left, view from above. Right, side view of upper portion. *(After Boas, 1955.)*

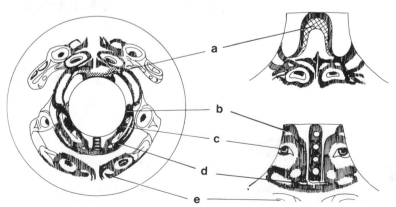

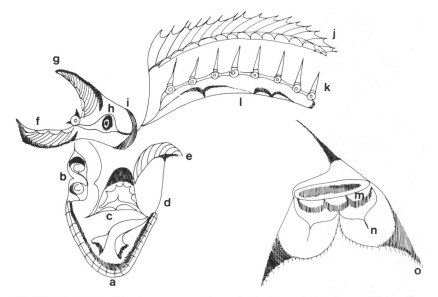

FIGURE 3-5   Kwakiutl representation of a halibut. *(After Boas, 1955).*

tomical locations. Figure 3–5 illustrates this final step in the process. Boas' interpretation of the parts of this particularly striking Kwakiutl design is as follows:

> [The figure] represents the halibut; (a) the mouth and over it the nose, (b) the eyes, (c) the bone of the top of the head and (d) the side of the head. In (e) are shown the gills; (f) and (g) represent the intestinal tract, and (h) is the part of the intestinal tract just under the neck; (i) is the collar bone, (j) the lateral fin, the bones of which are shown in (k). (l) is the clotted blood that is found in the dead halibut under the vertebral column; (m) represents the joint of the tail, (n) part of the bone in the tail, and (o) the tip of the tail (Boas 1955:205).

Carried to this extreme degree of stylization it is not surprising that Northwest Coast Indians themselves had problems interpreting their own art. There are numerous recorded instances of individuals, even highly regarded artists who, when presented with a piece they had never seen before, "explained" the meanings of parts of the figures in ways that contradicted other native interpretations of the same piece. For example, John R. Swanton (cited in Boas 1955:209), an early ethnographer of Northwest Coast culture, asked two different individuals for an explanation of the Haida housepost shown in Figure 3–6. Both agreed that the figure at the top of the post represented an eagle. But one told Swanton that the lower part related the story of a woman who was carried away by a killer-whale: Her face, he said, is shown just below the eagle's beak, and the large figure at the bottom is the whale. The face just above that of the whale stands

FIGURE 3-6 Haida housepost. *(After Boas, 1955.)*

for the whale's blowhole. Swanton was given a very different interpretation of the housepost by the second person, who maintained that the large face at the bottom was that of a grizzly bear, perhaps meaning a sea-grizzly bear; the small figure above its back was a "sea ghost," a character that usually rides on the back of a sea-grizzly bear. This person gave no explanation whatsoever for the small upper face.

Examples of multiple interpretations should not be overemphasized. Northwest Coast art relies upon elaborate and widely shared techniques of stylization. There is no question that the original maker of a piece, his apprentices, the patron for whom it was constructed, and other members of the immediate community knew the exact intended meaning of an elaborate carving or blanket.

Northwest Coast Art as Traditional Status Symbol

The preceding paragraphs have described the iconographic aspects of Northwest Coast art. In this style, individual pieces are conventional representations, usually of people or animals, and the works resemble, to a greater or lesser degree, the things they are supposed to represent. Often the iconic interpretations extend far beyond the piece itself. An individual mask, for instance, may be a visual token that recalls to the native viewer an elaborate folk tale, comparable to the way a picture (or carving) of Pinnochio would remind us of the whole moral tale associated with the little boy and his distinctively long nose.

But Northwest Coast art is also in some ways symbolic in the strict Peircean sense of the word. A piece carries with it a message that bears no palpable resemblance to the image itself: It is a "status symbol." The totem poles, houseposts, and most of the masks were signs of the high social standing of their owners. Even if a native viewer did not accurately decipher the iconic message of a given art work, he or she undoubtedly appreciated the social significance of the piece. The quantity and elaborateness of the works of art possessed by a person were public statements of the individual's relative position in the social hierarchy. As we know, members of Northwest Coast societies were vitally concerned with their relative social standing, so to them the symbolic messages transmitted via their art were far from trivial.

For us, these explicitly symbolic aspects of Northwest Coast art might be something of a disappointment. Some time ago Frederic Douglas and Rene D'Harnoncourt wrote, with regard to American Indian art, "The word *symbol* has always had a great appeal to buyers of Indian curios, who love to think they can purchase a mystery and a half with every souvenir" (1941:14). Although our own interest goes deeper than that of the souvenir hunter, we may share the hope that all symbols in art from small-scale societies conceal a "mystery and a half." But in the case of Northwest Coast art we have found that although individual pieces do indeed carry iconic and symbolic messages, these messages are hardly mysterious. A given item probably represented a specific person or animal; this being was probably associated with a folk tale that was largely of significance only to the family that owned it; and the only really symbolic message was its indication of the owner's social standing. It may be a puzzle for us, as nonnatives, to learn these meanings, but once discovered they hardly provide a key for an in-depth understanding of Northwest Coast culture as a whole.

But by now we are well aware of the enormous diversity that exists in art cross-culturally. If "mystery-and-a-half" symbols are not to be found in Northwest Coast art, then the symbolism of other art styles may meet our high expectations. The art of the societies of central Australia, such as the Walbiri, is a good candidate for such further study.

THE WALBIRI OF CENTRAL AUSTRALIA AND THEIR ART

The Walbiri live in a region that we Westerners might consider to be one of the least hospitable in the world, namely, the desert region of west-central Australia. In sharp contrast to the lush environment of the Northwest Coast American Indians, the Walbiri inhabit a region where water is found only in natural depressions in rocks in the ranges of outcrops and low-lying hills that run through their land, or else is collected from the bottoms of holes dug in dry creek beds into which water slowly seeps. Lacking agriculture the Walbiri traditionally derived their subsistence solely from gathering numerous kinds of vegetable foods and from hunting wild game. They resided in small, semi-nomadic bands that traveled from water hole to water hole, living at each for as long as local supplies of water, food, and game lasted. Eventually their travels would bring them back to their starting place, and the cycle would begin again. This pattern of constant circling from place to place is a recurrent theme in both the mythology and art of the Walbiri.

Between 1956 and 1958 Nancy Munn spent 11 months living near a group of about 375 Walbiri who resided in the vicinity of a government settlement at Yuendumu. Munn concentrated her study on Walbiri art and religion, and the rich data she collected have appeared in numerous publications (Munn 1962, 1964, 1970, 1971, 1973, 1974).

Much of Walbiri art is concerned with the people's religious beliefs, a complex subject in itself. Munn's summary of Walbiri religion will suffice here. The Walbiri, she states,

> have a typical central Australian totemic ideology involving belief in innumerable ancestral beings whose travels created the topography of the country. Many of these are personified aspects of the environment such as rain or honey ant; but others are wholly human or nonhuman.
>
> The ancestors and the times in which they travelled are called *djugurba,* a term that also means "dream." Walbiri men say that the ancestors, sleeping in their camps at different sites, dreamed their songs, graphic designs, and ceremonial paraphernalia. These phenomena record their travels, and the gist of Walbiri views on this matter seems to be that they also dreamed the world they created in their travels; as one man suggested, they dreamed their track (*yiriyi*) (Munn 1974:195).

A final feature of Walbiri society of relevance here is the "lodge," a ceremonial group composed of all initiated males in one locality who are related to each other through male lines of kinship. Each lodge has associated with it certain totemic ancestors. The relationship is a reciprocal one, with the lodge members feeling that they both influence, and are influenced by, the ancestors to whom they are related. In practice, an ancestor oversees the ritual ceremonies performed by members of its associated lodge, and the lodge members are responsible for caring for the symbolic paraphernalia used in the ceremonies.

Walbiri Art

The Walbiri provide convincing evidence of the pan-human importance of art. Despite the barrenness of their physical environment, the simplicity of their technology, and the sparseness of their population, they produce art—indeed, art of considerable variety and abundance.[1] Walbiri work in the following media: sand drawing, body decoration (using grease, pigments, and the fluff of certain plants and animals), wood, and stone. The latter two media, used only by men, are incised with designs and often rubbed with colored pigments. Elaborate headdresses are also made.

Art occurs in a wide variety of cultural contexts in Walbiri society, ranging from the mundane to the sacred. At one extreme are the informal drawings made in the sand by individuals as they sit on the ground talking or gossiping with each other. Munn (1973) remarks that the Walbiri "regard sand drawing as part of [their] valued mode of life, and as a characteristic aspect of their style of expression and communication. To accompany one's speech with explanatory sand markings is to 'talk' in the Walbiri manner" (p. 58).

More formalized are the "sand stories," told primarily by women, recounting traditional tales of the activities of the ancestors. In addition, both men and women use specific designs for body decoration. Accompanied by the appropriate songs and ceremonies, these will attract members of the opposite sex, or will increase the likelihood of a fertile union. As one man explained, a young married woman "might be painted on the

---

[1]If Walbiri culture has an artistic deficit, it lies in the low level of art specialization that exists in Walbiri society. Apparently all adult Walbiri can (and do) create graphic designs, and Munn makes no references to native standards for judging the relative virtuosity of the makers of designs. Mountford (1961:7), in discussing Australian native art generally, remarks that "all aborigines are natural artists; I have yet to meet one who would not or did not want to paint." But then he goes on to say, "Naturally, some are more skilled than others and take more care" (1961:7). Munn, however, says with respect to Walbiri sand story designs, "There were few married women at Yuendumu who did not have at their command a number of such stories and who could not recount them with fluency, expressiveness, and skilled use of sand graphics and gesture signs" (1973:63).

breasts at a *yawalyu* ceremony to 'make her breasts large' and to 'make the milk come,' that is, to encourage pregnancy" (Munn 1973:43).

The final Walbiri use of art is in the ceremonies performed by men for such important activities as initiating boys into adult manhood, ensuring the procreative powers of the society as a whole, and so on. All of these events require decorated paraphernalia, some pieces of which are created especially for the occasion on which they are used, others being stored by the men in secret locations for use in subsequent ceremonies.

Walbiri Representation

If you look at Figures 3–7 and 3–8, which show several individual Walbiri designs, you might guess them to be purely ornamental with no clear-cut meanings attached to them (like the lines and circles of chrome that decorate most automobiles), or else purely abstract symbols having meanings but not resembling the things they represent. Munn has shown, however, that neither of these guesses is correct: The designs are actually iconographic.

Walbiri art, whatever the medium, uses a single iconographic technique whereby each one of a small number of elementary figures is given

a   b   c

FIGURE 3-7 Elements used in Walbiri sand story figures. (a) Grove of trees. (b) Dancer(s). (c) Nest, hole, water hole, fruits or yams, tree, prepared food, fire, upright fighting stick, painting material, billy can, egg, dog (when curled up in camp), circling movement, encircling object. *After Munn, 1973.)*

FIGURE 3-8 Walbiri representation of a tree. *After Munn, 1973.)*

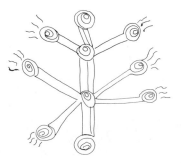

one or more meanings. Figure 3–7 shows three of the elements that women use in telling their sand stories. Note that while the wavy horizontal line (a) has only a single meaning, the circle (c) has 14 meanings and can in fact be used to represent any closed roundish object or any nondirectional, encircling movement.

Note too that if we use our imaginations a little, in every case the element bears some similarity to the item or action it represents. For example, element (b) is in practice drawn by putting the finger in the sand and drawing it down, making scallop after scallop, a movement that resembles the repetitive step-by-step movements of dancers. Or, to take another example, the circle represents a fighting stick—but only one that is sticking in the ground and is thus standing upright. (By contrast, a fighting stick that is lying flat on the ground or being held in a horizontal position is represented by a straight line.)

These elementary Walbiri designs may be used individually or they may be combined to make more elaborate figures with more specific meanings. Figure 3-8, for example, represents a tree. Note that only three elements—straight lines, circles, and wavy lines—are used, and since each may have more than one meaning depending upon where it occurs in the total figure, the elements can be used to represent an unlimited number of items or actions.

A representational system such as that of the Walbiri has both advantages and disadvantages. One might perhaps object that the system is too ambiguous: How is a person to know if a particular circle is intended to represent a water hole, a hill, a tree, or some other roundish object or movement? In practice this is not necessarily a problem because the representational context of the figure usually rules out all but the intended meaning. In the Walbiri case, other media may aid in specifying the intended meaning. For instance, as a woman tells a story she often gives some accompanying verbal narration of the tale so that others (including the anthropologist who is struggling to follow the proceedings) can tell which circle is a water hole, which a hill, and so on. Thus, in the more down-to-earth usages of the Walbiri system of iconography, contextual clues effectively prevent misinterpretation of designs.

The question of ambiguity takes on a new significance, however, for the designs that are used by men for ceremonial purposes. The rituals themselves fall into several categories, but the most important are those from which women are excluded. These include the circumcision and initiation of young men into the adult men's lodges, and the *banba* ceremonies performed by lodge members to insure the procreative power of the group as a whole.

Objects used in these rituals are decorated with figures that are categorically called *guruwari;* Figure 3–9 shows three *guruwari* designs as

FIGURE 3-9 Three Walbiri drawings on paper. (a) Drawing of a ceremonial ground design, ceremonial boards placed around the sides. (b) Drawing of Rainbow Snake design. (c) Drawing of a Honey Ant board design. *(Photos courtesy Nancy Munn.)*

drawn on paper by Walbiri with whom Munn worked. These are made using the system described above: Individual elements are given one or more meanings, and these simple elements are combined to create additional meanings. In the *guruwari* designs, the possibility of multiple meanings is not a liability. Rather, in the minds of Walbiri men, it is an asset that broadens the significance and enhances the power of the designs. A given pattern, by conveying several meanings at once, symbolically demonstrates the interdependence of the individual meanings. The term *guruwari* is itself an example of this. The word refers to a specific design—the actual pattern on a ceremonial object that depicts an ancestor and his activities during the Dreaming. But *guruwari* also refers to the ancestor himself and to his power of enhancing fertility and regeneration. Munn describes this power as "an essentially abstract or invisible potency left by the ancestors in the soil as they travelled through the country. *Guruwari* are both the essential visible forms and the essential invisible potency of the ancestors" (1973:29). In still other senses, *guruwari* refers to the ancestral spirit that enters a woman when she becomes pregnant and stays inside the infant when it is born. When the child grows up it shares this *guruwari* with other members of its lodge. Thus, in the mind of an adult Walbiri, *guruwari* refers to the decoration on a tangible ceremonial object, and it is simultaneously equated with the essence of one's own life and the quintessence of the lodge's procreative power. And, most importantly, each of these meanings is strengthened through its association with the others.

Many *guruwari* designs, because they represent the activities of individual ancestors, include marks indicating the footprints or the tracks left by the ancestor as he travelled through Walbiri country. Here, too, the duality of meaning is valuable:

> When a man identifies conventional prints as *guruwari*, he may mean that they depict the footprints of the ancestor, and therefore are his *guruwari*, or he may be indicating that the prints are a particular ancestral design. Actually, for Walbiri, the one tends to imply the other. . . . Here we meet again with the circle of reality and reference so characteristic of Walbiri thinking: designs are among the marks made by ancestors in the country and they also *represent* such marks (Munn 1973:126).

Munn suggests that in addition to the iconic meanings of Walbiri art that have just been described, the drawings also have more abstract, symbolic meanings. She notes that the stories told in each genre often have recurrent themes. Thus, for example, stories told by women are ostensibly accounts of the mythic activities of the ancestors. But in fact they are seldom fabulous accounts of the deeds of superhuman beings; rather, they tend to be homely tales of individuals who leave camp to gather food and then return to camp, who visit with friends and relations, who have families, and so on. That is, the stories depict the actual day-to-day activities that are experienced by Walbiri women themselves. These tales originate in women's dreams and, as Munn puts it, they are narratives in which "daily experience is, in effect, 'rerun' under the guise of ancestral experience. Its meaningful quality here comes to the fore: Life patterns are validated by being presented to the dreamer as 'tradition,' and yet are still constituted directly within experience" (1973:113).

Whereas the women's chief concerns, both in their daily life and in their art, are the practical problems of food and family, the men are preoccupied with problems of a sociocultural and cosmological nature: the relations between one kin group and another; the pattern of a local band's cyclic migration from water hole to water hole through the universe of the central Australian desert; and, most importantly, the ascertainment that the current generation of Walbiri will be followed by another generation. These concerns are mirrored in the art and stories of the Walbiri men. For them the recurrent theme is one of travels by the mythic ancestors through the land now inhabited by the Walbiri, always spontaneously emerging from the earth, traversing their route, and—like mortal Walbiri—ultimately returning to the earth.

Does Walbiri art have any additional symbolic significance? Some time ago Géza Roheim, an individual with a unique background in psychoanalysis and other areas, visited Australia. Based on what he saw, Roheim (1945) suggested that the symbolism of the central Australian peoples is primarily concerned with sexuality, with the many circles and straight lines representing vaginas and penises. Munn reports that Walbiri do indeed assign explicitly sexual meanings to some of the lines and circles in their art, but her more in-depth study of Walbiri thought reveals that the art is concerned with regeneration on a deeper level: It reflects the society's concern about its continued day-to-day existence and procreative powers, condensing several levels of Walbiri thought and action into a single icon. "It is as if," Munn concludes, "this figure constituted Walbiri life experience in time abstracted to its simplest, most general pattern. In the design system this abstract 'shape of space-time' provides the unifying format for the concrete variance of the species world" (1973:221).

Munn's analysis reflects a growing trend toward the application to art of the approach known as structuralism, as developed in cultural anthropology by Claude Lévi-Strauss, Victor Turner, and others, and in linguistics by Roman Jacobson, Noam Chomsky, and others. The goal in every case is to discern the deeper structural patterns that underlie the surface phenomena of behavior—artifact, cultural tradition, or well-formed sentence. This trend is discussed at length in the account of James C. Faris's analysis of Nuba personal art in Chapter 5.

The discussion in Chapter 2 of the functions of art in small-scale societies noted that art often helps maintain the cultural stability required for a society's continued existence, and that one way in which this is accomplished is through art's reflecting—and validating—the traditional underlying values and patterns of thought of the society. The present discussion of Walbiri iconography and symbolism leads to this same conclusion. Much of Walbiri art "merely" tells stories, but viewed as a whole, from the structuralist perspective of Munn (and her mentors, Turner and Lévi-Strauss), the narratives are actually only a single story—the story of Walbiri culture; and the art is a composite picture of Walbiri sociocultural thought. Both the daily and the cosmic experience of Walbiri life is, to use Munn's graphic phrase, "pumped into" Walbiri art; and from there it is pumped back into the imagination and consciousness of every living Walbiri.

For our present purposes the importance of this mechanism is that it is based on symbolism. Walbiri graphic designs have various kinds of meanings associated with them, ranging from the explicit and iconic to the implicit and symbolic. As vessels for cultural meaning they are sweepingly important for Walbiri society as well as for our own understanding of Walbiri culture.

UNIVERSAL SYMBOLS?

A discussion of symbolism in art would not be complete without reference to the question of universal symbols, that is, of specific figures that are found in all cultures, each figure having everywhere associated with it a single meaning or a cluster of closely related meanings. At the outset it should be noted that this is a controversial question, and whether or not a particular person feels that universal symbols exist seems sometimes to depend more on the person's disposition than on being convinced by firm and compelling evidence on the issue. One of the most annoying aspects of the debate over universal symbols is the lack of agreement as to just what sorts of evidence would serve to resolve the question of whether or not universal symbols actually exist.

Freudian Iconography

Much of the interest in the subject of universal symbols and icons derives from the psychoanalytic movement that began in the early twentieth century. Sigmond Freud contended that part of an individual's imagery often has iconographic meanings: The long nose that one visualizes in a dream, for instance, may be both a nose and a phallus. In his earlier work, Freud apparently believed that such imagery was personal and idiosyncratic, but by 1910 he had shifted his search in the direction of universal icons (Spector 1972:96), asking questions such as: Is a dream about a nose always and everywhere phallic?

This search has met with only mixed success. It appears that there are genuine cases of sexual iconography in the imagery of some other societies. For example, Munn's Walbiri informants candidly admitted that among other things their designs have explicitly sexual interpretations. They generally equated circular or ovoid figures with women or mothers and long, pole-like elements with men (Munn 1974:199).

There are, however, two difficulties with a narrowly Freudian approach to the imagery of other societies. First, thorough fieldwork in a given society often reveals that libidinous symbols are only part of the picture: Asexual imagery may be very important, too. As mentioned previously, the Freudian interpretation of Central Australian art that Roheim made was not inaccurate—it was simply incomplete. To ignore the facts that, in addition to their sexual meanings, Walbiri circles stand for water holes and lines stand for paths is to miss the wider significance of the figures for Walbiri culture as a whole.

The second difficulty with a narrowly Freudian interpretation of artistic imagery is that for every piece of confirming evidence for cross-cultural existence of sexual icons, there are one or more cases that do not fit the pattern. Thus, for example, although the snake image is manifestly phallic to the Freudians, Mundkur (1976) has recently surveyed the cultural contexts of the widespread snake or serpent motif in the Americas and found that it was only rarely associated with sexuality or fertility.

Inasmuch as the sexual figures in question are icons, bearing some resemblance to the things they represent, rather than symbols, it is not surprising that cross-cultural similarities do occur. Sexuality and reproduction are literally vital topics in all societies, and although some cultures deal with these subjects explicitly (cf. Mountford 1960, Rawson 1973), in others representation may be less literal; and if this latter approach is used the resultant images must inevitably be Freudian icons of a sort.

The important conclusion to draw, I believe, is this: When approaching the art of any society, one may legitimately ask, "Might the Freudian model be helpful in explaining the meaning of traditional imagery?" On the other hand, it is much less useful to ask, "How can I make this society's imagery fit the speculations of a turn-of-the-century Viennese physician?"

Jungian Symbolism

Although Carl Jung was an important early member of the psychoanalytic movement, he parted ways with Freud in 1913. In his later days Jung professed no doubts that universal symbols exist; indeed, the notion was central to his entire view of psychology. Jung felt that all human beings, no matter what their cultural background, held in their minds a share of the "collective unconscious."[2]

The collective unconscious was never explicitly defined by Jung. He claimed, in fact, that its undefinability was one of its characteristic qualities.

---

[2]Members of small-scale societies, however, were held by Jung to be in more intimate touch with the collective unconscious (cf. Jung 1964:24,52). Cultural anthropology was not Jung's long suit, and until his death he clung to the view, proposed in the early 1900s by Levy-Bruhl, that members of small-scale societies indulge largely in "prelogical" thought. A romantic, however, Jung believed that such thought was generally healthier than the "logical" thought of Westerners.

But whatever it is, Jung's collective unconscious includes the mysterious "human spirit" that reveals itself in all normal individuals, as well as much unconscious information that seldom, if ever, comes to the surface of human thinking and behavior. It does, however, emerge in certain human symbols, and this is where Jung's interests begin to coincide with our own.

Like the collective unconscious itself, such symbols are never realized in their totality, but rather, Jung says, they have "a wider 'unconscious' aspect that is never precisely defined or fully explained. Nor can one hope to define or explain it. As the mind explores the symbol, it is led to ideas that lie beyond the grasp of reason" (Jung 1964:20). Approximations of symbols do, however, emerge from certain kinds of human activity, including dreaming, fantasizing, and the creation of art.

The universal symbols hypothesized by Jung and his followers are more abstract than those of Freud, and their meanings are inevitably imbued with a mystic aura. For example, Aniela Jaffé has claimed the circle, or the sphere, to be

> a symbol of the Self. It expresses the totality of the psyche in all its aspects, including the relationship between man and the whole of nature. Whether the symbol of the circle appears in primitive sun worship or modern religion, in myths or dreams, in the mandalas drawn by Tibetan monks, in the ground plans of cities, or in the spherical concepts of early astronomers, it always points to the single most vital aspect of life—its ultimate wholeness (Jaffé 1964:240).

The difficulty with a sweeping thesis such as Jaffé's is that its validity cannot be tested. The non-Jungian may object that, although some circles do indeed symbolize unity and self, there are at least some circles that do not. For example, isn't the roundness of Eskimo igloos determined more by factors of design than a psychological sense of oneness? Or, are Navajos more "centered" because they live in round hogans, compared to their Pueblo neighbors who live in square dwellings? And, the objector may continue, some symbols of unity are neither circles nor spheres. (In Arabic numerals a straight line—"1"—represents unity, while a circle—"0"—represents either nothingness or is merely a place holder.) But the Jungian advocate may brush aside these objections: Whether they know it or not, Eskimos' igloos do reaffirm the oneness of Eskimo psyches; Pueblo Indians may live in square houses but their ceremonial structures are round; and the Arabic numbers can be discounted as a trivial exception that proves the rule. Or the objection might be turned around upon itself so that the circular zero figure, balanced as it is between positive and negative numbers, does indeed symbolize the real position of unity while the linearity of "1" reveals its departure from the perfect selfhood of zero!

What is one to conclude from an Alice-in-Wonderland argument such as this in which symbols can mean whatever partisans wish them to mean? Only, I believe, that the generality of the Jungian model of symbolism is too broad to be amenable to proof.[3] Most contemporary anthropologists would agree with Raymond Firth's remark about mentalistic theories generally:

> The description of subjective experience, of thought and feeling pattern, is inferential, and should be supported by systematic reference to empirical observed behaviour. And I am willing to assert that this must be so, if anthropology is to maintain its claim to deal with symbolic process on a comparative basis (Firth 1973:85, 86).

The cross-cultural quest for symbolic themes in the unconscious and subconscious realms is both fascinating and important for our understanding of human culture. Such a goal is at the root of one of the currently most viable areas of anthropology, the structuralism of Claude Lévi-Strauss and his followers. The structuralist approach requires both extensive ethnographic data and subtle analysis. Thus far structuralist methods have been largely confined to the topics of kinship, totemism, and mythology; a complete cross-cultural structuralist study of art has yet to be undertaken.

The "Heraldic Woman" Motif

Neither Freud's nor Jung's theories of universal symbolism has been supported by rigorous cross-cultural research, and both are virtually unprovable because of their vagueness. There have been, however, a few studies of iconic motifs with very widespread distribution. One of the most convincing of these studies is by Douglas Fraser, a cross-culturally oriented art historian.

Fraser examined a vast number of art works from all over the globe, from both recent and ancient cultures (cf. Fraser 1966, 1972b), and made an interesting discovery: A figure he calls the "heraldic woman" has appeared intermittently for nearly 3,000 years, occurring in many locations ranging from West Africa, to the Middle East, China, Southeast Asia, many islands of the Pacific, and North and South America.

---

[3]The flavor of disagreements about the application of the Jungian model to non-Western art can be sampled in volume 22, number 3, of the journal *Current Anthropology*. There, Victor Mansfield (1981) argues at length that circles pecked on rocks by pre-Columbian Mesoamericans served purposes comparable to Hindu and Buddhist mandalas. The article is followed by five pages of critical comments by other scholars, most of whom question Mansfield's theoretical approach.

The heraldic woman, as Fraser defines the motif,

refers to an image of a displayed female figure that is symmetrically flanked by two other beings. By "displayed" is meant a figure that holds its knees apart, exposing the genital area. The position of the hands, knees, and feet may vary somewhat. Femininity is made clear through the representation of the vulva or, in other instances, of the breasts. Symmetrical flanking may be said to occur when two beings, one on either side of the central figure, form mirror images or counterparts of each other (1966:36, 37).

Figure 3–10 shows five examples of the heraldic woman, taken from four different continents and Oceania. The similarities between them are amazing; it seems highly unlikely that the resemblance is purely coincidental because the figure is so elaborate. Unlike such Freudian symbols as noses, circles, and the like, the heraldic woman is unlikely to have been simply "stumbled onto" accidentally in each of the several dozen societies in which it was fashioned.

The most likely explanation for the widespread occurrence of the heraldic woman figure is cultural diffusion, whereby it was developed in one locality—probably early in the first millenium B.C. in Luristan, a region now included in modern Iran—and then was adopted by neighboring cultures, leap-frogging its way across continents and oceans. From Luristan the motif probably travelled both southwest (ultimately arriving in West Africa) and east. Fraser suspects that the easterly movement occurred via trade routes that connected the Middle East with the flourishing Asian cultures of the period—Late Chou in China and Dongson in Indonesia. From these oriental hubs, use of the design spread to the societies of the Pacific islands and, ultimately, to the western hemisphere. Some parts of this hypothesized journey have yet to be substantiated, but all of the currently available evidence fits comfortably into the theory.

The meaning of the heraldic woman design is more difficult to determine, as most of the specimens were created in nonliterate societies, long before the era of notebook-toting anthropologists. As far as speculation can carry us, however, it seems that the motif was always associated with one (or both) of two themes: Either the figure was a symbol of fertility, renewal, and regeneration, or else it was associated with a defensive power against sickness or danger in battle.

The heraldic woman is not a truly universal symbol, for there are many societies in which it does not seem to have occurred. (For example, figures in European art resembling the heraldic woman are few in number, are apparently not of great symbolic importance, and are always lacking in one or more of the formal features that define the heraldic woman.) Nevertheless, the scope of its distribution, and the apparent continuity of the

a   b

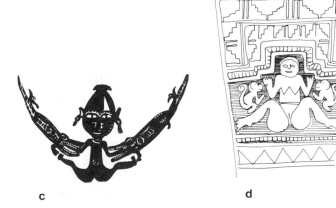

c   d

e

FIGURE 3-10   Five representations of the Heraldic Woman: (a) Bronze pinhead, Luristan (Iran) *(David-Weill Collection)*. (b) Nootka house painting, Vancouver Island *(Originally redrawn from photos in Provincial Archives, Victoria, B.C.)*. (c) Solomon Islands paddle (detail) *(Wilkes Expedition, U.S. National Museum, 2653; originally redrawn from photo by C. Schuster)*. (e) Lintel from a Bamileke chief's house, Cameroon *(Originally redrawn from photograph from Musee de l Homme, Neg. no. 31.607)*. *(All after Fraser, 1966.)*

meanings associated with it, do make the heraldic woman motif a fascinating topic for study.

The crucial question with regard to the distribution of the motif is *why?* Why was this particular design so attractive to people in such diverse cultures that they were prompted to incorporate it into their own indigenous art styles? And why did it remain unchanged for nearly 3,000 years? These questions are truly enigmatic. As Lévi-Strauss has remarked with regard to another geographically widespread artistic pattern, "Stability is no less mysterious than change" (1963:252).

Following Jung's theories of the collective unconscious one could contend that the popularity of the heraldic woman results from its symbolic representation of some primal theme that is present in the minds of all humans. Fraser argues against this approach, noting that the two components of the heraldic woman had had a long previous existence. Justifiably, he asks:

> If the theme [of the heraldic woman] is so natural, why did it take the Ancient Near East (perhaps the most creative cultural matrix ever known) so long to synthesize the two elements—the [displayed] woman which dates back to at least 6000 B.C. and heraldic flanking which begins about 3000 B.C.? The two were not combined until after 1000 B.C. and even then only in a marginal area under extraordinary conditions (Fraser 1966:79).

If a Jungian explanation is unconvincing, we are still left with the puzzling question of why the heraldic woman design, once created, spread through so many different societies. We can note, along with Fraser, that the genitals may be an arresting sight for members of societies in which their viewing is generally taboo. And, beyond that, the relation between female sexuality and the vital issue of reproduction is natural, not arbitrary. But how to account for the constancy of the details of the heraldic woman design? Further research may shed some light on the question, but since most of the information about the cultural context of the design and its diffusion is irretrievably lost to the past, a complete and certain answer may never be ours.

In the end, perhaps the only safe generalization that may be made regarding symbols universally is that they can, and usually do, convey subject matter of great social and cultural consequence. Victor Turner has observed (1966) that the colors red, white, and black play important symbolic roles not only among the East African Ndembu, whom he studied in depth, but also in many other of the world's cultures. This, he suggests, is because blood is everywhere red, semen and milk are white, and excreta and rot are black. And Turner's theoretical assertion has received empirical support in Adams and Osgood's finding (1973), that the color red does, like blood, prompt strong feelings among members of most cultures. Life and death, as well as reproduction and social identity, are issues that deeply concern all people. Various peoples construe these issues in differing ways, but art is quite often pressed into service as a channel through which these issues are expressed.

PORTFOLIO

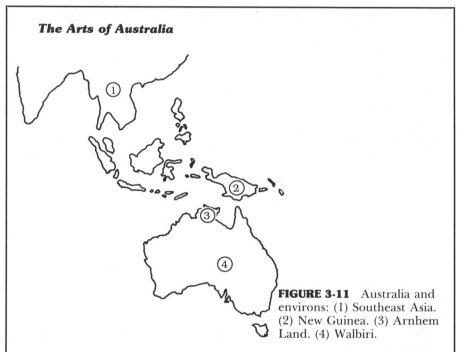

The Arts of Australia

FIGURE 3-11   Australia and environs: (1) Southeast Asia. (2) New Guinea. (3) Arnhem Land. (4) Walbiri.

To the eyes of a Westerner, the native peoples of Australia may appear to be about as remote as any inhabitants of the earth. Living in small, semi-nomadic bands, they exploit their harsh environment with the simplest of technologies: The women use digging sticks and grinding stones to obtain and prepare food from the earth; the men employ spears and boomerangs to bring down game.

But a closer look reveals the distance between "us" and "them" to be considerably less than one might at first think. For one thing, from the time of the first humans up until the relatively recent discovery of agriculture, *all* people subsisted on hunting and gathering, so in the longer scheme of things our industrial economy is little more than a recent aberration. Moreover, any supposed cognitive gap between native Australians and people of the West disappears when one considers the ingenuity that permits the Aborigines to survive in an otherwise inhospitable land despite the simplicity of their technology.

And anyone who persists in feeling a mistaken sense of intellectual superiority will be properly humbled by an effort to fathom the remarkably complex kinship systems that Aborigines use with perfect ease.

However, even though we do share a close affinity with the native peoples of Australia, the fact remains that they live in the smallest of small-scale societies, and this alone makes Aboriginal art interesting for cross-cultural analysis. Also, an account of Australian art is particularly pertinent here because it is preeminently symbolic: Pregnant with meaning, art from Australia resonates with powerful, sacred associations. Finally, Australian art is visually arresting to the eye, conveying a graphic force that has few equals.

The media of Australian visual arts are diverse. Like other seminomadic peoples, Aborigines capitalize on the most portable of all media, the human body itself. Scarification and body painting are supplemented by decorations (Figure 3–12) such as head-, arm-, and waist-bands as well as elaborate headdresses. Also, some groups produce paintings on large, flat sheets of bark from the stringy bark tree (Figures 3–13, 3–14, and 3–15); and tens of thousands of paintings on rock walls have been documented throughout the continent. These fundamentally two-dimensional styles are also commonly mapped onto three-dimensional utilitarian items such as spear-throwers and bowls (Figure 3–16).

Many bands of Aborigines produce genuinely three-dimensional art objects, the most important of which are *tjurungas*. These ritual objects are flat, oval, or circular slabs of wood or stone, from 2 inches to 18 feet in length, often bearing complex painted and incised patterns. (Traditionally, Aboriginal sacred art could be viewed only by initiated adults. This taboo is still in effect in some parts of Australia,

FIGURE 3-12 Australian Aboriginal pendent, with incised figures. *(Courtesy Field Museum of Natural History, Chicago.)*

FIGURE 3-13 Australian Aboriginal bark painting, by Barrduguppu, a member of the Gunwinggu tribe. X-ray wallaby showing heart, lungs, diaphragm, and liver, all by common convention. (Elementary anatomical information such as this is common knowledge among hunter-gatherer peoples.) *(Courtesy Edward L. Ruhe.)*

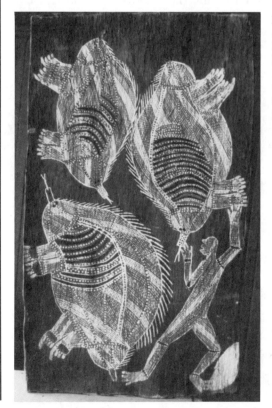

FIGURE 3-14 Australian Aboriginal bark painting, by Mandarrg, a member of the Dangbon tribe, born ca. 1925. Dreamtime hunter with spear, about to attack a spiny ant-eater (echidna). *(Courtesy Edward L. Ruhe.)*

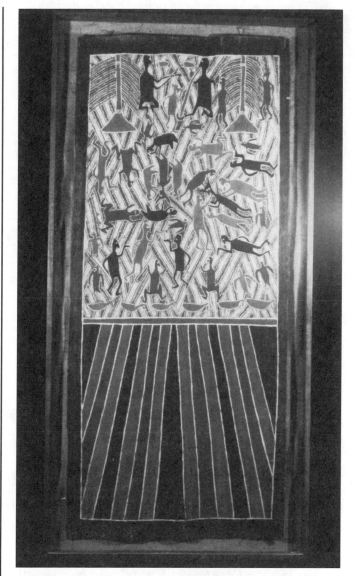

FIGURE 3-15 Australian Aboriginal bark painting by
Mathaman, a member of the Riraidjingu group in
northeast Arnhem Land. Corroboree at Munumbarlwui,
the way-station visited by the Riraidjingu dead on their
way to Bralku. The site is on Melville Bay, west of the
former mission. The dust raised in the late afternoon
dancing creates the rainbow-like design depicted on the
bark. At the top are musicians playing clapsticks and a
dronepipe with a paperbark pad used as a mute. Two
spirits, Bunbulama and Wuluwaid, greet the newly
arrived soul, who is depicted as a horned figure and
shown twice. Dowo trees and two types of birds are also
portrayed. *(Courtesy Edward L. Ruhe.)*

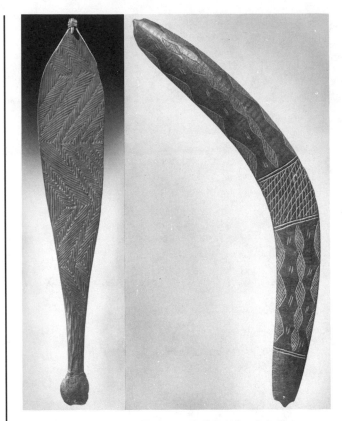

FIGURE 3-16 Decorated Australian Aboriginal non-sacred items. Left, spear thrower; right, boomerang. *(Courtesy Field Museum of Natural History, Chicago.)*

so no photograph of *tjurungas* will be provided here, although the reader may see *tjurungas* in some museum collections and in numerous older books.) In some regions carvers make wooden heads or full figures of anthropomorphic and animals subjects. Elsewhere they incise large designs into live trees or use earth, sand, and logs to produce huge high-relief sculptures on the ground.

Australian art begins with naturalistic subject matter—humans, animals, or components of the environment such as waterholes or even winds; but a distinctive subjective vision elevates these subjects to a heroic level. For example, a kangaroo may be depicted in such a way that its vital organs are visible, an indication of the animal's life-giving vigor (Figure 3–13). A common technique of stylization is to allow a few features to stand for the entire subject. For example, parallel, zigzagging lines may represent waves and, by extension, a particular river.

Although much Aboriginal painting is characterized by the use of dots, dashes, or parallel straight lines to fill in design areas, various localities and time periods have distinctive styles that can be categorized into regions and subregions (see, for example, Stubbs 1974).

The motivations behind Aboriginal art also vary from place to place, but most art is made to fill the needs of religious observances. The basic premise of Aboriginal religion is that long ago, during a period known as the "Eternal Dreamtime," mythical beings wandered through the countryside. The spirits' activities created many notable features of today's landscape, such as waterholes. Also, in their travels the Dreamtime spirits brought into existence a primordial abundance of plant and animal life, human beings, and many human institutions such as ritual, song, and the principles of descent. Religious practice is based on the belief that the Dreamtime spirits still exist today, and that by recounting the stories of their past travels (that is, by singing or reciting traditional myth) and by reenacting their activities (in the form of religious rituals), the original, harmonious, and prosperous state of the world will be perpetuated. The details of ritual practices vary, but everywhere they are the responsibility of totemic groups.

Our knowledge of the underlying philosophical principles of Aboriginal art is best for the region of north-central Australia called Arnhem Land. There, art has two primary uses: increase and initiation. *Increase magic* is meant to ensure the availability and growth of food supplies. For example, carved wooden poles and bull-roarers shaped like animals guarantee the fertility of the species that they represent.

If *increase rituals,* with their requisite arts, are intended to perpetuate the primordial abundance of nature, *initiation ceremonies* are meant to sustain the realm of the human spirit. Here, too, art is needed, providing a major means whereby initiates into totemic groups learn the mysteries of the Eternal Dreamtime. Dance and song are important, but the deepest meanings in initiation rituals reside in carved wooden poles, ground sculptures, bull-roarers, and, most powerful of all, *tjurungas,* which are believed to actually embody the Dreamtime spirits.

Thus, Australian Aboriginal art is simultaneously religious and utilitarian. Created to obtain thoroughly pragmatic ends—perpetuation of the environment and human society—it accomplishes its goal through supernatural means. Aboriginal art provides a conduit through which mortals convey their needs and wishes to the everpresent Dreamtime spirits. In the extreme, the decorated Aboriginal dancer actually becomes the spirit he impersonates, an identity that is more powerful and more real than his mundane life.

Through art, Australian Aborigines come into immediate, intimate, and genuine contact with the all-important spirits of the Eternal Dreamtime. Art in many cultures has a spiritual component, but rarely is this motive as important as among the native peoples of Australia.

CONCLUSIONS

Symbolism is a broad subject that has relevance for our understanding of many human endeavors, ranging from social structure and politics through religion and ritual to language and art. It is a difficult topic to grapple with because, though the symbols themselves may be tangible, the meanings they carry are often intangible and elusive. The distinctions that Peirce made between index, icon, and symbol are still useful tools for discussion, helping us avoid confusion as we discuss the various ways in which figures are attributed meaning.

Not all art in small-scale societies is intended to convey specific meanings. The geometric pattern that colorfully decorates the sides of a pot or basket may be just that—decoration, conveying no more meaning than patterns on most American men's neckties. Careful fieldwork, however, sometimes reveals that patterns that we outsiders cannot decipher are indeed iconic representations of specific things, beings, actions, or ideas. The complex figures that characterize Northwest Coast art are a case in point: No matter how seemingly fragmented and distorted the design, the maker intended it to portray certain individuals or animals, and he had at his command a repertoire of techniques for carrying out his culture's style of iconographic art.

The art of the central Australian Walbiri has some parallels to that of the Northwest Coast in that specific objects, individuals, and their activities are represented iconographically. But whereas the only additional meanings associated with Northwest Coast designs is their function as "status symbols" for their owners, Walbiri symbolism has a deeper significance: Walbiri art symbolically reflects life and belief, both on the level of individual day-to-day activities and interests, as well as on the level of larger spatial, sociocultural, and cosmological issues.

The subject of universal symbols is fascinating; part of its attraction perhaps lies in its implied promise to provide a basis for shared understanding between all people regardless of their cultural diversity. Unfortunately, little substantial headway has been made toward rigorously establishing the existence of such symbols. The biggest stumbling block has been the vagueness with which the supposedly symbolic figures and their meanings have been defined.

There have, however, been a few well-documented studies of widespread graphic motifs. The heraldic woman, for example, has turned up on four continents and throughout the Pacific, always seemingly associated with one of two sets of related meanings. Careful studies such as Fraser's pursuit of this motif will lead to a better understanding of the process of cultural diffusion and of the appeal of such figures.

Symbolism is an iceberg whose tip is obvious, whose massive importance can be guessed at, but whose submerged features are currently either inaccessible or else accessible only at the cost of a great outlay of effort and ingenuity. In the past, very little enlightenment has been provided by either the tough-minded scientist with a penchant for classifying and quantifying, or the armchair romantic with a weakness for grand but unverifiable theories. The modicum of insight we now have has come from pursuing a middle course between these two extremes.

GUIDE TO ADDITIONAL READINGS

As noted at the beginning of this chapter, symbolism is a subject that concerns writers not only in anthropology but also in a number of other disciplines. Anthropologists themselves have in recent years found it very profitable to consider cultures as symbolic systems and to analyze them accordingly. Firth (1973) and Geertz (1973) both provide useful overviews of the most important attempts in this direction. Notable ethnographic and analytic efforts are the many writings of Lévi-Strauss, Victor Turner, and Mary Douglas.

The iconography and symbolism of Northwest Coast art is discussed in Boas' *Primitive Art* (1955:186–298); and this material is brought up to date by Bill Holm (1965, 1972, 1983) and Erna Gunther (1962). Munn's *Walbiri Iconography* (1973), along with her shorter papers (1962, 1964, 1970, 1971, 1974) constitutes an anthropological *tour de force*.

Other significant attempts to apply structuralist concepts to art appear in Leach (1974) and in Faris's treatment (1972) of Nuba design, discussed later in Chapter 5. Hanson's analysis of Maori symbolism (1983a,b, 1985) and its relation to fundamental themes in Maori culture is also of considerable interest.

Mundkur (1976) discusses the serpent motif, a theme which, like the heraldic woman, is distributed across several continents. The feline figure has received similar attention (see, for example, Benson, ed., 1972).

Other works of interest on art and symbolism (or iconography) are Paula Ben-Amos's "Men and Animals in Benin Art" (1976b), Forge's "Art and Environment in the Sepik" (1971), and Flam's "Some Aspects of Style Symbolism in Sudanese Sculpture" (1970).

Standard works on Australian Aboriginal art are Berndt (1964, 1976), Elkin, Berndt, and Berndt (1950), and McCarthy 1938 (and later editions).

CHAPTER 4

The Artist's Life and Work

The preceding chapters have discussed art as cultural artifact (Chapter 2) and art as meaning (Chapter 3), but what about art as the product of one person's—the artist's—creative activity? After all, one component of the definition of art we are using focuses on the artist: Art results from a particularly skillful individual's work in one of the visual media. What, then, of the highly skilled individuals? Where do their abilities come from; what motives prompt them to make art; what status do they have in their society; how do they go about their work?

This personal aspect of art from small-scale societies interests laypeople and anthropologists alike. Over 50 years ago Franz Boas exhorted his students, "We have to turn our attention first of all to the artist himself" (1955 [orig. 1927]:155). However, with few exceptions, Boas' dictum went largely unheeded until the 1960s. Since then a number of anthropologists (and art historians interested in non-Western art) have lived with, and recorded the activities of, artists in a number of small-scale societies. Nevertheless, there are still major gaps in the literature. First, the relative abundance of studies from Melanesia and from West and Central Africa makes all the more noticeable the unfortunate shortage of studies from the remaining parts of Oceania and Africa, to say nothing of Australia and the Americas. Second, virtually all the artists described to date have been men (notable exceptions are Bunzel 1972, O'Neale 1932, and R. Thompson 1969), but women are artists too, and our general level of ignorance of female artists in small-scale societies is lamentable.[1] Finally, even if a field-worker spends several years in a particular society, he or she will probably not be there long enough to follow the long-term development of individual artists. These shortcomings of the extant literature should be borne in mind by anyone attempting to draw cross-cultural conclusions.

Although we clearly are not operating in an area of perfect knowledge, neither are we in a state of total ignorance. Some very interesting information about artists in small-scale societies has been collected. This chapter presents it in two sections, discussing first the development and training of the artist and the artist's place within society, then turning to the artist's work techniques, tools, and materials, and the compensation received for producing works of art. (Several closely related topics are not presented here but are dealt with in subsequent chapters. Chapter 5 discusses the psychological aspects of the artist's training and the interplay of old and new ideas in the creative process. The last chapter of the book notes some of the similarities and differences between artists in small-scale societies and those in the contemporary Western world.)

THE ARTIST'S LIFE: TRAINING

How does a member of a small-scale society become an artist? This section will deal with this question in general terms, often illustrating particular points by looking at the development of an individual artist, Chukwu Okoro, a master carver among the Afikpo of West Africa.

The Sexual Division of Labor in Art

Adult women and adult men are accorded different social identities everywhere. Just what these identities are, and the extent and nature of the disparity between male and female roles, depends on the locality, of course, but nowhere do men and women maintain identical statuses. This being the case it is not surprising that a sexual division of labor is found in virtually every society's art. There is women's art and there is men's art, and the differences between them are usually significant.

For one thing, the media available to artists are usually sex-specific. For example, male Northwest Coast artists carved (and painted) wood, horn, and stone to produce "totem poles," masks, boxes, and many other ritual and utilitarian items. Female artists in the same tribes did not carve at all; weaving and basketry were the media of their aesthetic expression. An equally clear-cut division of labor is found in most cultures, and sometimes it reaches surprising proportions. Among the West African Yoruba, for

---

[1]The relative numbers of male versus female artists in small-scale societies are unknown. In the past, most researchers have been men and they have, for various reasons, tended to focus on male artists. Throughout this book I have avoided using "he" and "him" with reference to artists except when the person in question is male.

example, although both male and female weavers are found, the former use a horizontal loom to weave narrow bands of material whereas the latter use vertical looms to weave cotton fabric. Each sex has its own guild, and exceptions to their respective specializations were nonexistent in traditional times.

Although the sexual division of labor varies from one culture to the next, some patterns do exist (Murdock and Provost 1973:207; Burton, Brudner, and White 1977:231; cf. Teilhet 1978). Working with hard materials such as wood, bone, horn, shell, stone, and metal is usually the exclusive domain of men; and, with rather more exceptions, women tend to work in softer materials, such as clay, fiber, and leather. Admittedly, societies differ in the strictness of such specialization (cf. Parezo 1982), but the reason for the existence of the patterns remains unclear. Does the male penchant for hard substances derive from their using such materials in making weapons and hunting tools whereas women's usual duties require softer materials such as baskets for food storage and leather for clothing? Or might differences of male and female modal personality be involved, as suggested by one feminist writer (Teilhet 1978:99)? In any case, Crowley (1968:431) has noted numerous exceptions to these patterns, such as the fact that pottery is a male craft in Europe, India, and Central Africa, whereas most West African and American Indian potters are women, so the maxim "gender isn't destiny" applies in art as elsewhere.

Sexual differences in style are almost as common as differences in medium. Some time ago Ralph Linton noted the "curious fact that where a free, naturalistic style and an angular, geometric one coexist in the same culture, the former is practically always executed by men, the latter by women" (Linton 1941:44). Again, the Northwest Coast provides a graphic example. There, male carvers utilized a curvilinear style to portray people and animals, utilizing the elaborate iconographic techniques described in Chapter 3. By contrast, female weavers and basket makers used a linear style to create nonrepresentational designs and, occasionally, to depict plants and inanimate objects. (Compare, for example, the Tlingit baskets shown in Figure 4–13 with the Tlingit mask of Figure 3–1.) The male/female dichotomy was carried to the extreme in the case of the Tlingit's Chilkat blankets. When the women made them for themselves, they used abstract, geometric designs. Blankets worn by men, however, traditionally bore figures of humans and animals. Denied the right to draw life forms, the women weavers copied figurative designs that men drew on boards (Goldberg 1978).[2]

[2]Exactly the opposite pattern occurs among the Peruvian Shipibo. There, too, women are weavers and men are carvers, but Shipibo women alone can draw the complex and highly valued geometric patterns for which their pottery is famous. Therefore, when a Shipibo man wants to carve, say, a sword-club, he must prevail upon a woman to draw a design on it, and then he incises the design into the wood's surface (Roe 1979:200). It is probably no coincidence that women have unusually great political and economic influence in Shipibo society and that this, too, is the reverse of the situation found in the Northwest Coast.

There are numerous other places where men tend to work in a naturalistic art style that includes figures of humans and animals, in contrast to the nonfigurative, geometric designs of women. In North America it occurs not only on the Northwest Coast but also in the Plains, the Great Basin, and among the Navajos of the Southwest; and in Africa, the Ashanti and groups in the Cameroon Grasslands show the same pattern.

Again, more than one hypothesis has been put forward to explain this phenomenon. The technical qualities of various media could be a factor inasmuch as figural sculpture is easier to execute by men in their carving than by women in their weaving. Also, if it is true that (1) most religious specialists are men; that (2) males, and their rituals, are primarily focused on interpersonal relations and hunting, that is, on humans and animals; and that (3) art generally reflects the deep concerns of its makers, then the prevalence of male figurative art styles is understandable. Or on a different level still, perhaps such art is made as a compensation for the fact that men, unlike women, cannot give birth to real human figures. All three of these arguments have obvious shortcomings, and once more the answer must await future, cross-cultural analysis.

The contrast between female and male identity sometimes has an unexpected influence on an artist's status. Consider, for example, the fact that the king of the Ashanti Confederacy, whose golden stool was discussed in Chapter 2, has his own, personal woodcarver, a man whom he calls *me yere*, "my wife." Harry Silver (1980) has suggested that this surprising term of address is used because Ashanti carvers are, at least in some respects, symbolically equal to females. For example, when a kingly stool is made, the carver produces the physical stool but the stool's spiritual identity is believed to come from the king, a process that parallels Ashanti assumptions about male and female contributions to conception and birth, according to which a baby's body comes from its mother, its soul from its father. More broadly, the matrilineal Ashanti view women as being responsible for perpetuating the clan's flesh and blood; and in a like fashion, carvers have the important duty of making royal regalia that give tangible continuity to the clan as a political body.

This example raises the inevitable issue of the politics of the sexual division of labor in the arts. From a political perspective, any division of labor has the potential for both good and harm. At least in theory, specialization leads to increased efficiency. For example, to some extent the technical excellence that is apparent in Northwest Coast carving and weaving is contingent upon the sexual division of labor whereby a woman can devote all her time and energy to mastering weaving, and a man to improving his skills of carving.

However, roles that are socially different are usually roles that are politically unequal, and such is often the case with art. Men dominate public life in most cultures, and their superordinate position carries over into the arts. Thus, Northwest Coast males generally dominated the social arena, and male arts overshadowed female arts in that men's carvings had more institutional significance than did women's weavings and baskets. And within the genre of Chilkat blankets, those woven with men's anthropomorphic and zoomorphic designs were more treasured (apparently by both women and men) than the geometric blankets worn by women. Or, to cite another example of the asymmetry of male/female involvement in art, among the Maori of New Zeland, whereas women wove cloaks but were expressly forbidden to engage in the male craft of carving, men were permitted to weave if they so desired (cf. Teilhet 1978).

The political dimension has affected not only art itself but also the study of art in non-Western societies. The majority of fieldworkers, and the natives who have assisted them, have been male. As a consequence women's art is significantly underrepresented both in the literature and in museum collections. When anthropology is defined as "the science of man," it is usually assumed that "man" is meant to refer to the whole human species and not just the male sex. One would hope that future research on non-Western art will help make this assumption more nearly a reality.

Who Becomes an Artist?

At one time or another each of us probably has wondered about the origin of artistic talent. Why is it, say, that I might have some musical ability while my good and otherwise able friend is tone deaf? Or why are your drawings of things easily recognizable while another person's best efforts need captions to help the unfortunate viewer make sense of them? As in all "nature-nurture" problems, there logically seem to be only two alternatives: The individual may either be born with talent, or else it may be acquired after birth through exposure to the person's sociocultural environment. The trouble is that upon closer examination neither of these two explanations seems very plausible. If talent is inborn then it must be transmitted genetically, but genetic research has yet to isolate an "artistic talent" gene. On the other hand, environmental explanations, such as formal and informal teaching and exposure to certain kinds of experiences, seem unable to account for the wide range of human variation, extending as it does from the child prodigy to the person who is "all thumbs."

If we ourselves are uncertain as to whether artistic talent is inborn or acquired after birth (or both), the same disagreement prevails cross-culturally. At one extreme are those societies in which it is believed that all individuals begin life with equal artistic abilities and that quirks of experience alone lead a few people to develop their talents to an extraordinary degree. Thus, for example, Crowley, whose account of the Central African Chokwe was mentioned in Chapter 2, says, "Every Chokwe considers himself at least a potential artist" (1973:222). A similar view is held by the Anang of Nigeria, where John C. Messenger did fieldwork. He found that not only could all men carve but that they could not understand the sense of his questions about the possibility of some youths failing to learn to carve (1958:22). The Anang attribute the exceptional skills of the rare carver of genius to fate decreed by spirits, but why these spirits smile on one person and not another remains an unanswered question.

A similar situation prevails among contemporary Eskimos in northern Alaska. Many men carve, but, as Ray notes, the carver himself is "the first to become realistic and to explain that the reason he carves so well is because his father began teaching him when he was very, very young" (1961:26). Indeed, Eskimos attach so much importance to parental training that of one who could not carve it was said, "He did not have a father" (1961:26).

The Afikpo of Nigeria have more ambivalent views with regard to the origin of artistic talent, as evidenced by the life history of Chukwu Okoro, a master Afikpo carver. (Simon Ottenberg's account of Chukwu appears in his excellent 1975 monograph, *Masked Rituals of the Afikpo: The Context of an African Art*. Ottenberg's book provides a great wealth of data, and interested readers are encouraged to go directly to it for additional information on Afikpo art and culture.)

Chukwu was a little over 50 years old when Ottenberg talked with him in 1960. Describing Chukwu's childhood, Ottenberg relates,

> Chukwu's father died when he was a year old and his mother remarried shortly after that. Both his father and stepfather were farmers. Chukwu believes that as a young boy he was "ordinary." He liked to fight and wrestle. He and his friends caught crickets and grasshoppers, pulling off their wings and roasting them or making grasshopper stew; they also caught and cooked rats and mice. They built miniature playhouses, played in the boys' house (ulote) in the compound, and took part in various children's games. Chukwu never went to school (Ottenberg 1975:67).

Teenage Afikpo boys are members of a mock secret society patterned after that of the initiated men. They stage masked plays, making their own masks for the performances. Chukwu's special artistic abilities were becoming apparent by this early time: The masks he made were, he says, the most popular ones; and in addition to masks for himself he made extra masks that he sold to other boys, "at a price of three medium-sized yams" (Ottenberg, 1975:68). Why was Chukwu specially blessed? When pressed on the point, Afikpo individuals fall back on supernatural explanations: "Skills are sometimes believed by Afikpo to pass down through reincarnation. Chukwu is a reincarnation of a former secret society priest. . . . While this man was not a carver, his association with the Mgbom secret society . . . puts Chukwu within a special group of ritual experts" (1975:69).

Finally, there are many societies in which artists are explicitly believed to be born, not made. The German ethnographer Carl Schmitz has reported that in the Sepik River area of New Guinea, one of the most fertile sources of art in the world, women believe that an infant born with the umbilical cord wrapped around its neck is destined to become a great carver (Schmitz 1962:xv, cited in Biebuyck 1969:14). Similarly, Margaret Mead (1971:137) has noted that the Mundugamor of the Sepik believe that, although such a birth is a prerequisite of becoming an artist, it does not ensure that the child will necessarily become one, conceding that training is also necessary.

Speaking from his experience in West Africa, William Bascom notes,

> Whether a boy learns quickly or slowly and whether or not he becomes a successful carver or a poor one is explained by the Yoruba in terms of personal destiny (*iwa*) assigned to him at birth by the Sky God (*Olorun*). If an apprentice can do better than his teacher, people know that his skill was given to him by the Sky God. . . . Soon after a child is born, the parents consult a diviner (*babalawo*) to learn about its destiny, and in order to achieve it, an individual may have to sacrifice to the Sky God at various times during his lifetime when instructed by a diviner to do so (1973:68).

In some cases the supposedly inborn artistic talent is a mixed blessing. The Gola of Liberia, for instance, feel that anyone who excels in the arts—not only carving, but also singing, dancing, music making, and story telling—was born with what we ourselves would call a "creative personality." But, according to Warren d'Azevedo, who worked among the Gola in 1956 and 1957, a child whose unique behavior indicates that he has special creative abilities,

> is an immediate as well as a potential danger to his family and fellows. He may be the agent of malevolent forces which bring sickness and death. He may be in league with an angry ancestor or a subversive soul from a rival lineage or chiefdom. Sorrow and fear surround such persons, and they may die young through the violence of some supernatural agency or of the righteous community itself. . . . If he achieves a degree of success in the world, and brings honor to his family and community, it is believed that he has mastered these forces and turned them to benevolent ends (1973b:283).

Thus, folk explanations of the source of artistic ability parallel our own beliefs: Some are convinced it's inborn while others prefer to look for causal factors during the individual's life. Of course, folk explanations are merely attempts to give culturally satisfying answers to thorny problems, and such accounts may or may not reflect what truly occurs. Although it is a less satisfying answer, the actual situation surely must be that *both* inborn and environmental factors play a part in determining one's artistic abilities. The factors that combine to form what we call talent—inventiveness, hand-eye coordination, self-discpline, and so on—are highly plastic traits, reflecting both nature and nurture in varying degrees. The only real problem lies hidden in the phrase, "varying degrees." As in the Western world, it is very common for artists in small-scale societies to be the son or daughter of an artist. But until we develop a reliable method for objectively measuring talent or a means for quantifying the aesthetic value of individual works of art (neither of which is likely to happen in the foreseeable future), there is no way to determine how much of the individual's abilities derive from his or her biological heritage and how much from sociocultural factors.

The Artist's Training

Given that at least part of the artist's competence is acquired from his or her cultural environment, how does this process take place? How does the artist acquire the motor skills and the knowledge of tools, materials, and traditional aesthetic values that are the prerequisites of being an artist? As might be expected, these questions do not have a single answer: There are various learning methods, ranging from informal self-teaching to highly formalized systems of apprenticeship.[3]

The importance of informal learning is significant, even in societies in which aspiring artists apprentice themselves to a master. Consider, for example, the man who is an expert carver. As a child, long before he attempted his first art work, he had probably used woodworking tools for other purposes, such as gathering firewood for his family's hearth. Also, he and his young friends probably had been making their own wooden toys for some time. The motor habits acquired in these extra-artistic chores eventually were adapted to artistic activities.

The skills gained through informal channels of learning are usually thought of as being generalized and diffuse, but a team of psychologists has shown that some well-defined cognitive abilities are also involved (Price-Williams, Gordon, and Ramirez, 1969). The psychologists gave tests to 12 boys living in a Mexican village well known for its pottery making; they then compared the test results to those from another group of 12 boys living in a nonpottery-making village. It was found that the boys from the pottery-making village performed consistently better than the others in realizing that manipulating a given piece of clay—for example, starting with a ball of clay and rolling it out into a long cylinder—does not change the amount of clay present.

In addition to "learning by doing," there is a high likelihood that the neophyte artist watched the members of an older generation of artists pursuing their craft. (An important exception to this rule occurs in those societies in which artists work alone—by preference, in secrecy enforced by supernatural stricture, or because they wish to guard their trade secrets.) In any case, the young person certainly heard adults discussing art, picking out the strengths and weaknesses of individual mature artists and their works.

Informal learning is illustrated by the artistic development of Abatan, a Yoruba woman famous in her native Nigeria for her pottery, mud sculpture, and poetry. Although both her mother and maternal grandmother

---

[3]For the most part, only the social and institutionalized aspects of art training are discussed in this chapter. The cognitive level of aesthetic instruction is dealt with in Chapter 5.

were also potters, Abatan received "no formal training, no deliberate lessons. She absorbed, very gradually (*díè-díè-díè*), technique and inspiration from constant observation of Agbédèyí [her mother] at work" (R. Thompson 1969:157). Abatan began making pottery herself when she was 12. Significantly, at first she only made items intended for everyday use—undecorated clay containers for food and water. Gradually her repertoire grew to include traditionally decorated pieces; but, as she reported to Robert Farris Thompson, she was "between thirty and forty when she accepted and successfully finished the most demanding commission of all, the *awo ota eyinle*," a large, earthenware vessel of central importance to shrines of the cult of Eyinle, one of the major gods of the Oyo Yoruba (1969:157). (One of Abatan's *awo ota eyinle* is shown in Figure 4–1.) With

FIGURE 4-1   Ceremonial vessel, made by Yorubu potter, Abatan. (*Courtesy National Museum of Natural History, Smithsonian Institution.*)

the creation of an *awo ota eyinle*, Abatan, whose first lessons came from watching her mother at work, attained the status of master of ceramic art.

A final note with regard to informal means of acquiring artistic skills concerns travel, an activity that is often mentioned as an important source of new ideas for artists in small-scale societies. For example, the young carver among the New Guinea Abelam who is looking for commissions may, if he pursues his kinship ties, find himself working with artists in villages five or more miles away from his home. Although this is not a great distance topographically, there is such a diversity of art styles in this area that the would-be artist is exposed through such travel to a far greater range of approaches to art than he could possibly get if he only remained in the village of his birth (Forge 1967:78–79).

The Liberian Gola place a very high value upon travel to strange and distant places as a means of artistic development:

> Such travel is thought most likely to provide dramatic success and is a romantic and adventurous theme of Gola legend. It is said that very few can become great among their own people, but everyone knows of the marvelous exploits of those [artists] who have gone away and returned after many years, rich in money, wisdom, and followers (d'Azevedo 1973b:288).

Clearly the belief that talented youths can profit from travel is not limited to the administrators of student exchange programs in Western colleges and universities.

Although informal channels of art instruction are important everywhere, many societies provide additional formalized instruction to those young people who are especially inclined to become artists. Often the teacher is an older, close relative of the aspiring artist—a parent, aunt, or uncle, for example. Such arrangements have been reported among people in the Eastern Solomon Islands of Melanesia (Davenport 1971:400), the Asmat region of New Guinea (Gerbrands 1967:170), the Nigerian Anang (Messenger 1958:22) and one group of artists among the Bangwa of West Cameroon, West Africa (Brain and Pollock 1971:44). The advantages of learning from one's near relatives are obvious: They live close at hand and instruction is free. One candid African artist told Himmelheber (1963), "I did not want to become a carver. I would have preferred to become a weaver. But since my uncle was a carver and was willing to teach me for nothing, my father ordered me to learn this trade" (p. 84).

The flaw in such a system is equally obvious: If only a few individuals attain the status of master artist, then not all aspiring artists can have a master as a parent, or even as a distant relative. This problem grows as societies get larger and more stratified and as the skills of the artist become increasingly specialized and different from the techniques used by nonartists (d'Azevedo, personal communication). A solution to the problem lies in providing some means whereby young artists can get instruction from master artists to whom they are not related. A simple method used by some neophyte Afikpo carvers is to work independently and then take the masks they've made to a known carver and ask for his suggestions (Ottenberg 1975:75).

Often, however, the relationship between student and teacher is institutionalized, with the young person formally becoming an apprentice to the master. The duration of the apprenticeship may or may not be culturally prescribed; payment to the master may come before, during, or after the training period, and may take the form of goods (food or trade items), services (helping in the master's household or with some part of the artist's work), or both.

Having noted these possible variations that exist from one society to another, let's take a more detailed look at art training in a single society—the Chokwe of Central Africa.

Becoming a Chokwe Artist   As noted previously, the Chokwe and their art have been described by Daniel Crowley (1971, 1972, 1973), who conducted fieldwork with the Chokwe of Shaba (formerly Katanga) Province, Zaire. Chokwe art is attractive to Westerners—specimens have found their way into numerous collections; and it is diverse, practiced in the media of wood, iron, clay, leather, bark cloth, and fiber. Some of it is used for religious or magical purposes, but much Chokwe art is secular.

Every Chokwe man considers himself a potential artist, but only a few are recognized experts who pursue art semiprofessionally and derive part of their income from making art items for sale to other Chokwe. (Even these individuals grow their own staple foods as a supplement to their art-derived income.) All Chokwe boys, at some time between the ages of 7 and 15, go through a formal initiation called *mukanda*. The affair lasts three months or so, and during that period the boys get their first instruction in the visual and performing arts—as well as in the subjects of sex, religion, and magic. Boys who show special aptitude in making the bark cloth and wooden masks for which they are responsible may, after the conclusion of the *mukanda,* seek out a well-known carver for further instruction.

For such aspiring artists, Crowley says,

> the choice of carving teacher is based on convenience and family connections. Among the artists studied, many had learned from their father, but a large number had also been taught by maternal uncles or maternal grandfathers, since many rural Chokwe are matrilocal. Older brothers, nonrelated older boys and age peers were also mentioned as teachers. Most of this education is casual and unpaid, but sometimes a formal apprenticeship relationship is set up when a carver is otherwise unwilling or when there are a number of boys requesting training (1973:234).

When a formal apprenticeship is arranged between a young Chokwe carver and a master, payment to the master takes several forms: Sheep and goats are the most common medium of payment, but cash may be given too. And, of course, "the boy is expected to do all the hard work, gathering suitable materials, finding trees of the right size and species, sharpening tools, and what is more important, taking over the hated agricultural labor every Chokwe must do for sustenance" (Crowley 1973:234). The boy receives expert instruction (and, later, the prestige of having worked with a well-known carver), and there are some fringe benefits too: "Chokwe boys are glad to get away from their family elders, finding the carvers demanding in labor but lax in discipline, and enjoy the camaraderie of the other apprentices" (Crowley 1973:234).

Finally, with regard to the Chokwe case, some interesting signs of the times might be noted. Crowley (1973:235) reports that some young Chokwe now get art instruction from the Ecole des Beaux Arts in Lubumbashi (formerly Elizabethville) and at European missions.

Art Training in Small-Scale Societies: Final Remarks

Before passing on to the next topic, it seems appropriate to take stock of the material relating to the training of artists in small-scale societies. It is clear, first of all, that learning *does* indeed take place; the artist is not a free spirit who spontaneously puts knife to wood to produce striking works of art, but rather one who has thoroughly mastered tools and techniques, has an intimate understanding of the capabilities of materials, and, most importantly of all, has internalized the aesthetic values of the culture in which he or she works.

Second, there has never been any doubt as to the importance of informal learning—of watching master artists at their work, of transferring into art work the skills that were first acquired in play, subsistence activities, and so on. Nevertheless, the subject has received insufficient study.

Third, formal art instruction occurs in many societies, with many variations in the actual arrangements. Although more is currently known about formal teaching methods than about informal techniques, there are still many interesting questions to be answered. For example, Ralph Linton suggested some time ago (1941:43) that apprenticeships tend to occur in those societies in which an economic benefit accrues to individuals with special training in art. There is now enough data to put Linton's educated guess to the test—at least for Africa.

Finally, the training that has been discussed above deals largely with artists' skills. But what about their sensibilities—how do they acquire the artist's vision? This topic will be touched upon in Chapter 5: Suffice it here to say that this question is at least as important as the ones we have been dealing with in the present chapter.

THE ARTIST'S LIFE: THE FRUITFUL YEARS

What is it like to be a recognized artist in a small-scale society? How is one regarded by fellow society members? What are the rewards of being an artist, and how does the artist fit into the larger cultural milieu? Despite their intrinsic importance, these questions have just about as many answers as there are small-scale societies—or, even worse, as many answers as there are individual artists. But while every group and every artist is ultimately unique, some patterns can be discerned.

The Social Status of the Mature Artist

Because of artists' special skills, they are almost universally thought of in some special terms; most societies have some sort of stereotype of the "typical artist." Just what that status is varies widely cross-culturally, but a polarity does seem to exist: In many societies the artist is a highly respected individual, while in many others the artist is relegated to the lower rungs of the social ladder. Let's look, first, at a few cases in which the artist has a relatively high social status.

Often the artist's high position in society is only an indirect result of artistic activities. Northwest Coast carvers, for example, were generally accorded a relatively high social standing, but apparently this was because some of the pieces they carved could only be made by members of certain secret societies. Artists were initiated into the societies, and as a result of their membership they were looked up to by others. Although the "totem poles" and other items he created were very important for his fellows, the Northwest Coast carver seems to have received no material fringe benefits from his profession: He had no special privileges, wore no special clothes, and, interestingly enough, he had "no extra orientation to the supernatural in spite of his continual engagement in portraying supernatural beings" (Hawthorn 1961:63).

Sometimes the relatively elevated position of artists results from the economic aspects of their profession. Thus, for instance, a woodcarver in the Asmat region of New Guinea often has a somewhat better house than other people because the men he has carved for are obliged to help him build it, and their assistance results in his having a bigger house (Gerbrands 1967:36). Likewise, while he is engaged in a carving commission his patron will hunt, fish, and pound sago for him. While carving for festivals he and his family often get extra delicacies—"the hind foot of a pig, the tail of a crocodile, and especially the larvae of the capricorn beetle, the most ambrosial of all" (Gerbrands 1967:36).

In many New Guinea societies, and through much of the rest of Melanesia, men are avid "social climbers," each trying to surpass the other in gaining prestige. The ultimate goal in many societies is to become a "big man," that is, one who has gained enough prestige and political influence to get others in his village to provide goods for the feasts he gives and to generally accede to his will. In many groups one becomes a "big man" only through fairly ruthless economic and political maneuvering, but in others art provides an alternative avenue to success. In the above-mentioned Asmat region, high social standing is accorded to the successful artist—success being measured by the number of commissions he successfully executes. And in Abelam society, a man who is known for his artistic abilities, who can speak reasonably well, and who can grow satisfactory yams for exchange with his trading partner is considered a "big man." Significantly, though, the Abelam individual who becomes a "big man" through artistic expertise tends to be of a different temperament than other "big men" in that he is a less aggressive entrepreneur (Forge 1967:73).

Finally, there are some cases in which artists are revered simply because they *are* artists, rather than because of the social importance of the items they produce. For example, the Bush Negroes of Surinam, in northeastern South America, give much credit to persons who excel in any of the arts—the skilled carver, the exceptional singer or dancer, the outstanding story teller: All are said to be literally "favored by a god" (Herskovits 1959:52). Similarly, the Anang of Nigeria, like the Bush Negroes, admire artistic merit in all its forms. But as previously noted with regard to the Anang, a prestige-bringing artistic temperament is viewed as a mixed blessing: The artist's creative spirit may get the better of him and bring him harm, perhaps even an early death. Messenger records that one artist

> was compelled to discontinue carving for us as the result of almost nightly attacks by female witches, who forced him to copulate continuously and scratched his body during orgasm. We often dressed wounds inflicted on him by these beings, and he and others suffering from their assaults came to us for medicines to alleviate the various illnesses visited on them (Messenger 1973:103).

If some societies put their artists on a pedestal, others are much less charitable in their estimates of artists. No clear pattern has yet emerged to explain which view a given society will take. For instance, although artistic skill is a means of upward mobility among the above-mentioned Asmat and Abelam people in one part of Melanesia, just the opposite is the case in another Melanesian society. In New Ireland, an island in the Bismarck Archipelago off the northeast coast of New Guinea, adult males also aspire to become "big men." Here, however, the competitive game is played principally with native shell money. Being a carver of the ceremonial objects called *malanggans* does give a man some prestige, but Philip Lewis claims that "it is quite possible that of all the specialist roles [in New Ireland society], that of carver was most likely to have been a *cul de sac* on the road to becoming a 'big man.' Carvers spent more time at their work and thus had less time to pursue other 'big man' activities" (Lewis 1961:74). Prestige in New Ireland societies seems to come despite one's being an artist rather than because of it: In an early study of New Ireland, Hortense Powdermaker (1933:109) reported that the carver in one village was a "nonentity," whereas the carver in another village had much prestige—not due to his carving, but because of his extensive knowledge of *malanggans* and folk tales and because of his position in his clan.

Worse than being a dead end on the road to success, the practice of art may even be considered a useless waste of time. The Fang of western equatorial Africa, for example, feel that responsible grown men should be occupied primarily with providing for their families and protecting the interests of their own lineages (Fernandez 1973:200). But Fang religious belief requires the production of reliquary sculpture, so someone must take time off from workaday activities to carve the pieces. Those who develop skill in carving are not, however, highly regarded. Fernandez sums up their status thus: "They rarely participated in debates in the council house though they occasionally contributed caustic commentary and ribald impieties from the peripheries. The contributions were appreciated, but carvers were not infrequently referred to as *okukut*—good for nothings" (1973:202).

The Fang carver is not alone in his status as a "good for nothing." His counterpart in Dahomey, West Africa, "seldom has the prudence to amass any wealth by his work—a very reprehensible fault, indeed, in the light of generally accepted native values" (Herskovits and Herskovits 1934:128).

The Afikpo mask carver, such as our friend, Chukwu Okoro, is viewed in a similar light. He is often "considered a person who is foolish or silly; he is doing a 'funny thing' but nothing very serious"; his is "lazy man's work" (Ottenberg 1975:66).

A final possibility with regard to artists' status is that they may constitute a distinct social caste. We Westerners tend to think of the artist's status as one that is achieved rather than ascribed—that is, that the individual works his or her way into it, rather than being born to it. But such is not necessarily the case. Vaughan (1973), in one of the few in-depth accounts of an African blacksmith caste, notes that among the mountain Marghi of northern Nigeria members of the smith caste are viewed by other Marghi as a breed apart—not so much inferior or superior: just different. Their separateness reflects both their monopoly on metalworking and other cultural differences that set them apart from nonsmith Marghi.

To conclude this discussion of the social status of the accomplished artist in other societies, a few summary observations are in order. First, it is noteworthy that the artist seems everywhere to *have* some special status. Whether artists are looked up to or down upon, they are inevitably the focus of a special set of social beliefs and expectations. This fact may be overlooked in societies in which, say, all men display some proficiency at wood carving. But even in cases such as this, the expert carver, the person acknowledged to have significantly greater technical skill or more sophisticated aesthetic sensibilities, is inevitably thought of as somebody special.

Just how special, and whether the artist is considered "favored by the gods" or a "good for nothing" or something else again, varies widely, as does the extent to which art works reflect the personal and unique style of their makers.[4] In all likelihood the variation is not random, but probably reflects some other aesthetic or, more likely, social factors. It is probably significant, for example, that in two of the societies (New Ireland and Fang) in which artists are not accorded a high status, the individuals merely make the art works and have no special role to play in the use of their products.

Karen Field (1982) has made one of the few cross-cultural studies of artists' status by comparing the stereotypes of artists in the United States and among the Gola of Liberia. Field begins by pointing out that, despite many obvious differences, Golan and American economic systems have one important and fundamental feature in common, namely, that in both places the production of surplus goods has resulted in the emergence of distinct economic classes. This in turn has led to class consciousness as well as a widespread desire for upward mobility. In such a setting, artists occupy unusual positions: Their products do not contribute directly to the all-important material economy, and although the ownership of art is an emblem of membership in the highest classes, the creative thought necessary for artistic excellence runs contrary to the dominant value of conformity that informs non-artist society. Field believes that because of the parallels in their economic milieus, Golan and American artists are accorded similar roles and statuses. For example, both derive their livelihood, meager though it may be, from an elite patronage. This also explains the similarities between the personality stereotypes of artists found in both cultures, where artists are typically thought to be hostile to many of the culture's values, unstable but inspired, and inept in making and managing money.

Motivation: The Rewards of Being an Artist

Making works of art is not an easy business; it requires materials, time, energy, and concentration on the part of the artist. (When Hans

[4]Thus d'Azevedo has suggested that "in some societies the identity and personality (style) of the producer adheres to the product and to some extent mediates its relative stature; in other societies the producer's identity is obliterated or usurped by those who commission the work or who take possession of it. Among the large-scale societies of West Africa the identity of great craftsmen is often an important factor in the value and appreciation of their work" (personal communication).

Himmelheber asked one African carver whether he would rather work at carving or farming, he got this reply: " 'Carving is hard work. I even prefer bush-cutting to carving. For when cutting the bush I may pause once in a while to talk to the girls, whilst in carving I have to think all the time whether I should proceed this way or that way' " [1963:85,86].) Why does the artist go to all the trouble? "The answer," Edmund Leach has succinctly remarked, "is 'partly for fun and partly because the public provides a market for his work' " (1961:34).

Fun may be part of the artist's inner motivation for working, although the word "pleasure," rather than "fun," seems more accurately to capture the satisfaction many artists derive from doing their work. The enjoyment may come directly from the act of making art itself, or else the process of making art may provide a haven from the workaday world of the artist's society. Thus Ottenberg remarks, "In the achievement-oriented, individualistic way of life at Afikpo, [the artist] is free to carve as he chooses, regulated merely by his own strong sense of tradition" (1975:67). Chuku, the Afikpo artist whose life and work Ottenberg studied most closely, "is a quiet and nonabrasive person in a society in which a good many men love to talk and argue and give forth with oratory. He lives in a small compound, distinctly separated from others in the village, that is itself a peaceful place, lacking the bustle of some of the larger compounds" (1975:74).

The artist may get other kinds of intangible rewards. The preceding section described several societies in which the artist's achievements bring prestige and high social standing within the community at large. And, insofar as the works take on a larger social importance, the artist can justifiably take pride in creating them. This can be particularly important if the products have religious significance: Through art the artist may be heir to all the emotional satisfaction that the supernatural realm can provide. (The romantic picture of the artist in small-scale society who works in religion-inspired rapture is, however, usually an overdrawn caricature.)

In addition to the possible pleasures of pursuing one's craft, the artist also often gets tangible rewards for his or her work—there is, in Leach's phrase, "a market." The artist can capitalize on the market for art work in one of several ways. If there are apprentices the master will receive goods, services, or both in return for instruction. More important, however, are the rewards the artist gets in exchange for the art he or she produces.

Chukwu Okoro, the master Afikpo carver in Nigeria who has been mentioned on several other occasions in this chapter, again provides a useful example. Afikpo carvers, you remember, are not held in particularly high esteem: Carving is "lazy man's work" in Afikpo society. Chukwu does, however, reap some economic benefits as a result of his artistic endeavors. The most important Afikpo art objects are masks worn by secret society members during the performance of the numerous plays that the societies stage periodically. (Figure 4–2 shows Afikpo masks in use.) When a secret society member intends to participate in a play, he approaches a known

FIGURE 4-2   Afikpo masks in use. *(Photo courtesy of Simon Ottenberg and the University of Washington Press.)*

carver such as Chukwu with his request for a mask. He may choose to commission a mask of his own, in which case he will pay the carver a small fee in cash or with some palm wine or tobacco. (It was Chukwu, remember, who even as a young boy was successful at mask making, selling his creations to other boys for "three medium-sized yams.")

There is, however, another option open to the Afikpo man who needs a mask. Some carvers have a stock of masks that they rent for ceremonial use. When Ottenberg talked with him, Chukwu Okoro had 30 such masks that he retained for periodic rentals. When a secret society member wants to rent one of them from Chukwu,

> he makes arrangements a few days before the ceremony in which he will use it. Chukwu has a boy in the compound . . . who receives a small commission for assisting when he is not around. Persons usually ask for a specific type of mask. . . . Chukwu usually does not tell them what to bring in exchange for the rental, only "something" if they ask, and he seems reluctant to put the matter on a strict cash or contractual basis (Ottenberg 1975:75,76).

In practice the cash payment is small, amounting to about 20 cents in U.S. currency, perhaps supplemented again by some palm wine or tobacco. (That amount, which pays for the use of the mask for only the few days during which it is used for a specific ceremony, appears to be roughly one-tenth the amount Chukwu would get for selling a comparable new mask outright.) Whether the mask is sold or rented, no ritual accompanies its transfer to another person, although Chukwu may give his client some advice on storing the mask or recoloring its surface before use.

Although a carver such as Chukwu may provide masks to several men before a big festival, mask making is far from a lucrative activity. Carving does not provide enough income to support artists as full-time or even half-time professionals; art work must be supplemented by subsistence activities such as farming, by trading, or by working in other traditional occupations such as carpentry.

Chukwu seems typical of many artists in small-scale societies who have been described in the literature. Carving is not a road to riches and power, but Chukwu—in his small shed at the edge of the bush (Figure 4–3), working quietly by himself at his own relaxed pace, or listening to the

FIGURE 4-3   Nigerian master carver, Chukwu Okoro, 1952. *(Photo courtesy Simon Ottenberg and the University of Washington Press.)*

gossip of his friends as they watch him at his work—seems to be living a life that is well suited to his temperament.

The Artist as an Integral Member of Society

One important aspect of the mature artist's life remains to be discussed, namely the extent to which the artist is an integral part of the community at large and the mechanisms whereby integration is effected. This topic is especially interesting because it is a major way in which artists in small-scale societies differ from their counterparts in the contemporary Western world.

The artist's ties with his or her surroundings are of various sorts. In the preceding discussion of artists' informal training, for instance, it was noted that the motor skills used in the production of art are often applied to other work. Subsistence activities and the making of utilitarian items both provide practice areas for art techniques. This is particularly important for the artist in small-scale societies since, as a less than full-time professional, the individual may go for long periods without actually working on art items. Thus the techniques used in making art seldom set the artist apart from the social milieu but rather are an extension of the skills that are used in the day-to-day life of the artist and by other members of the society.

There is an even more important way in which the artist is an integral part of society: He or she typically shares the same value system as the society's other members. This applies to both aesthetic values as well as to standards in other areas of life. This point should not, of course, be carried to extremes. The artist is not "just like everybody else." But even though the artist is special, he or she can seldom adopt a style of belief or behavior that is radically different from that of others in the society. The artist lives and eats with nonartists, sharing their beliefs about the supernatural, enmeshed in the same web of kinship relations, and so on. In direct contrast to the often-heard stereotype of the contemporary Western artist, with a bohemian life-style and eccentric beliefs, the artist in small-scale society is usually a well-integrated member of his or her group.

THE ARTIST AT WORK

The preceding sections looked at the artist as a social personage. Here we see the artist at work—selecting materials, using tools, actually making art.

Tools and Materials

One feature of small-scale societies is the relative simplicity of their technology, and this is reflected in the art that such societies produce. Most significantly, art in small-scale societies is based on a low-energy technology. The only source of power in most such societies comes from human muscle or from the heat given off by wood fires. The amount of energy available from these sources is minuscule by comparison to that which our own technology requires for such operations as sophisticated metal processing (mining, refining, alloying, casting, welding, etc.), chemical purification and synthesis (to produce and refine pigments, mediums, and so on), and other physical processes such as the production of large quantities of wood, paper, and canvas. As practiced today in our society, all these activities require energy in much greater amounts than is available solely from human muscle power and wood fires. In a sense, technology is only tangential to the artistic process itself, but unquestionably the nature of Western art would be drastically different in its absence.

The technology of art in small-scale societies is less complex than its Western counterpart in two additional ways. First, all (or most) of the materials used are derived from the artist's local area. This, of course, limits the range of materials available for the artist's use. (Granted that extratribal exchange of art materials is relatively common and that far-flung trade networks have sometimes existed in the past. Nevertheless, such importing of materials is the exception rather than the rule.) Second, the artist can seldom call upon the skills of others to supplement his or her own expertise. Apprentices and patrons may help with the less complicated parts of the work, but the artist obviously can never consult with a metallurgist, a paint chemist, or a lumber importer.

It must be stressed that the technological simplicity being discussed here is only relative, based on a comparison with Western society's elaborate methods. In absolute terms, the tools, materials, and methods used in small-scale societies are often ingenious. Again, Chukwu Okoro, the master Afikpo carver, illustrates the point.

Chukwu uses only two or three kinds of wood for masks. These species are apparently chosen for practical reasons: An analysis of samples taken from masks he carved revealed that they were all made from woods that are relatively light in weight and that have short, parallel fibers. Of these woods, Chukwu uses the lightest for masks that have no major projections; a stronger, somewhat heavier wood is used for masks that do have projections. If possible, Chukwu cuts wood for a mask as much as six months before he intends to carve it. This gives him time to soak the wood in water for a while before drying it, a process that Chukwu considers necessary to soften the wood for carving and also to prevent its splitting. Apparently the method works: Ottenberg remarks that "none of the masks that he made for me has cracked seriously; only a few have minor splits, although some of them are now twenty years old and have been through all sorts of climates" (1975:76).

In contrast to the pattern found among artists in many small-scale societies, traditional Afikpo carvers did not make their own tools. Chukwu himself now includes several Western items in his tool kit—a penknife, sandpaper, and so on. Previously, carvers got their tools locally from black-smiths. In Chukwu's father's time, carvers used the following tools:

1. A small adz called *atɔ*, short for *atufu* (to burrow out), a term used for a range of carving tools. This one had a wooden handle and was employed for general shaping and rough work.

2. A U-shaped blade of iron with wooden handles at both ends, also called *atɔ* and used to cut out the insides of the masks.

3. A long iron chisel, without a handle, again called *atɔ*, which was employed to carve out eyes, mouth, and other parts by being hit with a rock or a piece of wood.

4. A long, thin rod of iron, about 10 inches long and ¼ to ½ inch wide, called *ahia* (borer), which was heated in the fire and used to bore holes for the raffia attachment and for other purposes, as well as being used heated to blacken small surface parts of the mask.

5. A wide, flat piece of iron, or a machete, also heated in the fire and used to blacken larger surfaces.

6. Another machete was used to cut the original block of wood and for rough work on the mask.

7. A leaf, *anwɛrɛwa*, which is used when fresh, acts like sandpaper, being fairly fine-grained.

8. An iron needle, *ntutu*, about 3 inches long, for sewing up the raffia on the backing of the masks (Ottenberg 1975:76–77).

The traditional Afikpo tool kit, small though it is, is larger than that used by artists in many other small-scale societies. Yoruba carvers, for example, use only two knives and two adzes (shown in Figure 4–4), plus a larger adze for the felling of trees and an ax for splitting logs.

FIGURE 4-4   Yoruba carver's tools from Oyo, Nigeria. Sizes (top to bottom): 28 cm., 24 cm., 36 cm., and 41 cm. long. *(Courtesy Lowie Museum of Anthropology, University of California, Berkeley.)*

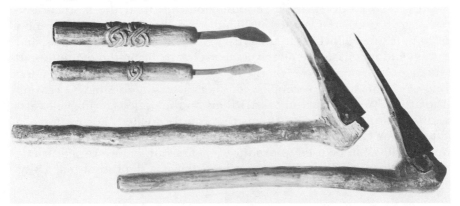

After carving is complete, Chukwu adds a raffia backing. Currently the raffia is purchased from traders; presumably it was produced locally in the past. The addition of color is the last stage in the creation of an Afikpo mask. Feathers were traditionally used as paintbrushes, sometimes supplemented by thin wood sticks or wood shavings. The traditional palette had four colors, each of local origin. Ottenberg describes their production as follows:

> **Black.** The traditional way to achieve this coloration is to blacken the surface with a very hot iron rod, a flat iron piece, or a machete. If the oil from a few roasted palm kernels is applied to a surface that has been blackened by searing, it becomes darker. . . .

> **White.** Traditionally *nzu*, a chalk mined at Afikpo, is used to add white to a mask. It is also produced in considerable quantities in nearby Edda Village-Group, from where it is traded to Afikpo. . . . Another white chalk sometimes used is *nzu ɛja*, which is mined at Afikpo. Although prepared in the same manner as *nzu*, it is not as smooth and fine. . . .

> **Yellow.** This coloring is traditionally made from the yellowish bark of the ɔkwoghɔ tree. . . . The bark is rubbed on a moist, flat stone, *npumɛ odo* (stone-*odo*), usually by women, and a substance comes off that dries into a powder and is kept in cake form. . . .

> **Red and orange.** The *uhie* color is traditionally made from camwood . . . by rubbing its wood (not its bark) on a moist, flat stone, *npumɛ uhie*, and collecting the powder, which is stored in cakes (Ottenberg 1975:81).

Considering the tools and materials that are used in Afikpo art production one by one, each is seen to be an ingenious utilization of something from the local environment. But considering the Afikpo art technology as a whole, the range is far narrower than that available to the contemporary Western artist.

A fundamental question regarding technology remains unanswered, however: Does the relatively limited range of tools and materials available in small-scale societies place a serious handicap upon the aesthetic expression of the artist? On the one hand it can be argued that the most important feature of art lies in the artist's skill, vision, and sensibilities, and that tools and materials are merely a means for realizing these quintessential qualities. Common sense, on the other hand, tells us that although the technology of art may be secondary to other factors, it does have a bearing on the artistic product, placing restrictions on the options available to artists and limiting the range of things that can be created. For example, a palette such as Chukwu's, with only four colors including black and white, unquestionably can be used to produce fine art, but a more varied palette opens up new possibilities. With regard to color it is significant that artists themselves in small-scale societies are usually eager to enlarge their palettes when possible. Chukwu, for instance, now gets blues, browns, and greens from imported paints and shoe polishes.

Perhaps the best answer to the question posed above is this: Primitive technology does indeed place some restraints on artists in small-scale societies, limiting the range of what they can do. But if art is thought of as the skillful manipulation of visual media, then even the simplest material cultures have some domains in which a high level of skill can be exercised; that is, even the least complex human technologies provide a sufficient basis for the production of valid art.

Making a Work of Art

Creating a work of art is a process that takes place on two levels, in the artist's mind as well as in his or her hands. Chapter 5 looks at the former of these two levels—the cognitive aspects of artistic production. The other level, the actual material creation of the piece, will be dealt with here. As has been the case throughout the present chapter, diverse small-scale societies exhibit a wide range of techniques. Again our approach will be to note the many possible methods and then describe in more depth the situation in one particular society.

In some societies artists are constrained by ritualistic restrictions. Our Afikpo friend, Chukwu, for example, can only work in a place where he won't be seen by women or by young males who have not yet been initiated into the secret society whose members use Chukwu's masks (Ottenberg 1975:72). (Navaho and Pueblo silversmiths sometimes also prefer to work in solitude, but not for ritual reasons. They merely want to avoid distractions, and some wish to protect their trade secrets, thereby keeping a partial monopoly on the market [cf. Adair 1944:92].)

A different type of prohibition is placed on the Anang carver: He should avoid sexual intercourse on the night before he begins carving a major piece because, the Anang believe, intercourse weakens one and diminishes a carver's skill, creativity, and desire to carve (Messenger 1973:109). But restraints such as these seem more the exception than the rule cross-culturally. As the Afikpo and Anang examples illustrate, they may be based upon beliefs about either the artistic product or the artistic process itself.

A second dimension of variation lies in the pace at which the artist works. Most Fang carvers, for instance, proceed in a leisurely fashion, interrupting work on a mask for several weeks or a month, whenever other duties such as plantation work beckon them (Fernandez, 1973:200). Two carvers told Fernandez that "a figure or a mask only took shape gradually, as the spirit moved the carver, and it could be rushed only at the sacrifice of its quality" (1973:200).

At the opposite extreme from the Fang are the carvers among the Anang and Yoruba. They typically work with intense absorption, going from the beginning right through the end of a project, pausing only long enough to appraise their progress occasionally or allow the completed work to dry (Messenger 1973; Bascom 1973).

The Abelam Artist at Work

Anthony Forge's description of artists among the Abelam of New Guinea's Sepik region can be used to breathe some life into the foregoing generalizations regarding the artist at work. Most Abelam art is made for use in the so-called tambaran cult, an institution into which young men are initiated by means of eight successive ceremonies that occur over a period of 10 or more years. Forge describes the cult and associated ceremonies in some detail (1967, 1971), but for our present purposes only a few features need be mentioned. During each of the eight tambaran ceremonies, initiates are shown art objects of one sort or another and are told that the objects are manifestations of a major class of spirits. (At each ceremony after the first, the initiates learn that the previously viewed objects were not actually the spirits themselves, but that this time they will see the "real thing.") During the last ceremony the initiates are shown the most sacred objects, and after that the whole process begins again, with the new cult members acting as initiators for the next generation of Abelam males.

The items shown to the tambaran initiates require extensive art production. The first ceremonies in the cycle involve painting only—on the floor of the ceremonial house and on flat wooden panels. Such panels are used in all eight stages of the ritual cycle, but in later stages they are supplemented by increasingly elaborate items carved in the round from softwoods. These too are painted, but painting and carving are always two distinctly different processes, carried out in different settings and manners.

Abelam painting is supervised by a man who is recognized for his artistic skills, but he is assisted by several other initiated men. The artist apparently has the whole design in his head before he begins. With materials at hand, he starts by outlining a design in white paint, using as a brush a single chicken feather, made pliable by bending. He may use some mechanical aids—a length of split cane to work out the proportions of a design relative to the panel upon which it will appear, or a piece of cane tied into a circular ring to serve as a template for curved lines. Usually, though, he works freehand, building up the design from one side of the panel to the other, or from the head of a sculpted figure downward.

When painting, the Abelam artist works with great speed, boldly laying out the white outlines of designs that are traditionally appropriate for the panel or sculpture he is working on. As soon as he finishes outlining a small part of the design he tells one of his more skilled assistants to go around it, painting a red or yellow line right beside the white one he has just put down. He himself continues, outlining more of the planned design with his chicken-feather brush, but keeping an eye on the work of his assistant, whose own work may be followed by that of another assistant, using another color. As the doubling, or trebling, of the design in one area is completed, the artist instructs yet another assistant to fill in remaining solid spaces with single colors, a duty that requires less skill than the painting of outlines. Even less skill is needed by the additional assistants who paint rows of dots or who work at making more paint. In all the artist is typically supervising the work of eight to ten helpers, in addition to drawing the outline of the design itself.

The swirl of activity attendant to Abelam painting stands in marked contrast to the quiet, contemplative atmosphere that surrounds the Abelam artist as he carves. He works in a place that is set off from the normal activities of the village, always in the shade to minimize the possibility of the wood's splitting. One assistant may be present to do some occasional minor task, but otherwise company and conversation are not welcome. A person interested in learning the carver's skill—whether he is a young Abelam man or a visiting anthropologist—must be prepared to spend a great deal of time silently watching the artist as he carves or as he simply sits thinking about the piece he is making.

Besides the strikingly different pace at which Abelam carving and painting are carried out, there are also differences in the ritual restrictions placed upon the artist. According to Forge, "Men who are going to participate in painting bleed their penes and must abstain from all sexual contact until after the ceremony; meat and certain vegetable foods are forbidden, but they can and do eat large quantities of the yam soup and finest steamed yams" (1967:75). By contrast, the artist as carver is under no ritual prohibitions whatsoever.

This account of the Abelam artist at work illustrates several of the generalizations made in the preceding section. It shows that the artist's work—his pace, his use of assistants, and so on—varies not only cross-culturally but may also vary within a single society. Interestingly, at least one art historian with no first-hand experience in Abelam culture feels that the Abelam practice of combining two distinctly different techniques is "unsuccessful"—at least in terms of his own aesthetic values. He claims that while "the painted designs of these forms . . . create an intense, spiritual quality, particularly in the faces, they produce an over-all visual excitation that tends to fragment the object both compositionally and expressively" (Wingert 1962:210). That native Abelam art critics would concur in this opinion seems unlikely, but Wingert is correct in his educated guess that Abelam art reflects two dissimilar styles of approach.

PORTFOLIO

The Art of the Northwest Coast

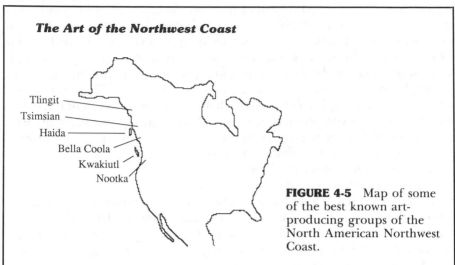

Tlingit
Tsimsian
Haida
Bella Coola
Kwakiutl
Nootka

FIGURE 4-5 Map of some of the best known art-producing groups of the North American Northwest Coast.

One of the most distinctive culture areas of indigenous North America stretched from Yakutat Bay in Alaska to what is now southern Oregon. Many individual tribes lived along this coast and on coastal islands, including, from north to south, the Tlingit, Tsimshian, Haida, Bellabella, Bella Coola, Kwakiutl, and Coast Salish (see Figure 4–5). In both quantity and quality, the pre-twentieth-century Northwest Coast was unquestionably one of the richest art-producing areas of the world. How did its inhabitants, who lacked any form of agriculture, manage to produce so much art of such impressive dimensions? The nonnative might look to the environment for an explanation; compared to the semi-arid Southwest, for example, the lush Northwest Coast seems well endowed with fishing, gathering, and hunting resources. But these food sources were erratic, with temporary surpluses in one location offsetting unforeseeable shortages and possible famine in another.

If the artistic richness of the Northwest Coast can be linked to any environmental factor, it is perhaps this unpredictability. Northwest Coast tribes coped with inequalities in food resources by maintaining an elaborate system for redistributing material goods. Each tribe had a hierarchy of slaves, commoners, and nobles; and men in the highest level competed fiercely with their rivals to see who could accumulate the largest quantities of wealth to publicly give away at ceremonies called *potlatches*. Potlatches ostensibly served as a means of gaining and displaying social status among noble families, but their practical consequence was the redistribution of unevenly available food, thereby providing some protection against the ravages of periodic famine. (After the arrival of European wage labor, potlatches became even more spectacular and included not just giving away but even destroying items of value.)

FIGURE 4-6   Haida village of Skidgate, Queen Charlotte Islands, British Columbia. *(Courtesy Field Museum of Natural History, Chicago.)*

FIGURE 4-7   Tlingit totem poles. *(Courtesy Field Museum of Natural History, Chicago.)*

If the rivalry for social status provided greater security for the people of the Northwest Coast, it also resulted in an abundance of art (Figure 4–6). When a particular village was blessed with an overabundance of food, its leaders inevitably shared their surpluses at a potlatch; and this ceremony, in turn, occasioned the commissioning of new and impressive works of art (Figure 4–7), both to give away in the potlatch itself and also to serve as public reminders of the hosts' generosity and greatness. As noted in Chapter 3, although the human and animal figures found in Northwest Coast art iconographically portrayed ancestors and mythic creatures, the overriding symbolic intent of the art was to flaunt the elevated social standing of its owners. Thus, from unexpected quarters—erratic food supplies and a class system based on competitive one-upmanship—came the motivation for creating a great deal of highly sophisticated art.

The link between art and environment is also seen in the artist's materials. Cedar forests provided straight-grained wood that resisted rotting; and spruce, yew, and other trees met the other requirements of the carver, as did bone, ivory, argelite, shell, copper, and slate (Figure 4–8). Sculptural media were often painted, and again the environment served the artist's needs: Iron oxides provided red and a mustard-yellow color, greenish blue came from oxidized copper, and black from soot or charcoal. These materials were used to produce art that included the monumental "totem poles," carved house poles, and painted house facades, accoutrements to ritual such as rattles and headdresses, and utilitarian items, including storage boxes, knives, ladles, and pipes.

Especially dramatic were the many masks produced by the various Northwest Coast tribes. Carved from wood, colorfully painted, and inlaid with copper or iridescent shell, they were masterpieces of ceremonial art. Some had movable lower jaws so that the wearer could open and close the mouth by means of a hidden string. Still more dramatic were the "transformation" masks in which two or even three faces were nested within one another. The outer mask, or masks, were carved and painted both inside and out and hinged at the sides so that, at the appropriate moment in a ritual performance, they could be opened to reveal another mask within (Figure 4–9).

FIGURE 4-8 Northwest Coast bowl in the form of a wolf. Slate with inlaid abalone shell and shark teeth. *(Photo Courtesy Field Museum of Natural History, Chicago.)*

FIGURE 4-9 Kwakiutl "transformation" mask, open. Vancouver Island, British Colombia. *(Courtesy Field Museum of Natural History, Chicago.)*

FIGURE 4-10 A Northwest Coast Chilkat blanket in the process of manufacture. *(Photo courtesy Field Museum of Natural History, Chicago.)*

Equally impressive were the Northwest Coast's traditional textiles and basketry. Best known were the distinctive blankets that may have originated with the Tsimshian, that reached their definitive development among the Chilkat subtribe of the Tlingit, and that were ultimately found as far south as Vancouver island. Chilkat blankets were made out of the wool of mountain sheep, shredded cedar bark, and, in some cases, hair from small herds of white dogs. Men's blankets contained a tripartite division, the middle zone of which portrayed human or animal figures (Figures 4–10 and 4–11), whereas women's

FIGURE 4-11 Northwest Coast chief, posed in traditional garb, including a Chilkat blanket. His carved headdress, with its yellow cedar bristles and cloth pendants, portrays a raven. On his baton can be seen crests of a sea lion, killer whale, devil fish, and dog fish. *(Courtesy Field Museum of Natural History, Chicago.)*

FIGURE 4-12 Haida woman making a basket using the suspended-warp technique. Massett, Queen Charlotte Islands, British Columbia. *(Courtesy Field Museum of Natural History, Chicago.)*

FIGURE 4-13   Tlingit baskets. Top, lidded rattle basket. Probably collected ca. 1900; 20 cm. in diameter *(Courtesy Kansas City Museum of History and Science)*. Bottom, unlidded basket, nineteenth century; 41 cm. high *(Nelson Gallery-Atkins Museum, Kansas City, Missouri, Nelson Fund)*.

blankets bore all-over geometric designs, a style also found in most Northwest Coast baskets (Figures 4–12 and 4–13).

The relative simplicity of media and technology found in Northwest Coast art contrasts with the high sophistication of its style. From the largest totem pole to a carving small enough to fit in the palm of one's hand, Northwest Coast art suggests power and vigor, qualities appropriate to the personalities of the proud owners of the art. The use of broad, sweeping planes gives even two-dimensional works such as blankets and the flat sides of boxes a sculptural quality, but this volumetric assertiveness is held in check by a highly sensitive treatment of the surface. There, painted and incised lines fill all empty spaces with either stylized features, such as eye designs indicating underlying joints, or with abstract patterns, including circles and flattened ovals that seem to be forced into the contours of rectangles (Gunther 1966:5). Another distinctive stylistic feature is the technique, described in Chapter 3, whereby a figurative subject is simplified, its components dissected and recombined in an arrangement determined by the shape of the available design field (see Figures 3–4 and 3–5).

Despite these area-wide similarities, no two tribes' art styles were exactly alike. The Kwakiutl, for example, are notable for their use of dramatic motifs that they flamboyantly carved in wood and outlined in vivid colors, whereas the nearby Haida specialized in smaller argelite carvings. Such regional variation reflects the availability of materials as well as differences in the religious themes that provide subject matter for the art.

The technical proficiency that characterizes Northwest Coast art reflects the presence of semiprofessional and even professional artists, a rare phenomenon among prehorticultural peoples. For a major work such as a large totem pole, a wealthy clan leader would seek a carver with an established reputation. Among the Kwakiutl, the commission would be announced with great public fanfare, a "down payment" made, and the artist, along with his family and assistants, would move into the patron's house and stay until the pole was completed (Gunther 1966:13).

But despite its elite sponsorship and the artists' specialization, Northwest Coast art was well integrated into the society at large. From the towering totem poles to items as common as carved hooks for halibut fishing, art pervaded the day-to-day life of every villager; and members of all classes understood the fundamental messages the art conveyed.

Recent years have seen a revival of artistic activity among many of the native peoples of the Northwest Coast. This welcome renaissance of a nearly forgotten art combines many traditional techniques, media, and subjects with a contemporary concern for ethnic identity and pride. Clearly, it builds upon a heritage of great artistic richness and vitality.

CONCLUSIONS

The task of all the sciences, the social sciences included, is to examine the world around us, to discover and describe patterns in its diversity, and, finally, to try to understand the fundamental principles that underlie these patterns. The cross-cultural study of artists thus far has been largely confined to description, but even here there are interesting variables that remain to be explored, such as differences in the rates at which art works are produced.

As a catalog of diversity, the present chapter should convince the reader that easy and certain generalizations about "the artist in small-scale society" should be viewed with much suspicion. There is enormous variety from one culture area to another, from one society to another within a single area, from one artist to another within a given society, and sometimes even between an artist's work in one setting and another. Some broad patterns can be discerned, however, and they are listed below. They are highly general and, for the most part, they tell us more about what artists typically aren't rather than what they are. Nevertheless, the generalizations have some value in that they are antidotes to some popular misconceptions about artists in small-scale societies.

First, this art is never anonymous. A given piece, by the time it finds its way into a museum collection in Europe or America, may seem that way to us, but this fault is ours: We may be ignorant of the maker, but in its society of origin the maker's signature is written all over the work. The exceptional person who creates art is inevitably recognized as being the possessor of special skills and abilities. The nature and extent of this recognition varies widely, but it seems to exist universally.

Second, art in small-scale society is nowhere a simple, untutored outpouring of emotion on the part of the artist. The society from which the art comes has traditional aesthetic standards, and the artist strives to meet these standards. In some instances the artist, once started on a piece, works with abandon, but even in these cases the product reflects much practice and forethought. As the case studies presented in this chapter have shown, any supposed parallel between the work of a mature artist in a small-scale society and the creations of children or psychotics in our own society is altogether spurious.

Third, the artist is not necessarily an impractical person, totally engrossed in art and oblivious to other matters. An important feature, indeed a definitive feature, of small-scale societies is the fact that no individual specializes full-time in any one activity. Thus, the person who is an artist is also by necessity a hunter or gatherer, a father or mother, and so on. The artist's personal status may range from that of a respected elder to a good-for-nothing but he or she is never an alienated rebel, marching to the beat of a different drummer. Thus, it is imperative that the artist be considered in the context of his or her own society and that art work be viewed in the context of the traditional values of the maker's fellow artists and critics.

Finally, the artist's social integration sets certain limits on the artistic freedom he or she has. Not only is the art work constrained by traditional tastes, but also the medium in which the artist works is limited. One source of limitation is technological: Only certain tools and materials are available to members of small-scale societies. But societies commonly limit the range of usable media even further. Often the limitation is sex specific.

The cross-cultural study of artists is still in its infancy; much research and analysis has yet to be done. Specifically, and as noted previously, more information is needed on female artists and on artists from places other than West and Central Africa and Melanesia. Also there is a serious need for descriptive studies of artists in prehorticultural societies such as those of the Eskimo, Kalihari Desert, and central Australian groups.

Description, however, is only the first step toward understanding. The search for patterns, and more importantly, the explanation of patterns, is a job that has hardly begun. Certainly there are many interesting issues to be explored. For example, what factors influence whether or not an artist receives extrinsic rewards for his or her work? And what sociocultural factors tend to promote a high level of artistic output in a society? This question has been asked for some limited areas (Houlihan 1972; McGhee 1976; A. Wolfe 1969), but a synthesizing, global approach might now be attempted.

There is, so to speak, an art to doing science. The art lies first in deciding which questions are important and interesting, and second, in selecting from these questions those that can profitably be pursued, given the information presently available or obtainable. The future should see some artful asking—and, one hopes, answering—of questions with regard to artists themselves.

GUIDE TO ADDITIONAL READINGS

Detailed accounts of individual artists in small-scale societies are few in number. Two symposia have been held on the subject; in both instances the papers that were presented have been published: *The Artist in Primitive Society* (1961), edited by M. W. Smith, has articles dealing with artists from several continents, while *The Traditional Artist in African Societies* (1973), edited by Warren L. d'Azevedo, confines itself to sub-Saharan Africa. Himmelheber (1960) also deals with artists from Africa.

Traditional African artists have been the subjects of several papers, with Carroll (1967) and Chappel (1972) discussing Yoruba artists, d'Azevedo (1966) dealing with Gola artists, and A. Wolfe (1955) briefly describing the work of an innovative Ubangi carver. Brain and Pollock (1971) provide substantial information on traditional Bangwa artists.

Culture areas other than Africa have received relatively less attention, although books and articles about art in particular societies typically give some information about artists' training, status, methods, etc. For the Americas, the classics by Bunzel (1972 [orig. 1929]) on Pueblo potters and O'Neale (1932) on Yorok-Karok basket weavers have been supplemented only by Ray's account (1961) of Alaskan Eskimo artists.

For Oceania, Gerbrands (1967, 1978) provides extended discussions of carvers in two Melanesian locales, while traditional Maori artists were described quite some time ago by Firth (1925).

A bibliography of published works on women artists in traditional societies appeared in volume 4, number 1 of *Heresies: A Feminist Journal of Art and Politics* (1978), and the same issue of the journal contains several of the articles cited in this chapter. Other interesting papers on the subject are Roe (1979) and Parezo (1982).

Holm has published (1974, 1983) an in-depth study of Willie Sea-weed, a traditional Northwest Coast carver. Other valuable studies of Northwest Coast art are Holm (1965, 1972), Holm and Reid (1975), Gunther (1962, 1966), Hawthorn (1961), Waite (1966), Siebert (1967), Wingert (1951), and Wyatt (1984).

CHAPTER 5

The Comparative Psychology of Art

From one point of view, all of human culture exists only in people's heads. From this perspective culture is composed solely of traditional rules, beliefs, and expectations, all of which are mental constructs; human behavior and artifacts reflect culture, but are themselves once removed from culture itself. A psychological definition of culture such as this one has some shortcomings: How, for example, is culture to be studied if it has only an abstract, cognitive existence? Nevertheless, such an approach clearly has applicability to the cross-cultural study of art: Traditional aesthetic standards, the artist's imagination, and the viewer's affective reaction to a work of art are of primary importance; the object itself and the skillful activities that went into its production are interesting, but they, again, are imperfect reflections of the mental processes and constructs that exist only in people's minds.

The present chapter surveys the current state of our knowledge of the psychological level of art cross-culturally. I have organized this highly diverse material into three general areas. First we will look at some of the ways in which the conceptual components of art are formed in the artist's mind in the first place; next, we will discuss the dynamics of the artistic imagination; and finally, we will consider the "psychology of the image" by looking at techniques of stylization and the "generative" approach to analyzing art.

BECOMING AN ARTIST: AESTHETIC SOCIALIZATION

One topic discussed in Chapter 4 was the mechanics of training young artists. But the overt process of training the hands is only one part—the easier part—of the story. What about training the mind? How are imagination, creativity, diligence, and so on nurtured in the neophyte's soul? Many parts of this question remain unanswered, but, fortunately, several cross-cultural studies now shed some light on this most important of questions.

One excellent source of information is Ruth Bunzel's *The Pueblo Potter: A Study of Creative Imagination in Primitive Art.* The fact that the fieldwork was carried out some time ago—the summers of 1924 and 1925—is in one respect a virtue: Today, most Pueblo potters make their wares for sale to outsiders, but this was less true in Bunzel's day, when pottery was still an important native craft. Not only did Bunzel interview potters in numerous villages, but she also became an apprentice potter herself. Her book provides a good account of the way in which the potter's art in the American Southwest is handed down from mother to daughter. (See this chapter's Portfolio for more information on Southwestern art, including the techniques used in Pueblo pottery.)

Much of Bunzel's training dealt with technical issues: where to get clay, how to prepare the clay for working, how to roll balls of clay out into long, slender cylinders and coil these into a vessel, and so on. This information is handed down from mother to daughter, partly through didactic teaching but largely by demonstration: As the mother goes through all the phases of pottery making her daughter watches, imitating her techniques, benefiting from her occasional practical hints such as a warning that the novice's pot will probably crack during firing unless the daughter does so-and-so.

The general principles underlying the pot's shape are apparently never verbalized by Pueblo pottery teachers. The woman may say, "It must be even all around and not larger on one side than another" (Bunzel, 1972:8), but more specific rules such as being certain that a jar's neck is two-thirds the size of its base, or that a certain number of strips of clay are needed to make a pot of the proper height—these are never stated by the teacher. When Bunzel pointed out such regularities, the potters agreed that they were generally true, but they said they had never noticed them before, much less included the principles in their instructions to their daughters.

Euroamericans might assume that making a pot provides two separate avenues for aesthetic expression—the shaping of the pot and the decoration of its surface. But in the minds of Pueblo potters, a pot's form is determined by tradition: In a given Pueblo there is only a small number of proper shapes, and virtually all pots made there conform to one or another of these shapes. Most Euroamericans find the compact gracefulness of the shapes of Pueblo pots very attractive, but their makers take the shapes more or less for granted. "Anyone," they told Bunzel, "can make a good shape, but you have to use your head in putting on the design" (1972:49).

If didactic teaching of general aesthetic principles was lacking for the shape of Pueblo pots, so also was it absent from instruction for the more individualistic activity of painting pots. One potter from the Pueblo of San Ildefonso told Bunzel:

> If I were teaching a young girl, I should tell her that she must be most careful with the polishing—not to scratch the pot and to make it nice and smooth. . . . In painting [designs] I should not tell her what to put on, but I should say to her: "Use your own brain and paint anything you like, only put it on straight and even." She would learn the different designs by watching the other women and by using her own brain and making the kind she wants (1972:61).

Another potter, a Zuni woman, explained to Bunzel how she would give a novice potter elaborate instructions for laying out decorations on a pot, utilizing the width of one finger as a unit of measure, and using her fingernail to mark on the clay the places where designs should be placed. The only nontechnical advice this woman would give a student was this: "The jar must be covered all over [with designs] but there should be plenty of white showing. I should tell her not to use too many small designs, because then it is too black and that is not nice" (1972:50). Bunzel herself discovered some principles that underlie pot decoration (such as an aversion to using certain designs together on a single pot), but these too were tacit, never explicitly taught to young potters.

Put designs on "straight and even" and don't use too many small ones—that is as far as Pueblo potters go in terms of explicitly teaching the next generation the aesthetic principles that underlie the traditional decoration of pots. Bunzel herself was frustrated by the sparseness of instruction: "When we started to paint, I was told once more to paint whatever I wished. When I insisted on more definite instructions, one woman, though amazed at my stupidity, said she would paint one of her bowls while I did mine, copying her design, stroke by stroke as she made it" (1972:61).

The most telling feature of this quotation is that the potter was "amazed" at Bunzel's "stupidity." We have no reason to believe that Ruth Bunzel was deficient in native intelligence, perceptual abilities, or motor skills; she did, however, lack one vital thing that was possessed by her Pueblo mentors and by everyone else who had ever tried to learn to make Pueblo pottery: She did not have a lifetime of intimate exposure to Pueblo pots. The only conclusion we can draw from Bunzel's account of Pueblo potters (and from similar reports from other societies) is that novices learn most of the principles of pottery making largely informally and unconsciously, by being raised in close proximity to pots, potters, and the technique of pottery making. The process whereby individuals, during the interval between birth and maturity, acquire the principles of their culture is known as *socialization;* and aesthetic socialization is obviously a crucial part of learning to become an artist.

Little is known about how the informal transmission of aesthetic standards from one generation to the next actually takes place. However, we can get some clues about the process by looking at analogies with language. After all, both art and language are means of conveying information; the messages may be explicitly straightforward or nebulously emotion-provoking; and the communication is made possible by imposing order on a natural medium in accord with a set of traditional rules—grammar in the case of sentences, stylistic conventions in the case of art.

For our present purposes the most interesting similarity between language and art is that each is transmitted from one generation to the next, usually with only minor alterations in its structure, and this transfer occurs without explicit, didactic teaching of fundamental principles. And, indeed, socialized individuals are only unconsciously aware of the rules themselves. Our own culture is unusual in that we do indulge in some explicit teaching of grammatical principles, with primary and secondary school teachers sometimes acting as if our civilization will stand or fall depending on whether or not members of the next generation are able to parse sentences. In fact, however, most children already "know", albeit unconsciously, a large number of complex grammatical rules before they even begin school. In societies that do not have a tradition of grammatical analysis and formal teaching, the rules for speaking "properly" are as numerous as in our language, but they remain largely implicit and untaught.

Thus, although the remark, "I don't know much about art, but I know what I like," is often derided as being philistine, in fact it reflects some very important features of the human mind: All of us, even in the total absence of formal training in "art appreciation," have acquired aesthetic standards; these values are derived wholly or partially from other members of our society and are acquired during the process of socialization; and most of us have difficulty verbalizing the rules in general terms. But however unconscious they may be, we can use the rules to evaluate the art works we see, allowing us to say with conviction, "I like this one better than that one." And, as in the case of grammatical standards for language, we have arrived at our aesthetic views despite the fact that no single work of art embodies the standards with absolute perfection.

How does one acquire such standards? Certainly extensive exposure to art objects is an absolute necessity, but beyond that nothing is certain. Does the young person unconsciously and independently deduce the basic principles? Is the human mind and perceptual apparatus "programmed" in some way so that certain qualities such as balance and symmetry are discerned with particular ease? And what is the role of offhand remarks by art cognoscenti who freely voice their opinion that one piece is a "better example" than another, but who fail to specify what it's a better example of?

We can, finally, return to the scene of Ruth Bunzel, in the summer of 1924 or 1925 sitting in the shade with a San Ildefonso potter, trying to learn how to paint designs on the sides of a hand-built clay pot. The potter is "amazed" at Bunzel's "stupidity" because all people—certainly any woman of Bunzel's maturity—could reasonably be expected to know a large number of individual design figures and also to share the views of others as to what decorations "look good" to San Ildefonso eyes. Thus, the San Ildefonso potter intended to have to teach Bunzel certain practical techniques; the rest she expected to take care of itself.

And, oddly, it does indeed take care of itself. After having gained a modicum of skill at making San Ildefonso designs, Bunzel went to a Hopi village to get instruction in Hopi pottery making. Again she was given clear instructions for the technical processes required to form a pot, but when it came time to paint decorations onto the vessel she was told to make a design "out of her own head" (1972:62). This she was able to do for pots that were uniquely Hopi in shape, but when she came to a round jar whose shape strongly resembled a type of pot common in San Ildefonso, the decoration she put on it was far more in the San Ildefonso style than in the Hopi style she was trying to learn. In retrospect, Bunzel observed, "Apparently in even so short a period of observation and imitation (ten days), I had assimilated the San Ildefonso style to such an extent that I unconsciously reproduced it when confronted by a vessel of the familiar proportions. *It must be by some such process that the traditional styles are passed on"* (1972:62, emphasis added).

The methods of teaching art in the Pueblos of the Southwest are paralleled by those described elsewhere. Apprentices to African carvers typically are given technical information regarding methods of production, but their aesthetic standards are acquired by virtue of their socialization into their culture, sharpened by watching their master as he works and by emulating his methods (cf. Himmelheber 1963:90–101); the same apparently holds true for African potters (cf. R. Thompson 1969:156). And, of course, methods of teaching art in Western society are not, in practice, greatly different. Much instruction consists of teaching technical skills, familiarizing students with "good examples" of work by artists whom the teachers admire, and criticizing students' art works in fairly general terms.

Other Sources of Artists' Ideas

Usually each generation of artists receives most of its aesthetic socialization from its elders. But other sources may play a role too. For example, in Chapter 4 it was noted that the artist may travel beyond the boundaries of his or her own group and, by so doing, acquire new techniques and inspirations. Chukwu Okoro, the Afikpo carver who was discussed at some length in Chapter 4, spent five years of his early life traveling and working at various jobs (Ottenberg 1975:68). Besides benefiting from the exposure to diverse art styles which his travels afforded him, these experiences provided Chukwu with some useful techniques. For example, unlike other carvers in his area, Chukwu makes a paper pattern before beginning work on a mask, and he uses pieces of reed or grass to check the proportions of masks as he works on them.

Whereas Chukwu traveled through space, some of the Pueblo potters interviewed by Bunzel had the unique opportunity to travel through time. About two miles from the Hopi village of Hano lies Sikyatki, an uninhabited mound that once was the site of an ancient Pueblo. The Pueblo is gone now, but the mound holds many prehistoric items. At the time of Bunzel's research, Hopi women regularly visited the mound to collect old potsherds; particularly fruitful were visits right after a rain, when a new crop of finds had been exposed. Do the Hopi women copy the old designs? Bunzel says they do not. Rather, the fragments of old pottery are merely a starting point which modern Hopi potters combine and modify as they see fit.

Ideas for art productions can come from traveling through space, through time—or from excursions through one's own mind, via dreams or other altered states of consciousness. The use of dreams as a source of artistic innovation has been reported in numerous places, but again Bunzel's Pueblo studies provide the richest single source of information. A Hopi potter told Bunzel, "One night I dreamed and saw lots of large jars and they all had designs on them. I looked at them and got the designs in my head and next morning I painted them. I often dream about designs, and if I can remember them, I paint them" (1972:51). Another woman, a Zuni, said, "Sometimes when I have to paint a pot, I can't think what design to put on it. Then I go to bed thinking about it all the time. Then when I go to sleep, I dream about designs. I can't always remember them in the morning, but if I do, then I paint that on the pot" (1972:51). (It should be noted that although some Pueblo potters use dreams as a source of design ideas, many others do not.)

Finally, there is the case of the Tukano, who live in the northwest Amazon region of Colombia. Like many of their neighbors, adult Tukano males regularly indulge in the ceremonial drinking of *yajé*, a hallucinogenic beverage made from a species of vine that is native to their region. Yajé plays an important role in Tukano mythology, and, as Gerardo Reichel-Dolmatoff has shown (1972, 1975), use of the drug is intimately related to the strengthening and legitimization of traditional Tukano social structure. Reichel-Dolmatoff's accounts of yajé, including his own experiences upon taking the drug, are fascinating, but the aspect of yajé that interests us here is the role it plays in Tukano art.

Tukano art takes the form of figures painted on housefronts, on musical instruments, and on utilitarian items such as pottery vessels, benches, and bark cloths. The figures range from clearly representational designs to geometric figures that are at most semi-iconic. What inspires these designs? The Tukano told Reichel-Dolmatoff, "These are the things we see when we take yajé; they are the *gahpi gohori*—the yajé images" (1972:104). The ethnographer gave several men paper and colored pencils and asked them to draw the images they had seen while under the effects of the hallucinogen; the result was a collection of figures identical to those included in traditional Tukano paintings. (When asked the meanings of the figures, the men attributed to each a subject that was related to procreation, kinship, or social structure in general.)

Dreams and hallucinogenic drugs may provide motifs that can be incorporated in art works, but one might well ask, what is the source of the stuff of dreams and hallucinations? The answer lies largely in culture itself. Consider the Tukano case, for example. Reichel-Dolmatoff (1972:110) notes that since infancy every Tukano male has been exposed to his society's art, so even before his first experience with yajé he knows what he'll probably see after he drinks the beverage. Also, during and after the yajé-drinking ceremony individuals commonly discuss the hallucinations they have, thus increasing the likelihood that yajé users will for the most part see just those visions that traditional Tukano culture prescribes, namely the motifs that occur in Tukano art.

Developmental Possibilities

Thus far we have talked as if becoming an artist were solely a matter of an individual acquiring skills, sensibilities, and values from the broader cultural milieus. Such external sources are obviously important, but what about the possibility that some components of artistic development spring from within artists themselves?

As noted in Chapter 4, the question of individual genius remains altogether baffling; but the discipline known as *developmental psychology* has had some success in illuminating another dimension of this problem. Inspired by the work of Jean Piaget, developmental psychologists have discovered that a child's mind does not undergo a gradual, steady process of growth. Instead, there seem to be distinct phases—periods of rapid acquisition of new cognitive abilities alternating with plateaus during which old skills are honed while yet-to-be acquired skills remain inaccessible. The hypothesized phases are fairly well defined and may be strictly programmed in a young person's mental development, just as are the changes of puberty in the process of biological development.

Most developmental studies have focused on young people's logical and conceptual abilities rather than on art, and most of their subjects have come from Western culture and thus shed no direct light on the cross-cultural study of art. A few recent investigations do suggest, though, that not only logical but also artistic abilities go through distinct phases. Howard Gardner (1973, 1980, 1981), in a major research undertaking known as Harvard Project Zero, has discovered five stages that Western children's artistic inclinations pass through from birth to age 20. Gardner believes, for example, that the ages seven to nine years represent the "heights of literalism," when, in contrast to the preceding and following stages, children want paintings to look like their subjects, poems to rhyme, and music to be harmonious.

Gardner makes no claims as to the presence of such phases in other cultures, but an interesting study by Alexander Alland (1983) has examined this very question. Alland collected drawings from groups of two- to eight-year olds in the United States, France, Japan, Taiwan, Bali, and the small Pacific island of Ponape. He found great consistency among the children's drawings *within* each culture, but marked differences *between* cultures. And, significantly, the intercultural differences increased with the age of the children, suggesting that cultural influences soon prevail over any pan-human commonality. Although Alland found no tendency for children everywhere to pass through specific phases of artistic development, such as making increasingly representational drawings, he does claim that the earliest drawings by children in all cultures reveal the presence of certain generalized and abstract principles, rules that Jacqueline Goodnow (1979) previously found among American children, such as the tendency to construct complex drawings by combining a small, conservative "vocabulary" of simple shapes.

The developmental study of art is itself in an early stage of development; and cross-cultural applications are even more tentative. However, both show promise of shedding useful light on the psychological dimension of art.

Copying

If, on the surface, art production is largely a matter of combining old ideas in a new way, then we should pause here to consider the extreme possibility: What about the case in which an individual copies a preexisting art object in an attempt to duplicate as precisely as possible?

Interestingly, such behavior is extremely rare. Even when the artist is specifically asked to replicate an older item, the result is almost inevitably an object that has been "personalized" in some way. For example, in 1950 when he was studying Yoruba carving in Nigeria, William Bascom came across a carved ceremonial staff that he wanted to buy. The owner did not want to part with the item but suggested to Bascom that he have Duga, a recognized carver, make one for him as it had been Duga who had originally carved the staff in question (Bascom 1969:114; 1973:74,76). Bascom did indeed commission Duga to carve a copy of the original staff, but the result

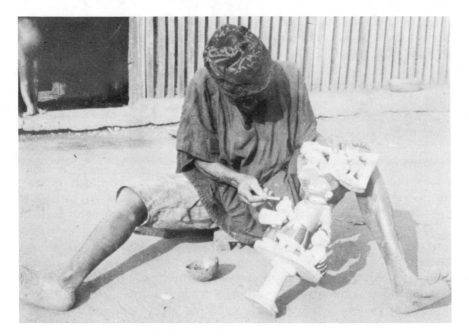

FIGURE 5-1   Master Yoruba carver, Duga of Meko, painting a ceremonial staff. Wood, 50 cm. tall. *(Photo courtesy Mr. and Mrs. William Bascom.)*

of Duga's efforts was not an exact duplicate of his earlier work. His new staff was, in the first place, larger than the original—perhaps because Bascom had promised Duga a good fee for his services. Also the new staff had several modifications in the details of its carving. Finally, Duga painted the staff with different colors than he had used on the first staff. The result was a staff (shown in Figure 5–1) that strongly resembled the original staff, but that had been modified by Duga in several ways as he worked on the commission.

Bunzel's study of Pueblo potters provides information on copying that is relevant. One Zuni potter told Bunzel, "I never copy the designs of other women. It is not right to do that. You must think out all your designs yourself. Only those who do not know copy" (Bunzel 1972:52). And, in fact, mature, traditional Pueblo potters do decorate each pot in a manner unlike any other pot. In some Pueblos the avoidance of copying even extends to pottery made for sale to outsiders: Bunzel watched three potters in the village of Isleta decorating wares that would later be sold in Albuquerque. They laughed and talked as they worked, but in less than two hours they completed 42 pots, each with a design unlike any of the others (Bunzel 1972:63). (Other Pueblo makers of trade pottery do, however, repeat designs; cf. Bunzel 1972:62).

The general absence of copying may strike the Euroamerican nonartist as puzzling. If the artist is technically able to make an exact duplicate and if preexisting art objects are recognized as being aesthetically effective, why not copy the old objects as accurately as possible?

One can only speculate as to the answer to this question, but several possibilities present themselves. The simplest answer is to assume that humans—or artists, at least—have a "creative urge," a desire to express themselves and their vision in constantly new and untried ways. Perhaps such a drive does exist, but the more importance we attach to it, the more difficulty we have explaining societies in which change occurs only very slowly. For example, the arts of ancient Egyptian civilization did evolve through time, but the rate of change was so slow that the nonexpert must look very closely to see the differences between a sculpted human figure from the Fourth Dynasty and one from the Eighteenth Dynasty, made over a thousand years later (cf. Spencer 1975:25–27). If a creative urge exists, there must be other, sociocultural factors that enhance or discourage its effect.

Our puzzlement about the general absence of copying in art results in part from our making an unwarranted assumption, namely that it is easier to copy a preexisting piece than it is to use the piece as a starting place for modification. There is only one way in which something can be accurately duplicated, but the ways in which it can be altered are limitless in number; at least in terms of skill, copying is more difficult than is innovation. Himmelheber reports being told this very thing by a Cameroonian artist (cf. 1963:106,107), and Bunzel makes the same point: Hopi potters "constantly invent new patterns . . . because it is as easy as painting the old ones and very much more enjoyable" (1972:57).

Finally, it might be noted that in highly stratified societies works of art often function as indicators of prestige. In such societies the careful copying of preexisting art works could be considered equivalent to counterfeiting, in that it results in increasing the supply of items that are valued partly because of their very scarcity. A taboo on "faking" is inevitable in such situations.

THE CREATIVE PROCESS

Surely there is more to the creative process than a simple, mechanical reshuffling of old concepts to arrive at novel ones. There must be, we Westerners feel, a spark of genius involved. Creativity is more than just synthesis; it is, in the phrase of an eminent psychoanalyst, a *magic* synthesis (Arieti 1976).

But what exactly is the nature of this "magic"? Given the personal and fleeting nature of the creative process, it comes as no surprise that the social sciences have discovered few "facts" about creativity. There is, however, a sizable body of opinion concerning the creative process. This body of opinion has its roots in classical Western thought, and many modern thinkers—philosophers, social scientists, and others—have contributed to it. For convenience I will refer to this composite theory as the "Western folk model" of creativity.

A folk model is a set of theories that is prevalent in a given population; it provides a means of explaining some phenomenon that is deemed to be important. It is supported less by empirical data than by the sheer intellectual momentum given it by a persistent need to make sense of the significant unknown. Not all individuals in the society necessarily embrace all parts of the folk model, but it nevertheless informs most people's thought on the subject in question. Whether or not a folk model is "true" is another matter: Some such models are simply not amenable to proof; others, like the Western folk model of creativity, are testable only in some of their details and then only with considerable methodological difficulty. So by labeling Western opinion regarding creativity a folk model, I am not saying that it is or isn't accurate, but simply that it is a widely held set of beliefs whose accuracy is as yet unknown.

Three salient features of the Western folk model of creativity are particularly interesting: First, the creative individual is considered to have a mental constitution unlike other people's: The artist may be described as merely "lacking common sense," or, in the extreme, as being mad. Second, creativity is thought to require a special sort of mental acrobatics. The visual artist, specifically, is believed to be able to use and manipulate visual imagery with more adroitness than non-artists. Finally, the Western folk model suggests that the creative process itself is characterized by what has been called "passion and decorum," that is, an alternation between concentrated, conscious mental effort and passive, out-of-awareness operations in the unconscious mind of the creative individual.

How well does the Western folk model of creativity stand up cross-culturally? If creative individuals (or if artists, as a subset of that group) in every society seem to function in accordance with the Western folk model, this would suggest that the model reflects some fundamental, pan-human processes. If, on the other hand, the Western folk model is soundly contradicted by the folk models of creativity found in other societies and by those aspects of the creative process that we can discern in the work of artists elsewhere, this finding would suggest that the Western folk model might have more limited applicability.

The following three parts of this section attempt such a comparison. As elsewhere, we are hampered by the sparseness of relevant data, and the results will necessarily be tentative. Nonetheless, most components of the Western folk model of creativity do have parallels in other societies.

The Madness of Genius

One salient theme in the Western folk model of creativity is that the process is somehow irrational. Plato wrote that the poet, for example, is "indeed, a thing ethereally light-winged and sacred, nor can he compose anything worth calling poetry until he becomes inspired and, as it were, mad" (quoted in Hatterer 1965:17). It was not until the Romantic Period, however, that the claim that the artist is "mad" was taken literally. Freud systematized this part of the Western folk model, claiming that the creative artist tends to be more sexually frustrated than others; creativity, by this view, serves as a means of substitute gratification. (The fact that the biographies of many creative individuals revealed them to have had active sex lives made even Freud have second thoughts about such a formulation. Cf. Trilling 1945.)

We saw in Chapter 4 that stereotypes of artists vary quite widely from one culture to another. The public image of artists in some societies do resemble to some extent the Western conception of the artist as divinely mad souls. The West African Afikpo, for example, generally consider their carvers to be "foolish or silly," and artists among the Fang, Dahomeans, and New Irelanders are considered such "good-for-nothings" as to be aberrant in their native cultures. Just the opposite is true, however, in the Asmat region of New Guinea and among the Bush Negroes of Surinam. Whether artists around the world are actually more or less mentally sound than their non-artist peers is uncertain; and given the difficulties involved in even defining neruosis in a way that is cross-culturally meaningful, it seems doubtful that such a conclusion can ever be substantiated.

There is, however, one feature of the psychoanalytic account of creativity that receives some support from the ethnographic data, namely the apparent correlation between creativity and short-term sexual abstinence. In many societies (for example, Anang, Abelam) a person engaged in creating a major art work is under a sexual taboo during—and, sometimes, preceding—the artistic activities. Presumably the reason lies in the channeling of sexual energies into artistic activities, but one wonders if the energy involved is mental, physical, or both, since sexual abstinence is also required in many societies for people engaged in endeavors that are demanding but non-artistic, such as participating in warfare, making difficult journeys, or—in Western society—participating in some professional sports.

The Role of Imagery

A second salient aspect of the Western folk model of creativity involves *imagery*. Psychologists have claimed that the artist has a superior ability to manipulate mental images and that creative individuals generally are abnormally skilled at "associational thinking." The twentieth-century English sculptor Henry Moore describes it thus: "The sculptor gets the solid shape, as it were, inside his head—he thinks of it, whatever its size, as if he were holding it completely enclosed in the hollow of his hand. He mentally visualizes a complex *form from all round itself:* he knows while he looks at one side what the other side is like" (1952:74). Moore's statement implies—probably correctly—that the artist's mental "picture" is not quite like a tangible picture one sees with the eyes. Rather, it is conceived in such a way that it can be simultaneously "seen" from more than one viewpoint. Is such a thing possible? Perhaps so. Moore goes on to say that one accomplishes this feat of mental acrobatics thus: The sculptor "identifies himself with [the sculpture's] center of gravity, its mass, its weight" (1952:74). That is, the conceptualization is only partly visual; in addition, it is tactile and kinesthetic. And while the non-artist finds it difficult to simultaneously *visualize* both the front and the back of an object, one can to a certain extent imagine *touching* front and back at the same time.

The role of imagery in the creative process has been noted among artists in several small-scale societies. An African carver's remarks to Hans Himmelheber are particularly vivid: This carver relied upon fetishlike objects for inspiration, rubbing his hands with them before beginning to carve. "This magic," he said, "shows me all the different forms of masks and spoons which men have ever made. They show up in my head *like something coming to the surface of the water*" (quoted in Himmelheber 1963:107, emphasis in original; cf. also Messenger 1973:113).[1]

Sometimes there is observable evidence that the artist had in mind a clear image of the finished product before actually beginning a work of art. For example, some of the intricate curvilinear designs carved by Maori artists on housepanels make sense only if one assumes that the carver first conceptualized a figure larger than the board itself, and then carved onto the panel only the part that would fit (cf. Linton 1941:47). Similarly, Bunzel reported that when potters in the Acoma Pueblo decorated small pots made for the tourist trade, they used traditional designs but instead of reducing them in size, they made the figures the same size as those that are drawn onto larger pots but used fewer of them on each pot (cf. Bunzel 1972:36).

Pueblo potters are generally quite explicit about the imagery required for the designs that are painted on pots. As noted previously, some potters report seeing designs in their dreams and then copying these onto the pots they are making. Others see designs while daydreaming and still others simply close their eyes and consciously summon up images of possible designs: "Whenever I am ready to paint, I just close my eyes and see the design, and then I paint it," a Hopi potter told Bunzel (1972:49). In some Pueblos, potters sketch tentative designs on the ground or on paper before beginning, but whatever their method, all Pueblo potters would concur with the Laguna woman who said, "Pottery . . . means a great deal to me. It

---

[1]This carver's fetishes are made by obtaining a certain type of leaf from a particular kind of bush, pulverizing it, mixing the powder with some other substances, and rolling the mixture into "little sausages with pointed ends." The compulsiveness of this ritual may strike us as being somewhat bizarre, but it differs little from the textbook writer who, before sitting down at his typewriter, obtains roasted beans from a particular type of tree, pulverizes them, mixes the powder with boiling water and other substances, pours the concoction into a special cup, puts the vessel on the corner of his desk—and then forgets it.

is something sacred. I try to paint all my thoughts on my pottery"
(1972:52).

One last interesting feature of Pueblo artistic imagery should be
noted. In some Pueblos (Acoma, San Ildefonso, and Hopi) two distinctly
different styles of decorating pots were in vogue during Bunzel's study.
But except under abnormal circumstances, the two styles remained separate, with no hybridization between them. Thus, like Beethoven, who composed his Seventh and Eighth Symphonies at the same time but never
allowed the themes of one to slip into the other, the Pueblo potter is able to
couch her images in one traditional style or another and execute the design
without interference from other information that is present and active in
her mind. Or, to return to the previously mentioned analogy between art
and language, the artist who has mastered working in two different styles is
like the bilingual individual who is fluent in two languages but who rarely
mixes both languages in a single sentence.

"Passion and Decorum"

What is the nature of the mental processes that go on in one's head
preceding and during the creative act? According to the Western folk
model, the process is often believed to be a combination of careful, disci-
plined conscious thought combined with apparently free wheeling, spon-
taneous work by the unconscious mind. As Jerome Bruner (1963:12,13)
has succinctly remarked, creativity requires both "passion and decorum." A
remark made by the photographer Henri Cartier-Bresson reflects this aspect of the Western folk model of creativity: "Thinking should be done
beforehand and afterwards, never while actually taking a photograph"
(quoted in Sontag 1977:53).

Solid cross-cultural support for this part of the Western folk model is
scant. There is abundant evidence that the artist goes through a process of
conscious planning and, once a plan is clearly fixed in mind, that the artist
executes it in a well thought out, "decorous" manner. But what of the
"passion" in Bruner's phrase? Is a period of incubation necessary before
new ideas come in an avalanche into the mind of the creator? Such a period
has not been reported, although in at least one instance (Goodale and Koss
1971) it has been looked for. There is a distinct possibility that the process
does occur but that due to its being entirely within the mind of the artist, it
has gone unnoticed or unreported to date by other ethnographers.

The infrequency with which an incubation period is noted cross-culturally may be due in part to the fact that the amount of novel thinking
required for making a given work is relatively small—a factor that impedes
all attempts, such as the present one, to look for cross-cultural correlates of
the Western folk model of creativity. Artists in small-scale societies seldom
have to wrestle with totally new or unfamiliar materials or techniques in an
effort to determine the most satisfactory application to their craft; and

although they seldom if ever copy an old piece, the extent to which a given work differs from its predecessors is often relatively small. Thus the strikingly innovative effort is doubtless an even greater rarity in small-scale societies than it is in complex ones. For lesser acts, the unconscious component of creativity is perhaps submerged in the total activity of art making, observable only in such situations as when an artist remarks upon completing a piece, "It's not exactly as I'd planned—it's better!"

The mind, in Shakespeare's phrase, is "a very opal," scintillating rays of pure colors from unexpected places at unpredicted times. Mineralogists have discovered the source of the opal's fire, but how far social scientists are from understanding the fire of the artist's mind! About the best we can do at the present is to spell out the two topics that are promising areas of inquiry. First, one would like to know more about how the artist acquires special cognitive abilities, how one becomes inbued with the aesthetic values of his or her society. How do we ourselves do this? Sometimes, as a young person, we are given overt aesthetic training ("Don't wear stripes and plaids together"), but more often the process of socialization is inexplicit, requiring the individual to deduce general principles, based on day-to-day experience.

Second, we need more understanding of the way in which the artist transmutes past experience into new and different works of art. Is the Western folk model of creativity valid—for all humankind or even for us? An answer to this question will be difficult to attain, but the closer we approach it, the closer we come to understanding what is probably the most fundamental issue in the human endeavor we call art.

REPRESENTATION AND STYLIZATION

Look at the West African masks shown in Figure 2–1. The masks portray some features that are common to the human face, but great liberties have been taken: The proportions are changed, ears are lacking, and so on. But why, we may well ask, are these changes made? Since there are at least a few pieces of art from small-scale societies (for example, the Northwest Coast mask shown in Figure 3–1) that give a photographically accurate rendering of the subject, the answer cannot be simply that the artist lacked the technical skills needed to make a more accurate mask. If the answer does not lie in manual skill, then it must be sought in the realm of psychology. Although many artists claim that they are merely making a reproduction of what they see, we must remember that the total aesthetic process includes two distinctly psychological phases: The subject is processed through the artist's visual and mental apparatus, and, later, through our own as we look at the object the artist has produced.

With respect to thinking about the general question of representation in art, two extreme positions are possible, and it seems wisest to avoid both.[2] On the one hand, a person could assert that, because no attempt at representation can be perfectly accurate, any talk of accuracy is senseless. But we are here speaking only of relative accuracy, and it is counterintuitive to hold that a color photograph of a particular individual is no more or less accurate than a portrait of the same subject made by a cubist painter. Granted that neither is a perfect representation, that the interpretation of even the best photograph requires knowledge of some arbitrary conventions, that the cubist painting may provide an insight into the subject's personality (as opposed to appearance) that may be lacking from the photograph, and that we may disagree as to which of two cubist paintings is more accurate—granted all these things, it still seems reasonable to assume that it is the photograph, rather than the cubist painting, that more closely resembles the image that falls onto the retina of the viewer's eye when he or she looks at the subject.

But equally untenable in the extreme is the opposite view, that is, the assumption that a given object provides a simple, straightforward subject to be copied by the skilled artisan. The piece of stone or wood in the artist's hand can never be *exactly* like the model; for better or worse, Pygmalion is only a character of myth, and stone is not flesh nor paint a passing blush on the cheek. The artist is, at most, an illusionist.

Patterns of Representation

Given that the artist must choose to represent some of the subject's features while (at most) implying the rest, what principles are the artist's choices based upon? Boas (1955:71,72) noted one dimension of choice, namely, that the artist may either attempt to portray the subject as it appears at a given moment from a single viewing point, or else the goal may be to depict those features of the subject that are, in the artist's opinion, most important. Since art is inevitably a cultural endeavor, it is little wonder that the latter approach is far more common, with artists acting as "editors of visual reality," using cultural relevance as a guideline for determining which features to emphasize and which to ignore. As Linton remarked, the artist's aim in small-scale societies is "to present his subject as he and his society think of it, not as he sees it" (1941:48).

If the artist uses this editorial style of representation, the features that are portrayed may be physically present but not visible. Thus, the so-called X-ray drawings of people and animals that occur in various places around the world presumably depict those inner organs that the artist considers to be particularly vital.

---

[2]Here, as on several other points in this chapter and in Chapter 3, I am making a case with regard to art from small-scale societies similar to the one that Gombrich (1972b) makes for Western art.

FIGURE 5-2   An example of subjective representation: "Noblemen and Attendants," Benin culture, Nigeria, sixteenth or seventeenth century. Bronze plaque, 37 cm. high. *(Nelson Gallery-Atkins Museum, Kansas City, Missouri, Nelson Fund.)*

Often, though, artists need not portray hidden traits such as the skeleton and internal organs; rather, they may choose which ones among the visible features to illustrate or emphasize. For example, the prominence of noses in masks made in the New Guinea highlands probably is a reflection of the importance that the local populations assign to the nose as a focal point of personal beauty (Paul Wohlt, personal communication). Or, to take another example, if a sculpture is to depict several people, and the subjects are generally thought to be of unequal social or cultural importance, then the artist may quite reasonably scale the sizes of the figures accordingly, making the most important person substantially larger than the others. Figure 5–2, for example, shows a bronze plaque, produced in the sixteenth or seventeenth century by Benin artists in Nigeria. The differences in size between the "nobleman" and his "attendants" does not reflect a difference in stature but rather in social importance.

Extreme Stylization:
The Case of the "Trobriand Medusa"

Although creation myths typically claim that humans were formed in the shape of their supernatural maker, albeit with important modifications, when humans portray supernatural characters in their art, the exact reverse occurs: Deities are made in human form, but, again, with important differences. The result may be a figure whose resemblance to humans is so tenuous that the uninitiated might interpret it as being completely abstract, having either a symbolic meaning or no referent at all. In the native's eyes, however, the resemblance is clear, despite the stylizations.

The best ethnographic examples of this come from Melanesia, the most interesting being Edmund Leach's attempt to explain the designs that were traditionally painted by Trobriand Islanders on the shields known as *vai ova,* which were used in warfare by the bravest and most distinguished Trobriand warriors. Before Leach advanced his theory the designs had been assumed to be nonrepresentational, and since their makers died long ago, a positive interpretation of their meaning is not possible. Nevertheless, based on ethnographic accounts of Trobriand mythology, Leach has argued convincingly that the designs are highly stylized representations of a winged anthropomorphic figure, most likely the "flying witch" that plays an important role in Trobriand supernatural belief. Leach suggests that the design emphasizes those parts of the witch's body that are believed to be most important, namely the anus and vulva, which emit highly dangerous forces. (It is these forces that give the figure efficacy upon a war shield and which prompted Leach to dub the figure a "Trobriand Medusa.") Figure 5–3 shows the hypothesized witch's figure on the right; on the left is the same figure as it appears on a shield, folded in upon itself so that some parts, such as the anus and navel, coincide.

Some writers have disagreed with the particulars of Leach's interpretation of the designs of Trobriand *vai ova.* Ronald Berndt, for example, has claimed that a more likely interpretation is that the figure represents "a male and female engaging or about to engage, in coitus" (1958:65). But the weight of evidence strongly favors Leach's fundamental assertion, namely, that the seemingly abstract *vai ova* designs are in fact representations of natural or (more likely) supernatural inhabitants of the Trobriand world.

Another Step in Stylization

Richard Salisbury (1959), in a comment on Leach's Trobriand Medusa paper, illustrates the results of stylizing a traditional figure to the point of its becoming a simple, geometric pattern. Working among the Siane of the New Guinea highlands, Salisbury noticed that two common

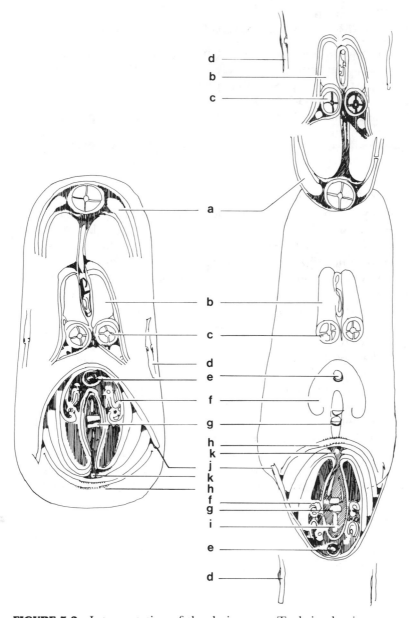

FIGURE 5-3 Interpretation of the design on a Trobriand *vai ova* shield *(after Leach, 1972)*. Left, design as originally painted on shield; right, design as conceptually "unfolded" to form Trobriand flying witch figure. Interpretation: (a) Wings and arms, (b) Face, (c) Ears and breasts, (d) Feet and hands, (e) Anus and navel, (f) Buttocks and, perhaps, Womb, (g) "Witch testicles," (h) Pubic hair, (i) Vagina, (j) Knee joints, (k) Clitoris.

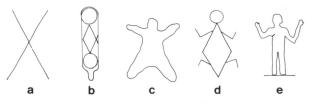

FIGURE 5-4 Design figures made by the Siane, New Guinea. *(After Salisbury, 1959).*

patterns occurring on men's shell headdresses and elsewhere were crosses and diamonds, as shown in Figure 5–4a,b. He was told that the cross designs were called *sirirumu,* the diamonds, *gerua,* and that both designs were love charms, helping the male wearer gain the sexual favors of women who looked at the designs. More explanation of the figures was not forthcoming, but one day by coincidence Salisbury happened to see two boys playing: One "stood with his back to the sun, his arms bent, and his hands held out on each side of his head at the level of his ears. The other boy was tracing the outline of his shadow in the dust" (Salisbury 1959:50). When the boys saw Salisbury watching them they obliterated the drawings and looked guilty, but eventually they told him that they had been drawing *gerua.*

Later, using this and other clues, Salisbury made line drawings similar to those shown in Figure 5–4c,d. When alone with his best informant, Salisbury revealed the drawings. The man's reaction, Salisbury writes, "was one of extreme horror and shock, as he shuddered and told me to hide them again" (1959:50). Salisbury suspected that the man's indignation was partially feigned, but through questioning he learned that the design shown in Figure 5–4c was considered to represent an opossum, and that it should be called *sirirumu,* the same as the name for the simple cross design. Figure 5–4d was said by the informant to represent a pig, but was called *gerua,* the name for the diamond pattern.

But if, in Siane thought, diamond shapes somehow stand for pigs and crosses for opossums, there still is the question of why the two designs serve as love charms and evoke such strong reactions among natives. The answer is that the opossums are closely associated with fertility and sexuality; and in other New Guinea highland societies, pigs are also associated with regeneration, although Salisbury fails to note whether this belief prevails among the Siane. In any case there is an equivalence between the diamond and the cross designs: Salisbury was told: "'Yes, they are both *sirirumu;* can't you see they are the same?' I asked him to explain and he held his hand over the right half of the design and then over the left half, to show how the two halves of the cross, if joined at the extremities, make a diamond" (1959:50).

This information reveals, generally, the elaborate psychological machinations that may underlie artistic production in primitive societies. Specifically, it explains why the diamonds and crosses on Siane men's headdresses are effective love charms. The figures are actually iconic representations of opossums and/or pigs, species which have a symbolic association with women and sexuality. Why not just decorate the headdresses with accurate representations of women? Because, Salisbury learned, "A naturalistic drawing of a woman would make any woman recoil in horror, and would have no practical effect, while a stylized design enables her to look at it for a long time, without realizing its significance—long enough for the design to have its magical effects" (1959:51). Thus, stylization may be motivated by attempts to partially conceal the referent of a representational drawing.

The artist may say, "I draw what I see," but "seeing" is anything but a simple process. Perceptual psychologists have demonstrated that when an individual looks at something the eye does not randomly scan about the whole scene, but rather it flits back and forth between a small number of information-rich points (cf. Noton and Stark 1971). More importantly, the incoming information is combined with information from the past as recorded in the person's memory. The resulting impression is thus an amalgam that is unique to the individual viewer, but with a strong admixture of conventions derived from the person's cultural heritage. If the individual is an artist, an attempt to realize this vision in an expressive medium will necessarily reflect both the personal and the cultural components of the image.

What factors determine the relative importance of the literal versus the conventional? The answer seems to lie primarily in art's function and in the cultural homogeneity of the society in which it occurs. Stylization can run rampant in a society that is so homogeneous that all its members are socialized into the conventions of its art. In practical terms, this would apply to a society such as the Australian Walbiri (described in Chapter 3), whose small numbers ensure a high degree of cultural uniformity, and also to larger societies that happen to be changing only slowly with the passage of time and which have an effective system of intrasocietal communication. Or, if art serves some function other than the explicit communication of culturally important information, it may be conventionalized to an extreme degree. Thus, as noted in Chapter 3, an elaborate work of art from the Northwest Coast communicated the elevated social status of its owner regardless of whether viewers could decipher the stylized animals and people portrayed in the piece. Otherwise, if the referents for the art works of a society are to be communicated to individuals who lack thorough aesthetic socialization, stylization must be kept within certain bounds: A work must give the less-than-perfectly socialized individual enough visual hints to allow accurate interpretation.

A GENERATIVE APPROACH TO AESTHETICS

As noted previously, art and language are much alike. For example, an actual art work is ultimately based on abstract ideas about style, meaning, and beauty; and in a parallel way the tangible manifestation of language, the spoken utterance, derives from abstract principles of grammar. Linguists have made great strides toward developing techniques to analyze the intangible precepts of grammar systematically. This being the case, one might well ask, can analogous methods be created to study art? Several scholars have attempted such an approach, the most extensive of which is James Faris's analysis of Nuba body decoration.

Nuba Personal Art

Faris spent 15 months living with approximately 2,500 southeastern Nuba in three villages in Kordofan Province, Democratic Republic of Sudan. The Nuba are agriculturalists who supplement their farming and herding with hunting and gathering. Nuba art takes the form of body decoration, with the application of paint and oil to the body, decorative shaving of the hair, and scarifying the body; jewelry is also worn by members of both sexes. The goal is to enhance one's natural beauty and give the impression of strength and good health. (Also, Nuba body decoration serves to mark an individual's age, kin group, and ritual status.) A great

FIGURE 5-5   Nuba men, decorated with several types of *toma* and *pacore* designs. They are watching tribal sport. *(Photo courtesy James C. Faris.)*

FIGURE 5-6 Nuba man wearing *nyulan* designs, radiating from his upper abdomen and from his forehead. Both representational and nonrepresentational linear designs are visible. *(Photo courtesy James C. Faris.)*

amount of effort is expended in obtaining the necessary materials for decoration, shaving off all pubic and body hair (both for appearance's sake and also to ensure the adhesion of pigment to the skin), and oiling and painting the body. Young men, aged 14 to 25, are the most avid body decorators, oiling themselves daily and painting new designs on their bodies every day or two (except during the busiest part of the agricultural cycle). This is no small task since the painting of the more complex designs requires an hour's time. As Figures 5–5 and 5–6 indicate, however, the results are striking, combining the beauty of the well-formed human body with effective, colored designs. (The excellent illustrations in Faris's book, many of them in color, make this point even more convincingly.)

The general aesthetic principles that guide Nuba body decoration are balance and symmetry, with the former taking precedence over the latter: Virtuoso Nuba body painters delight in making asymmetric designs that are brought into balance by skillful playing off, say, of a small dark area painted on one side of the face against a larger, lighter colored area on the face's opposite side. The natural symmetry of the human body is always the starting point, to be enhanced or modified in appearance by body painting. Needless to say, some Nuba are more skillful and attempt more difficult designs than do others, who limit themselves to the simpler patterns or just cover their bodies all over with oil and black pigment. An individual's decoration may fall short of perfection in one of two ways—either by being a poor execution of a satisfactory design, or else by making designs that, although they are well executed, are unorthodox and outside the realm of traditionally meaningful Nuba art. (The analogy with language errors should be made explicit at this point. The utterance of a sentence may be flawed in one of two ways: Either it can be poorly executed—with an unexpected sneeze in the middle of it, for instance—but otherwise grammatically well formed; or else it can break a grammatical rule, although its execution is flawless.)

Nuba Iconography

A great number of the designs used by Nuba men are nonrepresentational. The body, for example, may be divided into several parallel bands, drawn in a vertical, horizontal, or diagonal direction, with alternate bands being painted in contrasting colors. Such a design is named, but it is not intended to represent anything in the visible world. Other designs, however, are thought of as representing actual things—most commonly, particular species of animals. Some species are depicted simply by drawing their two-dimensional projection onto any part of the body. This method is also used to portray figures that are alien to this part of Africa. Faris drolly observes, for example, "My own visit introduced new sources of inspiration—I once observed the Middle-Eastern skyline, which is featured on the back of Camel cigarette packages, very accurately represented on a young man's back" (1972:18,19).

The most interesting of the Nuba styles, however, are those figures that are iconic, but in which representation depends partially or wholly upon portraying characteristic features of the subject's surface. The following discussion of Nuba art will be confined to figures of this sort.

Figure 5–7a, in Nuba body decoration, represents a particular species of poisonous snake, known by the native name *dēņā kwa*. Presumably the series of diamonds corresponds to the pattern of scales that characterizes this particular species. If the design is painted onto a wider part of the body, the *dēņā kwa* figure may be drawn in a wider version, as shown in

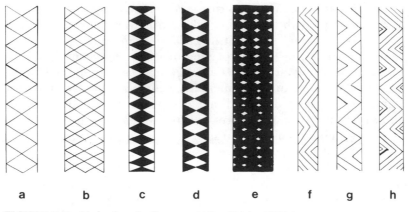

FIGURE 5-7 Nuba iconic figures. *(After Faris, 1972.)*

Figure 5–7b, with no danger of confusing viewers as to the figure's meaning. (Alternative figures with the same meaning are called "allophanes" by Faris.)

Such variations are, however, highly constrained. If, for example, the diamonds (or, as an allophane, the spaces between the diamonds) in the narrower *dēṇā kwa* design are filled with color, as in Figure 5–7c,d, it is no longer interpreted as a certain type of poisonous snake but rather it represents *ṇōrā*, or cowrie shells on leather strips. If, on the other hand, the wider *dēṇā kwa* is similarly filled in (as in Figure 5–7e) the result is a particular species of anteater! If the Nuba artist errs in making one of these designs the result may be a body decoration that is faulty as a whole, despite the fact that it is composed of units which are independently valid, in the same way that the utterance, "Colorless green ideas sleep furiously" is absurd for English speakers although the words that make it up are all in the common vocabulary and each word is of the proper grammatical type for the position it occupies.

As an example of this error, consider the design shown in Figure 5–7f, which represents another kind of poisonous snake, a type of python called *dēṇā kaperget*. If instead of the proper triple diamond an artist makes a double or quadruple diamond pattern, as in Figure 5–7g,h, however, the result is considered a mistake: It simply has no meaning.

A Generative Model of Nuba Figures

Generative linguists attempt to account for well-formed sentences by positing various kinds of rules which, if followed, lead to the production of such sentences. Faris has attempted to construct an analogous model to account for the type of Nuba designs that have just been described.

Nuba individuals attach no meaning whatsoever to elementary figures such as circles and simple zigzag lines—just as we attach no meaning to individual elements of sound such as "p," "t," or "k." Faris has discovered, however, that by choosing five basic elements and defining a few simple operations, all 65 of the meaningful Nuba designs can be generated. The elements Faris uses are: a pair of short, perpendicularly-oriented lines joined to form a right angle; the same figure rotated 45 degrees; a half-circle; a short diagonal line; and a short vertical line. Seven operations are necessary to generate any of the traditional Nuba figures (although for the creation of many of the figures some of the operations are unnecessary). Each of the operations is an algorithmic statement; that is, each gives directions for carrying out certain manipulations on what has been created up to that point.

The way in which the *ŋōrā* design (Figure 5–7c) might be generated illustrates the model that Faris has developed. The first step is to choose the color of the figure and its background color. Then, starting with the half-diamond shown in Figure 5–8a, we may follow one of the options of the "horizontal" algorithm, namely to duplicate the original element, but reverse it and place it adjacent to the original element, thus producing a complete diamond (Figure 5–8b). The next algorithm, "vertical," permits the same type of diamond formation, but this time in the vertical direction, thus producing a string of diamonds such as shown in Figure 5–8c. A series of at least four such diamonds is needed to avoid ambiguity; beyond that, the string could go on indefinitely. A subsequent operation permits the filling in of any enclosed figures, thus producing Figure 5–8d. One final operation, the framing of the string of diamonds by vertical lines along the left and right points of the diamonds completes the figure: The result is *ŋōrā*, the design for cowrie shells on leather strips (Figure 5–8e).

By making changes in the generation of *ŋōrā*, different legitimate Nuba designs are produced. If, for example, the shading had been omitted, the final figure would have been the now-familiar *dēŋā kwa;* a horizontal duplication before framing would have given *karaca,* the anteater. The

FIGURE 5-8 Generation of Nuba *nora* design.

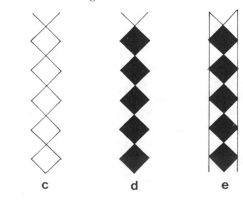

a   b   c   d   e

entire model can be reduced to definitions and algorithmic statements. Faris explores several of the implications of the generative approach, and the interested reader is referred to his original work for additional information on this and on other aspects of Nuba personal art.

Estimate of the Generative Model of Nuba Art   Faris's model of Nuba iconography has been discussed in some detail because it is the first full-blown attempt to apply to art some of the approaches that have been so widely heralded in linguistics. But what are we to make of the model?

First, some of the less damaging criticisms to Faris's thesis should be put into proper perspective. It may be objected, first, that even if such a model were valid, it leaves unanswered many other questions about Nuba art. A generative model of aesthetic production tells us nothing, for instance, about the sociocultural functions of the art in question. But this is an unfair criticism in that we can hardly hope to find any single theory that by itself explains everything we wish to know about art. Thus, Faris supplements his generative model of Nuba design by providing a traditional ethnographic account of other aspects of Nuba art and culture.

One could also object to the fact that although Faris has adopted a quasi-linguistic approach, he is copying a linguistic model that is more than a little outmoded by now, superseded by models that emphasize semantics rather than syntax. But this objection, too, is rather beside the point in that Faris's approach could be a major step in the right direction despite the possibility that it may benefit from future modifications.

The really serious objections to Faris's model are the same as those that have been directed at generative theories in linguistics. First, what is the "psychological reality" of such theories? Does the Nuba artist actually have in his mind, if only unconsciously, all the algorithms (or comparable algorithms) that are the heart of Faris's model? If so, does the artist actually use them as he creates designs or as he evaluates the designs made by others? For his part Faris (personal communication) claims that his model of Nuba personal art is meant only to be descriptive, that is, to be a process that can generate certain Nuba designs: Whether this process resembles the psychological processes that are the basis of Nuba personal art is irrelevant. But ultimately our interest must turn back from abstract, hypothesized models to living, breathing human beings who create art.

These questions lead to another sort of problem: What kind of evidence can support or disprove Faris's model? The tendency of Faris—and of most generative linguists—is to use simplicity as the major criterion for judging competing theories: Given two theories, each of which satisfactorily accounts for the data in question, that theory is preferable which does so most simply. But simplicity alone, unsupported by empirical evidence, cannot be trusted. What sort of empirical evidence can be adduced in such cases? The generativists (and quasi-generativists such as Faris) have yet to answer that, and indeed have yet to try to answer. (Dunn-Rankin's theory of how readers of English recognize letters and words [1978] has many interesting parallels with Faris's model of Nuba figures. Significantly, Dunn-Rankin has obtained some empirical evidence for the psychological reality of his theory.)

The approach of some generative linguists is to suggest that language is an intrinsic aspect of human mentality, the human brain being "wired," as it were, for operation according to the generative principles they have proposed. But this is itself a less-than-parsimonious solution, assuming as it does that the psychological level of human language operates (or is acquired) in a way that is fundamentally different from that of all other human behavior and of the rest of the animal kingdom. The problem is doubly difficult for Faris: Is the generative character of Nuba iconography proof that not only language but also art operates in a different psychological mode than does everything else; or are Nuba figures merely an aberrant extension of "linguistic thinking" into the realm of aesthetics? The success of future applications of linguistic models to art depends upon finding answers to these difficult questions.

PORTFOLIO

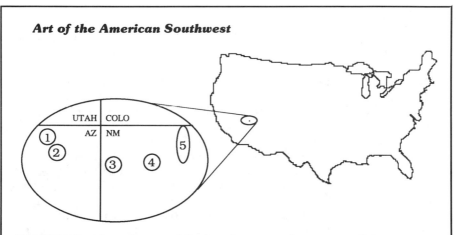

Art of the American Southwest

FIGURE 5-9 Map of some of the best known native groups of the American Southwest. The widely-spread Navajo people are indicated by 1; all others are puebloans: (2) Hopi, (3) Zuni, (4) Acoma and Laguna, and (5) the several eastern pueblos such as San Ildefonso, Santo Domingo, and Taos.

For most Westerners, art is just one part of culture, and often a small part at that. But for the native tribes of the American Southwest, art and culture tend to merge into a single, unified way of viewing the world. The Navajos, for example, don't seek beauty in a few, isolated objects; rather, according to one experienced field-worker, they expect every person to live in beauty and to radiate beauty personally in day-to-day life (Witherspoon, 1977:32). Such aesthetic worldviews provide a dramatic (and, some might feel, highly appealing) contrast to the hectic, postindustrial world that most of us live in. Certainly, they have prompted the creation of a great quantity of art works that are altogether arresting in their form and presence.

Well over a millennium ago a distinctive life-style emerged in the Southwest. Farming, rather than hunting and gathering, provided most of the food; people lived in permanent villages of apartmentlike dwellings made of adobe and stone that we now call pueblos; pottery-making and weaving were widely practiced, and a rich ceremonial life was evident. Many of these enduring beliefs and practices are still found in a score of Pueblo groups—the Hopi villages of northeastern Arizona, the Zuni in western New Mexico, and various tribes in New Mexico reaching as far east as San Ildefonso and Taos in the Rio Grande valley (see map, Figure 5–9).

Every Pueblo group is distinctive, but as a whole the Puebloans stand in marked contrast to the Athapascan-speaking Navajos and Apaches. Whereas Puebloans are ardent horticulturalists and depend primarily on corn, beans, and squash, Athapascans are closer to their hunting–gathering past and emphasize sheep raising; if the former live in populous clusters of cubical dwellings, the latter prefer round structures, with single, or only a few, families grouped together (see Figure 5–9).

But religion and philosophy are important for traditional Puebloans and Athapascans alike. The inevitable focus is on maintaining a harmonious balance between humans and the environment. In the seemingly inhospitable setting of the Southwest the native belief is that the diligent execution of appropriate rituals will cause supernatural forces to provide people with the things they need for long and positive lives.

Just as the religions of the Southwest are intimately involved with the environment, so too is the art by virtue of the differential availability of materials. Clay is abundant but wood is not; consequently, pottery is more common than wood carving, which is restricted to relatively small items related to ceremony. Naturally occurring minerals and plants provide many sources of color; and the result is turquoise jewelry, colorful sandpaintings and textiles, and painted masks. Native cotton served the precontact weavers' needs, but the sixteenth-century arrival of sheep was followed by a marked increase in the size and aesthetic significance of woolen textiles.

Looking specifically at the Puebloans, numerous *kachina* cults provide an integrating force, both culturally and artistically. Kachinas are supernatural figures who exercise control over the elements of the material world, from the wind that brings rain clouds, through the thunder and lightning that accompany a late spring shower, to the germination of corn that the rainfall encourages. Kachinas themselves are not continuous residents of the temporal world, but *kachina cults* are. At specified junctures in the annual cycle, cult members propitiate

FIGURE 5-10 Hopi kachina doll, Suy-ang-e-vif, "Left-handed Kachina." *(Courtesy Field Museum of Natural History, Chicago.)*

the spirits by carrying out elaborate and prolonged rituals that climax in daylong dances during which elaborately costumed cult members actually become the kachinas they are honoring. Part of the ceremony involves giving children dolls that replicate the appearance of the costumed dancers; and as the Hopi kachina doll in Figure 5–10 indicates, the decorated cult members are often spectacular indeed.

Kachina cult activities require art in virtually all media. Besides the carving and painting of masks and dolls, men weave multicolored sashes as part of their costumes; paintings may be made by cult members in their *kivas,* or ceremonial chambers; and special baskets are needed for food offerings—to say nothing of the song, music, and dance that are involved in kachina ceremonies.

But ceramics, a medium that serves both ceremonial and utilitarian needs, is the art form for which the Puebloans are probably best known. As was the case in the rest of the Americas, the potter's wheel was unknown in the native Southwest. In its absence all sizable vessels are traditionally made by rolling balls of clay into long, snakelike cylinders and then coiling these into pots of the desired shape, later to be smoothed by a stone, shell, or wooden paddle. After drying, a slip, or watery suspension of clay, is usually painted on part or all of the pot, followed by a design that turns white, tan, brown, red, or black

FIGURE 5-11 Water bottle from Cochiti Pueblo, made between 1770 and 1780 and decorated in the Kiua polychrome style. 49 cm. high. *(Nelson Gallery-Atkins Museum, Kansas City, Missouri, Nelson Fund.)*

FIGURE 5-12 Zuni storage jar, ca. 1875. Clay and paint; maximum diameter 36 cm. *(Nelson Gallery-Atkins Museum, Kansas City, Missouri. Gift of Miss Katherine Harvey.)*

when the pot is fired. During its 1,500-year history, the Pueblo tradition has produced a truly remarkable inventory of shapes and decorations, ranging from simple, bold, geometric motifs (Figure 5–11) to complicated patterns that include animal figures (Figure 5–12).

Moving from the Puebloans to the later-arriving Navajos, the influence of the former is clear in the latter. Nevertheless, Navajo art and culture are distinctive in many ways. For example, Navajo religion, like Pueblo religion, attempts to maintain the natural harmony and beauty of the world, but among Navajos the primary emphasis shifts from the fertility of the land to the health of the individual; and this goal is usually attained through Navajo "sings" that occur when needed, rather than as communitywide affairs governed by the solar calender, as among the Puebloans. In the Navajo context, the paintings often found on Pueblo kiva walls become "sandpaintings" executed on the ground, made in a style and in dimensions that transcend their Pueblo origins: The most elaborate sandpaintings require a full day's work by as many as 40 men and may measure 25 feet (8 meters) across (Figure 5–13).

Sandpaintings, and the songs they accompany, demonstrate the instrumental importance of art in the Navajo worldview: Misfortune, such as illness, is believed to occur only when something has upset *hozho,* the natural state of harmony and beauty in which the world was first created. But by chanting songs that retell the creation story and

FIGURE 5-13 Navajo *Yeibachai* (Night Chant) sing. *(Courtesy William R. Heick Photography, Mill Valley, California.)*

FIGURE 5-14   Navajo weaver, Harriet Cadman, carding wool in her hogan, 1953. *(Courtesy Laura Gilpin Collection, © 1981 Amon Carter Museum.)*

by illustrating selected episodes of the tale in sandpaintings, the world is restored to its primal condition of *hozho,* or balance, harmony, and beauty. Thus, art is the medium through which Navajos maintain the good world in which they live.

The weavings (Figure 5–14) that Navajo women make are as intimately tied to Navajo philosophy as are the sandpaintings made by men. Considerations of balance and harmony, the interplay between dynamic and static principles, and a subtle color symbolism govern Navajo weaving—and Navajo daily life in general.

Besides the Navajos, the other widespread Athapascan-speaking peoples of the Southwest are the several Apache groups. Their most notable art medium is coiled basketry, which is decorated with small, black, stylized human and animal forms.

Although the tribes of the Southwest retain more of their traditional lifeways than any other native groups in the United States, their contemporary cultures and arts do reflect numerous alien influences. The sheep that provide the Navajo weaver with her wool, the techniques of the silversmith (see Chapter 6), and even some aspects of the Pueblo kachinas are actually Western in origin.

But regardless of their antiquity, the arts of the Southwest are fascinating not only for their unsurpassed visual qualities but also for the aesthetic disposition of their makers. At the conclusion of the nine-day sing called "Shooting Way," Navajos repeat the words *Hozho nahasdlii, Hozho nahasdlii*. The long ritual has been successful and, in McAllester's translation (1980:211), "Conditions of beauty have been restored, Conditions of beauty have been restored."

CONCLUSIONS

Repeatedly throughout this chapter the most important issues have been left unanswered. Relevant information on each one can be discussed, but inevitably the most fundamental questions have been left in doubt.

The sparseness of sound information regarding the psychology of art is partly due to methodological difficulties: How are we to gain access to the psychological level of art? Contemporary academic psychology tends to focus on behavior, giving greatest emphasis to those topics that can be studied in the laboratory. Needless to say, the creative process hardly lends itself to such an approach. Alternatively, information can come from introspection, with individuals describing the way they believe they function psychologically. Some important insights can come from such reflection, but there is no doubt that many unconscious factors go into the creation of art.

An even more important source of difficulty stems from the proximity of the psychology of art to the philosophy of art and of human beings generally. Consider, for example, the problem of representation. The question "What does the artist portray?" presupposes that one has satisfactorily answered the question "What is real?" I myself skirted the issue by asserting that it seems more *useful* to assume that a material world exists and that, through our several senses, we apprehend this world with a greater or lesser degree of accuracy. But "most useful" does not—and should not—carry the same conviction as "truthful," and many thoughtful people, from Plato through Descartes to Chomsky, have claimed that the world of our senses is illusory and that only the abstract and timeless deserve the title of "reality." Neither logic nor experiment can resolve the debate. At best one can only assume that one position represents the best bet and proceed from there. But whichever route is chosen, there are problems in store. If one adopts the empiricist position, as I have tended to do, it becomes quite difficult to collect data upon the processes by which the artist acquires and acts upon general aesthetic principles, despite the fact that everything we know about representational styles leads us to believe that the artist does indeed do this. But to discard empiricism and embrace the rationalist position is, I believe, even more frustrating: We may concoct seemingly satisfactory theories, but how are we to test them if we deny their applicability to the mundane world of the senses? Perhaps, as Gregory Bateson has suggested (1972c), we should conceive art simultaneously in both literal and figurative terms—a mask, for example, *is* both a face and a piece of wood. When we concentrate solely on either one interpretation or the other the magic, the art, is lost. In terms of our affective reaction, this is no doubt true.

Ultimately, the issue is this: Can we conceive of ourselves in naturalistic terms, as members of a species that is unique but not different from other species in any supernatural way? And, having made this ego-shattering leap, can we then make any sense of our most distinctive trait, human culture? The answer lies, I believe, as much in our self-image and our motives for altering it as it does in the particular methodologies we develop.

GUIDE TO ADDITIONAL READINGS

Only a few psychologists have ventured into the area of art. Although their data come almost exclusively from Western populations, their theories potentially have cross-cultural implications. Access to the pre-1965 literature may be gained via Kiell's extensive bibliography, *Psychiatry and Psychology in the Visual Arts and Aesthetics* (1965). Reviews of more recent research appear in *Psychology and the Arts,* edited by David O'Hare (1981), with the articles by Lindauer, Eyesenck, and Gardner being especially useful. Winner's synthesis of the field (1982) is valuable for its treatment of not only the visual arts but also the performing arts.

Heroic, if not always successful, attempts by social science writers to construct large-scale theories relating to the psychological level of art are Kavolis (1972) and the writings of Otto Rank (1943, 1959). Howard Gardner (1973) has applied Piagetan structuralism to art and artists, while Getzels and Csikszentmihalyi (1976) have produced one of the few works that begins with empirical data and proceeds to develop nontrivial conclusions.

Finally, in the area of nonanthropologists writing, largely, about complex societies, mention must be made of the work of the art historian Ernst

Gombrich (1972a,b). Gombrich combines a vast knowledge of Western art with a toughness of mind and rigorousness of approach to examine important and interesting questions.

Except for the structuralists, few anthropologists have ventured into the psychological level of art, although the importance of the subject is widely appreciated. Forge's "Learning to See in New Guinea" (1970) offers some interesting insights, as does Bunzel's *The Pueblo Potter* (1972). Also, Lackey's account (1981) of a pottery-making family in Ácatlán, Mexico, provides an excellent account of the stages that neophyte potters pass through.

Besides Faris's Nuba work, other generativist analyses of non-Western art are Sturtevant's treatment (1967) of Seminole clothing and Flora Kaplan's study (1977) of folk pottery from the Valley of Puebla, Mexico. Also, the approach known as *structuralism*, while not narrowly generativist in nature, owes many of its assumptions and methods to linguistics. Claude Lévi-Strauss is the quintessential structuralist, and art provided grist for some of his early studies (see, for example, Lévi-Strauss 1963). Munn's work, cited in Chapter 3, uses this approach productively, as do the articles by Kaeppler, Korn, and Vastokas that appear in a volume edited by Greenhalgh and Megaw (1978), and many of the articles in Washburn (1983). Muller (1979) provides an overview of structural studies of art style.

Easily available sources on the Southwest are Dutton (1974) and the authoritative essays in volumes 9 and 10 of the *Handbook of North American Indians*, Sturtevant, ed., (1978, 1979). Among fieldwork-based studies of Southwestern art in its cultural context, Witherspoon's *Language and Art in the Navajo Universe* (1977) is particularly outstanding, although its account of Navajo philosophy should be supplemented by Farella (1984).

CHAPTER 6

Art in Transition

Change is problematic. A butterfly, dead and pinned to a specimen board, can be observed in minute detail, its parts dissected and studied at our leisure. But of course it isn't really a butterfly at all—it's a lifeless bundle of tissue, quite different from the free-flying butterfly of a summer's day. For the specimen butterfly the dimension of change has been removed: Artificially stopped in time, it no longer moves from shrub to flower to grass, and the egg-larva-cocoon-butterfly-egg cycle cannot run its course. Although it may be easier to study, by limiting ourselves to the specimen butterfly we ignore the real-world problems of locomotion and life cycle.

In the preceding chapters we have, as it were, pinned art to the specimen board and treated it as if it were a fixed, unchanging *thing*. But art is actually a *process*, always in flux, changing from day to day, generation to generation, and epoch to epoch. To breathe life back into art we must now look at it in transition. For convenience, this chapter deals first with changes in art that occur spontaneously within a traditional culture; the spotlight then shifts to the transformations that result when divergent cultures collide.

AUTONOMOUS CHANGE

Autonomous change, that is, change that does not result from contact with other societies but rather from processes within a given society, occurs everywhere and at all times. Most often it occurs slowly, but nevertheless it moves inexorably onward, with the aesthetic tastes of yesterday evolving into today's preferences, and so on into the future. This pan-human trait seems to extend even to our distant relatives, the apes and monkeys: Paul Schiller (1971) gave paper and pencil to a chimpanzee named Alpha every day for six months. Not only did Alpha adopt a fixed style of drawing on the paper, but as months passed the style evolved into a distinctly different manner of drawing. By our definition, Alpha was not making art, but the gradual change in her style illustrates the pervasiveness of autonomous change in all expressive cultures.

Because autonomous change is usually a gradual process, it can seldom be studied during the typical fieldwork period of one or two years. Indeed, under such conditions it may go totally unnoticed so that the strongest impression made upon the ethnographer is that the art of a given society is totally changeless. But our colleagues, the archeologists, are quick to remind us of the shortsightedness of our vision. Inevitably when they excavate a site that contains the remains of many generations of human habitation, archeologists find a succession of artifacts that evolved from one style of production or decoration to another.

Autonomous Change in Eskimo (Inuit) Art

Eskimo (Inuit)[1] art is a fascinating study in itself (see Portfolio at end of this chapter), but it also provides good examples of art in transition. Later we will look at the recent emergence of commercial soapstone carving in the Canadian Arctic, but our interest here concerns the gradual changes that occurred during the prehistoric period in the "winged objects" of northern Alaska (cf. Collins 1962, 1964).

Ten of these ivory objects are shown in Figure 6–1. Despite obvious differences in appearance, each one has a deep socket carved into its lower side; and on the opposite side of each there is a shallow pit or notch. Although it is only conjecture, probably the winged objects were attached to the butt end of a harpoon or dart. The harpoon or dart would have fit tightly into the socket, and the composite projectile would have been hurled by means of a spearthrower, the bone or ivory spur of which would have fit neatly into the small notch in the winged object. So used, the objects would have acted as a weight to counterbalance the heavy harpoon point at the other end of the projectile. This explanation of the use of the winged objects is given credence by the fact that modern Greenland

---

[1]Some of the native inhabitants of the North American arctic prefer to be known as "Inuit," their name for themselves in their own language, while others prefer "Eskimo." The issue is an important one, dealing as it does with the ethnicity and self-image of a sizable minority population. In the absence of a consensus among the people involved, I have chosen to use the terms interchangeably, giving equal time to both sides of the question.

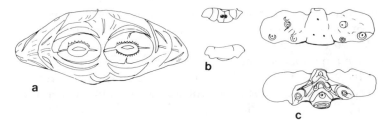
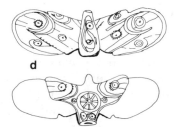

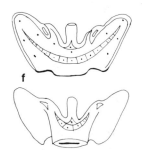
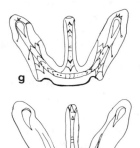
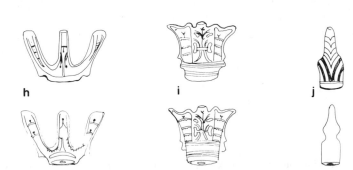

FIGURE 6-1   Prehistoric North Alaskan winged objects.
(After Collins, 1964.)

Eskimos are known to have used bone harpoon "wings" that served the same counterbalancing function.

The winged objects shown in Figure 6–1 were made over a period of more than 1,000 years; *a* is the oldest, dating from around 100 B.C., and *j* the youngest, from about 900 A.D. While all have the definitive traits of socket, notch, raised central portion, and (except for *j*) bilaterally symmetrical wings, the overall shape of the objects changed drastically during this time. Most noticeable are the modifications that occurred in the shape of the wings: Beginning as rather irregularly rounded extensions coming directly out of each side, they soon became more carefully shaped and began to sweep backward a bit. This trend continued, ultimately producing the gracefully formed specimens, *g* and *h*. With *i* the process was completed, the wings being swept back to the point of being joined with the central body; the two pairs of small triangular projections just above the base are all that remain of the outer wings. Finally, with *j*, the wings disappear completely.

Concurrent with these changes in shape, the decorations incised upon the winged objects were constantly changing. The oldest piece clearly has a face, probably human, carved on it: The eyes are obvious, but also visible are eyebrows, nose, and nostrils. Whether or not the decorations on the subsequent pieces were meant to be representational cannot be known, but the distinct stylistic changes that occurred are clearly apparent. Although many artifacts from various time periods must be examined before the patterns of decorative change become apparent, the winged objects shown in Figure 6–1 illustrate some characteristic changes. Consider, for example, the linear and circular elements that are used in decorating the objects. On *a*, in a style that was common during the Okvik period, the lines tend to be short, straight, and detached, many of them being doubled. With *c*, small double-edged circles become popular design elements, and, in *d* and *e*, the circles work themselves into elaborate patterns with lines being used to demarcate larger rounded design areas.

Object *f* marks the transition from a culture known as Old Bering Sea to that known as Punuk. Circles remained popular in Punuk, but with a difference. Old Bering Sea carvers engraved their somewhat irregular circles by hand, making them in various sizes, often with a double perimeter. Punuk carvers must have made their circles by using a stone bit in a hand-twisted drill, because their circles are uniform in shape, usually about an eighth of an inch in diameter, and never concentric. Later, with the circles reduced to incised points, sinuous linear designs became dominant, resulting ultimately in the rather geometric patterns on the last winged object, *j*.

The winged objects from northern Alaska prove that no matter how remote a society, or how simple its technology and sparse its population, its art styles change with the passage of time.

Stylistic Change and "Culture Drift"

As noted at the beginning of this chapter, the study of change tends to be very difficult, and the gradual evolutionary process that typifies autonomous change is especially elusive.

Of course, cultural anthropologists are not the only ones with this problem: Linguists are faced with similar difficulties in studying the gradual changes that occur in languages, and physical anthropologists must try to explain the genetic changes that are random in nature rather than attempts to better adapt to the environment. In both these situations, the notion of "drift" has shed some light on the process of change. Drift occurs in an entity that is always subject to change, and in which any individual change is random in direction, rather than being determined by a prevailing, external principle. With the passage of time such an entity will change in a way that is unpredictable in direction but that is substantial in degree as it undergoes successive, random changes.

A good illustration of how drift might work is found in the prehistoric winged objects from northern Alaska. Some of an object's features are not subject to drift because the implement's usefulness as a harpoon counterweight depends upon them. Among these are its socket, the opposite pit or notch, and, of course, its weight. None of these features may be substantially altered without reducing, or even negating, the object's practical value. None of these instrumental traits is subject to drift; and, in fact, none of them did change during the 1,000-year history of their manufacture.

In contrast, the shape of an object's wings apparently has little effect on its efficacy as part of a harpoon. The earliest known objects had wings that were fairly wide and came out at right angles to the body of the object. From this shape, any of a number of changes could have occurred: The wings, for example, might have become more narrow but continued to stick out at right angles; or they could have become wider but shorter, causing an increase in the overall width of the object; or, finally, they could have—and in fact did—change by becoming more round in shape, the back edge being curved more than the front.

If we were to make prototypes of each of these three possible modifications of the wings and do systematic testing, perhaps using a wind tunnel, we might find one of the designs to be more efficient than, and hence preferable to, the other two models. But in practical usage any such differences would be so slight that the prehistoric Inuit probably would not have noticed them. Consequently, any one of the three (or more) possible alterations was equally likely.

But, for some reason that we'll probably never know, it was the third style of wing that did come into fashion. Its shape became the norm for the moment, although as the centuries passed, it too was subject to alteration in any of several ways. For one thing, it might have been changed back to the preceding shape of wing, but other possibilities presented themselves too: The wings might have become longer, shorter, or wider. In fact the change that occurred was an increased curving of the back edge of the wing, giving it the beginnings of a "swept back" appearance.

And so the process went, with change following change, as the years and generations passed. The same was true of other noninstrumental features of the winged objects, such as their incised decorations. Through the process of drift, they too inevitably changed in substantial, yet unpredictable ways.

Whence Drift?

As noted in Chapter 5, copying very seldom occurs. Moreover, the transmission of artistic skill from one generation to the next inevitably results in at least minor changes in style. Thus, for example, Davenport (1971:385) could see clear differences between the work of two carvers in the Eastern Solomon Islands, despite the fact that each had learned his craft from men who themselves had been apprenticed to the same master carver. These factors alone—the near universal absence of copying and the changes that occur in the process of aesthetic socialization—are enough to ensure that the prerequisites of drift are fulfilled: Each piece of art differs from all others in one or more ways, and the direction of change is unaffected by considerations of practicality.

The likelihood of drift occurring is even greater in societies where there is not only an aversion to copying but an actual premium on novelty. Tiwi artists, for example, carve impressive mortuary poles and although they conform to some traditional restraints on media and form, within these limits artists thrive on originality (Goodale and Koss 1971). Similarly, the East African Pakot consider novel things to be "pretty," and thus constantly encourage native artists to shift their methods of aesthetic expression (H. Schneider 1956). In these and many other societies the pattern seems to be this: The artist and the artist's audience like works that are a little—but not too much—different from the things that have gone before. If the difference is too great, they—like most of us—balk at accepting the change.

Why do many people prefer a modicum of novelty in art? Several reasons may be adduced, the most mundane of which are mere practical considerations. For example, one Pueblo potter told Bunzel that she always made her pots just a little different so that when she took food to festivals in them she would be able to recognize hers among all the others when the festivities were over and it was time to collect the empty pots and go home (Bunzel 1972:65).

Another possible motivation for novelty lies in the realm of politics and economics. In highly stratified societies there is always the danger for the powerful that the symbolic system publicizing their importance will be debased when commoners copy their symbols. One way for the elite to prevent this is to equate originality with quality, with the proviso that only those innovations accepted by the elite themselves are improvements—all others are simply "bad art." (The same end can be accomplished, of course, by requiring "fine" art to be made only in rare media—precious metals or stones, hard-to-find dyes and fibers, high-fired porcelain, and so on.)

Needless to say, motives such as these may also occur on the more benign level of personal interaction. In societies that value individuality, people may be prompted to create unique art works simply because they find pleasure in seeing a statement of their own identity made manifest and public.

An additional explanation for the widespread appreciation of artistic innovation might be suggested. A very important trait of the human species is its adaptability. We have come to dominate the globe (at least for the moment) by our inventiveness and our ability to adopt new cultural practices if they improve the life chances of us and our children. The tendency has been to remain largely true to traditional ways while simultaneously making small alterations here and there. This process of "cautious innovativeness" may lead to major cultural changes as the centuries roll by.

Whether this seemingly pan-human tendency for judicious creativity is instinctual, learned, or both, it does have a clear value for human survival inasmuch as innovativeness in art could be looked on as providing a practice area for the development of skills that pay off in the pragmatic world of subsistence and protection from life-threatening dangers. Thus, for example, humans often create what Ravicz (1976) has termed "ephemeral" art, that is, art objects that deteriorate or are destroyed soon after their creation, simply because we benefit more from the process of making art, with all the practice it provides in cautiously innovative thought and work, than we do from keeping a piece of art for passive appreciation indefinitely into the future. Art, so the argument might go, offers an area in which we can play with experimentation, to some extent "discovering how to discover" without risking life and limb.

Although there are good reasons why innovativeness, in moderation, is fostered in the arts of many societies, we should not lose sight of the fact that the countervailing force of conservatism is always potent. Again, there are good reasons why this is the case. For example, while some innovation may benefit the powerful in stratified societies, too rapid change would undermine the status-conveying capacity of art. Some elites have decided, as it were, not to take any chances and have attempted to prohibit innovation. In traditional Maori (New Zealand) culture, deviations from the traditional were considered to be evil omens; and Firth (1925) has claimed that Maori carvers were summarily executed if they happened to create a novel pattern, even if the innovation occurred by accident.

Another restraint upon innovation stems from the affective response that art prompts. At least part of one's emotional reaction to a work of art is based on previous aesthetic experience. Thus, a work of art that is quite unlike any other a viewer has seen will probably be difficult to appreciate, unless a strong value is placed on innovation for its own sake. For example Alvin Wolfe (1955) has described an Ngombe carver who began making figurines, items that had not previously been included in the Ngombe artistic repertoire. Although the carver and his peers believed that the figurines made him a more successful hunter, the new art form was considered something to be curious about but not to be imitated. As of the end of Wolfe's fieldwork, no other Ngombe carvers had taken up figurine making. Bunzel, in her work with Pueblo potters, had similar findings. She took with her numerous photographs of pots from various locales in the Southwest. When she showed them to the potters of a given village, the women took seriously those pots of their neighbors that had many similarities to their own, avidly discussing what were, in their view, the pots' strong and weak points. A few potters went so far as to incorporate into their own pottery some features they had seen in the photos of their neighbors' pots. But the photographs of pieces from more distant Pueblos brought a totally different response: The potters laughed at them—and promptly lost interest in them.

ART AND CULTURE CONTACT

The preceding section discussed autonomous changes in art—the ubiquitous modifications that spring from within a single society. But even more common are those changes that occur as a result of contact between two different groups. If humans are inveterate innovators, they are even more prone to "borrow" attractive ideas from others.

An extreme case of artistic borrowing is exemplified by the masks of the West African Guro (cf. Himmelheber 1963:105,106). The Guro constitute a unified tribal group, but they have two distinctly different artistic styles: One has been borrowed from the Baulé, the Guro's eastern neighbors, while the other strongly reflects the art of the Senufo to the north of the Guro.

Of necessity the best documented instances of change resulting from culture contact are those in which a small-scale culture is influenced by Euroamerican culture. Around the globe, Western explorers, traders, missionaries, and bureaucrats have made their presence felt in the native societies they have encountered.

Every instance of artistic change due to acculturation is unique, but some order can be found in this diversity by noting two variables that are applicable to all such situations (cf. Graburn 1969, 1976a:5–9). The first

TABLE 6–1 Typology of Art Production, with Examples.

DESTINATION OF ART FORM

		Fourth World Society	Other than Fourth World Society
ORIGIN OF ART FORM	**Traditional Fourth World Society**	*Traditional Art* Eskimo "winged objects"	*Commercial Fine Art* New Guinean shields made for sale to outsiders
	Synthesis of Native and Alien Traditions	*Reintegrated Art* Kuna *molas*	*Novelty Art* Contemporary Inuit soapstone carving
	Other than Fourth World Society	*Popular Art* Navajo jewelry made for local sale	*Assimilated Fine Art* Inuit prints Navajo jewelry made for sale to outsiders

(Adapted from Graburn, 1976a)

question we may ask about art produced in a Fourth World society concerns its origins. Two extremes are possible: Either the art is a modern-day continuation of traditional art, with no significant changes in subject matter, medium, or style; or at the opposite extreme, the Fourth World[2] society may have adopted an art form from the First, Second, or Third World Society that has impinged upon it, borrowing subject matter, media, or styles that were totally absent in the precontact situation. Clearly many instances will fall somewhere between these two extremes, with a Fourth World society, say, combining new tools and materials with traditional styles and subjects to produce a wholly unique art form.

A second dimension to be noted is the intended market for the art of Fourth World societies. On the one hand, art may be made for local use, valued by the native population for its aesthetic merit according to their own standards. Alternately, members of a Fourth World society may have begun to create art for sale to outsiders. The buyers may be visiting tourists or professional dealers who buy goods in large or small quantities, ship them to Western commercial centers, and display them or sell them for a profit. Again, a middle position is possible: Navajo silver jewelry, for example, was for a long time made both for local consumption and for sale to outsiders.

Given these two variables, it's easy to use them to construct a table into which most Fourth World art can easily be fit. Graburn has done this and

---

[2]When small-scale societies come under the influence of complex ones, they are inevitably transformed into qualitatively different entities. Following current usage, I will refer to such groups as "Fourth World" societies. ("First" and "Second" World refer, respectively, to Western noncommunist and communist nations; the "Third World" is made up of the many emerging nations around the globe.)

suggested names for the resulting categories (1976a:8); with a few minor modifications, his system will be used through the remainder of this chapter. Table 6–1 includes ethnographic examples to illustrate each of the categories.

"Reintegrated Art:" Kuna Molas

Mari Lynn Salvador has described a definitive example of "reintegrated art," that is, an art form that emerged from the culture contact situation as a synthesis of ideas from native and alien cultures and that has now become integrated into the matrix of the Fourth World society. Salvador did fieldwork among the Kuna (Cuna) of the San Blas Islands, off the Atlantic coast of Panama, focusing primarily on the attractive *molas* that are made there primarily for local use.

Molas have become part of the everyday dress of Kuna women, being used as front or back panels of blouses. Contemporary molas are made of two or three layers of brightly colored cloth. Patterns—either geometric designs or representational figures—are cut out of the top layer or layers and the pieces are stitched together to create handsome works of reverse appliqué such as the one shown in Figure 6–2.

FIGURE 6-2 Kuna *mola*, San Blas Islands. Reverse applique, cotton cloth; 37 cm. long. *(Collection of the author.)*

Before the arrival of Europeans, a major Kuna art medium was personal decoration in the form of body painting and jewelry; molas did not exist. But the contact situation brought with it two things: an ethic of personal modesty that required the covering of most of the body with clothing, and relatively easy access to factory-made cloth, needles, thread, and scissors. By the late nineteenth century, Kuna women were wearing dark, short-sleeved chemises over underskirts that were painted with geometric patterns. When bright-colored cloth became available, instead of painting their underskirts, women invented the technique of cutting designs out of the lower portions of their long blouses and sewing these onto their underskirts, producing proto-molas. The modern mola came about as the garments were shortened, causing the reverse appliqué decoration to move upward to the fronts and backs of the blouses (Salvador 1976a,b; Stout 1947).

Thus, the technique of mola work is a synthesis of an alien medium with native aesthetic expression and ingenuity. The decorations that appear on the molas are similarly eclectic: The two-layer geometric molas resemble designs used in precontact body painting and traditional Kuna basketry. Other molas have representational figures depicting political, recreational, and religious themes—the latter itself being a syncretistic combination of native and Christian belief. Fads in mola design and subject matter come and go. In the 1960s the most popular were "missionary molas" that depicted Bible stories, the Crucifixion, and so on. These eventually fell out of fashion and few women now wear them.

The relatively young art of mola work has become an integral part of Kuna culture. Fine molas are a source of pride for the family of the maker, and their production provides an expressive outlet for Kuna women. Not all women are equally skillful at mola work, and an elaborate set of criteria exists for judging molas. Some of the standards concern workmanship: In Salvador's words, "The sewing must be carefully done with matched thread, no stitches showing, and no raw edges. Lines have to be even, thin, and equally spaced" (1976a:172). Other standards relate to aesthetic values: Large areas around representational figures should be filled in with straight lines or geometric patterns; patterns should be balanced; the top layer of material must be all one color—usually red; all colors should be intense, not muted; and the contrast between different colors must be carefully worked out (cf. Salvador 1976b; see also Hirshfield 1977).

Molas have also taken on an economic importance for the Kuna. Because women's tastes frequently change, molas often go out of style before they are worn out. Molas have become popular purchase items for tourists, and for years Kuna men have taken molas to sell in cities on the mainland. A few women now make "tourist molas" for sale directly to outsiders, but these molas are sometimes "made quickly at the expense of the accepted quality criteria. Women who make them are often criticized and the problem of 'tourista molas' has been discussed at the Cuna congress" (Salvador 1976a:180).

But commercialization has not had a uniformly adverse effect on quality. In 1966 the *Cooperative de Mola de San Blas* was organized, partly as a means of marketing the dresses made by women in a sewing school started by Peace Corps volunteers in 1963. The molas they produce are of the finest quality, partly, Salvador says, because the members take pride in the work they do for the Co-op, and partly because the products are under the scrutiny of a strict quality-control board composed of the most skillful mola makers.

The Kuna molas illustrate one possible result of a small-scale society's encounter with the West. They represent a felicitous blend of the traditional and the alien that benefits both parties—the Kuna in now having a new art form that plays an important role in their culture, and us in our being the recipients of strikingly handsome (if often secondhand) works of art.

COMMERCIALIZATION OF ART: A NAVAJO EXAMPLE

The evolution of Kuna molas is relatively simple by comparison to the developments that have occurred in many other small-scale societies as a result of contact with the West. The following two sections describe two of the more interesting and better documented cases—that of silversmithing by the Navajo and the commercialization of art among Canadian Eskimo groups.

The Development of Navajo Silversmithing

John Adair has studied the pre-1944 evolution of silversmithing among the Native Americans of the Southwest. Like Kuna molas, silversmithing is a relatively young art form among Navajo and Pueblo artisans. Sometime around 1859 a Navajo named Atsidi Sani first learned the craft from Mexican smiths living in New Mexico. When he returned to Arizona, his Navajo and Pueblo neighbors provided a ready market for his silver jewelry and decorated functional items such as horse bridles. Atsidi Sani did not produce a great quantity of work himself, but he did teach the craft to his four sons, and they all became prolific silversmiths and taught the skill to others.

Since then, Navajo silversmithing has undergone constant development. Some changes have been the result of new techniques, such as the insetting of turquoise; others reflect new tools, such as metal stamps that produce small, repetitive patterns on silver. As is typical of the culture contact situation, Navajos did not adopt alien ideas indiscriminately but rather selected those things that fit best into the traditional system. For example, the iconography of the Franciscan missionaries in the Southwest provided a large inventory of designs that smiths could incorporate into their silverwork, but the one that became most commonly used by Zuni smiths was the double-barred cross motif. To the Spanish missionaries the design stood for Saint James, the patron saint of Spain, but its popularity among the Zuni was due to its similarity to the traditional representation of Dragon-Fly, a figure that had been popular in Zuni art long before the arrival of the Spanish.[3]

Navajo Silver as "Popular" Art

Silver ornaments imported from Mexico had been prized in Southwestern societies long before the development of local silversmithing. Because Navajo smiths could easily tap—and expand—this market, the new craft caught on quickly, making it an example of what Graburn (1976a:7,8) classifies as "popular" arts, that is, arts introduced from outside the society but which, in their adoptive form, are also appreciated within the population.

Fine silverwork is held in high esteem in contemporary Navajo communities. Individuals—both men and women—wear their silver with pride; Adair found that a common means of one Navajo complimenting another is to remark on the quantity and quality of that person's jewelry. And silver jewelry is not just a means of displaying wealth; it also plays a role in the ongoing economic system, for pieces may be pawned at the trading post when the owner is temporarily in need of money or other goods.

But the silver worn by Navajos does more than fill economic needs; it's also an art form, valued for its beauty and judged according to a set of standards that, though they have shifted through time, are commonly held throughout the Navajo population. At the time of Adair's research, silver bracelets were felt to need one or more turquoise settings to be attractive: Deep, clear, robin's egg blue stones were preferred. Tastes in design have shifted from the simple bold designs popular at the turn of the century to the more elaborate styles in the 1920s; finally, at the time of Adair's research, there was a swing back toward jewelry with more simple symmetry and elegance. Transcending these changes in fashion, however, was a constant seeking of fine workmanship: Navajos rarely wear sloppily made silver jewelry.

---

[3]The Dragon-Fly icon is exceptional in that most of the designs used on Southwest silver are nonrepresentational, despite the claims to the contrary by some Anglo traders who know that their white customers will pay more for a piece if told that its decorations hold some supernatural meaning in the mind of its maker (Adair 1944:104).

Navajo Silver as "Assimilated Fine Art"

Silver jewelry is not only a popular art among its Native American makers, but also among Anglos, making it an example of Graburn's category of "assimilated fine art." This side of the art's history is an interesting tale in itself.

Tourists from the East were expressing interest in buying "Indian-style" silver as early as 1899, but the pieces then being made for Navajo and Pueblo buyers were considered too heavy to carry back home and wear in society. Seeing a potential market, Herman Scheizer, head of the Fred Harvey Company's curio department, bought a supply of silver and turquoise and farmed it out to various traders, asking them to have Navajo smiths make jewelry that was lighter in weight than that made for local use. The technique was a commercial success, with the Harvey Company—and later others—selling the new-style jewelry to people touring the West on the Santa Fe Railroad. By the mid-1920s Navajo and Pueblo smiths were selling large quantities of the lighter-weight jewelry.

The development of an outside market for Navajo silver has influenced the craft as a whole. New tools and techniques have been introduced to hasten production; torches have commonly replaced natural fires and blowpipes as a source of heat for soldering, and mechanical rollers are used by some full-time smiths. These aids do not noticeably alter the quality of the final product and are used not only on silver made for sale to Anglos but also on silver intended for local use.

The difference between the two markets is, however, kept in mind with respect to style and workmanship. Both smiths and traders typically believe—probably rightly so—that most nonnatives feel authentic silverwork should look old, with tarnish in the crevices of fine work. Tom Burnside, Adair's principal informant, artificially oxidized the pieces he made for sale to Anglos by first heating them and coating them with a tarnish-producing chemical, and then buffing them to leave only the grooves darkened. (By contrast, jewelry made for local use is not artificially tarnished, for Navajos take pride in bright, new-looking silver.)

The most important difference between the jewelry produced for export and that made for local use results from the buying methods of the traders. Usually tourist jewelry is bought from smiths by the ounce, giving little or no premium for careful craftmanship. As one would expect, this practice encourages some smiths to turn out work as quickly as possible with only minimal regard to quality. Another unfortunate outcome of the commercialization of Navajo silver lies in the fact that if a certain style proves popular and can be mass-produced, in all likelihood a nonnative entrepreneur somewhere will begin manufacturing jewelry that imitates the successful Navajo handmade work. As early as 1910 a Denver firm was imitating Navajo jewelry; and it is not unknown for curio dealers to manufacture "Indian-made" silverwork, drawing upon Navajo and Pueblo urban immigrants as a source of cheap labor for their factories.

COMMERCIALIZATION OF ART: THE CANADIAN ARCTIC

Navajo and Pueblo silversmiths found their first customers among their own people, and despite growing sales to Anglos, that market has remained important. Figurative soapstone carving by Canadian Eskimos is also new, but the native market for these works is nil, and this craft provides a good example of yet another type of transformation that art can undergo in a culture contact situation.

Changes in Inuit Art

Compared to the gradual changes that occurred in the North Alaskan winged objects during the thousand years of their known evolution, the events in the Arctic's recent past have been tumultuous indeed, especially in northern Canada, a region that Europeans have continually explored and exploited for some time. For example, an early traveler named Nevins described how he and his fellow sailors anticipated meeting the "Esquimaux" of the Hudson Bay region, "speculating upon what we were likely to get from them" (1847, quoted in Martijn 1964:559). What Nevins got, in fact (in addition to prized fur pelts) were small ivory and bone carvings depicting animals and canoes.

Sales of Inuit ivory carving gradually increased, but its distribution was erratic. The situation began to change dramatically, however, in the autumn of 1948 when a young Ontario artist named James Houston returned from a painting trip in the north with several figurative pieces that Inuit carvers had executed in soapstone, rather than the traditional ivory. The response in Montreal to these sculptures was so encouraging that during the next summer Houston purchased about 1,000 more items at Port Harrison, Puvungnetuk, and Cape Smith. The Canadian Handicrafts Guild mounted a show of the work, and within three days every piece was sold!

The Canadian government quickly became interested in the sale of Inuit art, seeing its potential for increasing Inuit employment and for improving living conditions in a territory that was very depressed economically. Within three years Houston had taken a civil service post and was coordinating a sizable network of carvers; meanwhile the Canadian government organized an extensive promotional campaign to expand the market in Canada, the United States, and Europe. Later, Canadian Eskimos learned printmaking techniques and created their own cooperatives to provide some protection in a market otherwise dominated by the Hudson's Bay Company.

Although Eskimos still suffer hardships, soapstone carving has ameliorated their economic situation somewhat. Graburn (1976b) estimates that in the mid-1970s art sales were bringing over $2 million annually to Eskimos, increasing the average household's income sixfold over 1949–1950 levels. Money received from art production now pays for snowmobiles and outboard motors, which Inuit now rely on for carrying out their subsistence hunting and fishing activities.

Soapstone Carving in Perspective

There has been much heated debate about how Inuit soapstone carvings compare to traditional Inuit sculpture. In the opinion of some, such as James Houston and others interested in selling the contemporary work and in increasing outsiders' respect for traditional Eskimo culture, the differences between the old and the new are minimal. Edmund Carpenter, however, has taken the extreme opposite view, claiming that much post-1948 soapstone sculpture is "Western-designed, Western-valued, and some of it Hong Kong-made" (1971:166).

Polemics aside, several features do differentiate the two art forms. First, in making soapstone carvings, Inuit artists must subordinate their own religious and expressive needs, which were ably met by their traditional arts, and focus instead on the tastes of Euroamericans. This change obviously reflects two different approaches to making art, but before we facilely condemn the contemporary Inuit carver's commercial motives we should remember that Western artists, in the interest of gaining a livelihood, have often yielded to the wishes of their patrons (cf. Cameron 1983). Second, modern Inuit sculptors work almost exclusively in soapstone and serpentine, media previously used only for utilitarian items such as seal-oil lamps. (Apparently the shift away from carving in the traditional medium of ivory was prompted by Houston himself.) Third, whereas precontact sculptures were small enough to fit easily in the palm of the hand, most soapstone carving is substantially larger in scale. And finally, modern soapstone sculptures typically portray animals and human figures, complete with clothes and facial details, often engaged in an overt activity such as hunting, although none of these traits were present in earlier sculptures.

But there are also marked similarities between contemporary soapstone carving and prehistoric Eskimo art, with its subtle and well-crafted three-dimensional portrayals of traditional subject matter. Indeed, the transitions that Eskimo art has undergone illustrate a central theme of this chapter, namely, that art is always and everywhere in a constant state of flux, with the work of every period both building upon and going beyond its predecessors.

Whether one likes or dislikes Inuit soapstone carving, it is unquestionably an important part of the art world of the Canadian Arctic today, as Eskimos themselves are quick to admit. Valuable research by Nelson Graburn has revealed that Inuit aesthetic tastes combine the old and the new. Most soapstone carvers still show traditional admiration for pieces that are smooth, well made, and use some ivory for special effects; but they have adopted Euroamerican preferences for elaborate pieces that portray complex scenes. Indeed, if traders did not discourage such works because they are easily broken in transit to the south, more would be produced today (Graburn 1976b; see also Graburn 1971, 1972, 1976c).

THE MESSAGES OF TOURIST ART

The reality of modern times is that many Fourth World artists now produce art for nontraditional markets. In some quarters such art is still ignored or disparaged, but a few scholars have begun to undertake serious, sophisticated research to study its inner workings. Bennetta Jules-Rosette's African work is perhaps the best example of this.

During numerous visits to the Ivory Coast, Zambia, and Kenya during the 1975–1982 period, Jules-Rosette interviewed about 200 artists, often conducting follow-up interviews and sometimes videotaping them at work. The artists represent varied media and production methods, but all produce work for sale to tourists. In gathering and analyzing her data, Jules-Rosette has adopted a semiotic approach that views art as a process of communication—hence the title of her book, *The Messages of Tourist Art* (1984).

The semiotic model is useful because "message" implies a "sender" (the artist) and a "receiver" (the buyer of the art), and in "tourist art" an important discrepancy exists between the two. The artists that Jules-Rosette interviewed are "image creators who attempt to represent aspects of their own cultures to meet the expectations of image consumers who treat art as an example of the exotic. . . . For image consumers, the exotic makes sense only when translated into the terms and preconceptions of their own cultures" (Jules-Rosette 1984:1). Sometimes the gap between artist and buyer can only be bridged by intermediaries who "explain" the art to tourists and then interpret the buyers' responses to the artists. (In the Ivory Coast, such intermediaries are called "Charlies," and are usually Wolof from Sénégal and Hausa from Nigeria.)

Jules-Rosette's research reveals that despite popular belief, tourist art is not necessarily mass-produced by inexperienced workers. In the cases she studied, commercialization has led to increased specialization, which results in a higher quality of workmanship than found in traditional settings. And contrary to the "conveyor-belt fallacy," tourist art may also be more individualized than indigenous art, often being produced by artists who singlehandedly carry out diverse tasks that, in traditional settings, would have been executed collectively.

Nor do tourist artists slavishly follow the tastes of buyers alone. Their livelihood requires profitable sales to outsiders, of course; but like everyone else, tourist artists also seek the esteem of their peers and of others within their community. A Lusaka painter told Jules-Rosette, "Granted, it's the Europeans who buy our art. But we don't produce for the Europeans. We want our own people to understand what we produce" (1984:226). Considerations of the marketplace require innovations in technique and subject matter, but the makers of tourist art have their own standards too. Jules-Rosette delineates six stylistic traits, such as a rhythmic quality and luminosity, that she believes informs all visual art made in Africa today. And although the themes of commercial art's subject matter may seem to be designed only to tell foreigners what they want to hear, African tourist art carries messages to Africans themselves. It typically represents a culture's shared identity and values; and sometimes it also embodies an implicit critique of present-day conditions while conveying a nostalgia for the past.

By taking seriously the phenomenon of tourist art, Jules-Rosette has examined a dilemma that faces artists in many Fourth World societies— and, for that matter, most artists in the West, namely, how to remain true to one's own aesthetic and cultural standards while trying to make a living in a world that thrives on commerce and practicality.

THE DYNAMICS OF ART AND CULTURE CONTACT

Kuna molas, Navajo silver, Inuit sculpture, and African tourist art all exemplify a worldwide phenomenon. Wherever small-scale societies have fallen under the influence of colonizing nations, their traditional arts are inevitably changed. Simple extinction of old forms may be the result, in which case we can only mourn their passing. But in many instances traditional skills and aesthetics, although significantly modified, are maintained or increased in their importance. (The Central African Fang's estimate of their own indigenous reliquary sculpture has increased considerably since they learned that Whites not only want it but, in fact, buy it from each other for tens of thousands of dollars [Fernandez 1973:218n.].) With reports of individual art works from small-scale societies bringing prices of over a quarter of a million dollars, there is little doubt that Western influence will continue to have a marked effect and that the future will only bring increased commercialization of these arts. And in many cases the native populations do not seem reluctant to change. As Graburn has remarked, Fourth World peoples "may *want* to change" (1976b:12).

Factors that Influence Acculturation

Four different kinds of considerations—economic, social, cultural, and artistic—have a bearing on the course taken by acculturation in a given society's art.

The hand manufacture of art makes sense *economically* in many Fourth World societies, where a surplus of labor accompanies a lack of capital, although ensuring reliable and fair channels of distribution presents a serious problem. Obviously, a prerequisite of the commercialization of art is that its makers want the goods that money from art sales can buy. In the Canadian Arctic, for example, Euroamericans arrived just as Eskimos were experiencing difficulties with their traditional means of subsistence. At first, the Inuit natives traded fur pelts to supplement their food supply, but when that market proved to be erratic, they turned to commercial art production.

Social and personal factors also play an important role in the process of acculturation. Some individual must introduce both the idea and the technique of commercialization. Outsiders are often responsible: Missionaries, Peace Corps volunteers, and anthropologists themselves have all been instrumental in doing this in various societies.

Often, though, the individual responsible for the introduction is someone who is a member of the culture, but only minimally so. For example, Kiste (1974) has described the plight of the Bikinians, who were removed from their Pacific atoll when the United States government decided to test nuclear warheads there. While relocated on the island of Kili, they were aided by James Milne, an islander of mixed Micronesian-European descent. Drawing on his knowledge of both traditional skills and Western markets (gained from living in Hawaii and going to the University of Hawaii), Milne designed a woman's purse that could be made from materials readily available on Kili. Woven by Bikinian women, the "Kili Bag" became a popular purchase for Americans who lived in or visited the Pacific. (Unfortunately, logistic problems and the departure of Milne led to a collapse of the industry.)

Cultural factors also play a part in the acculturation process. It has been suggested that some traditional societies are more predisposed to adopt market-oriented techniques, whereas others show less interest in exploiting such an innovation.

Ruben Reina (1963) has described a case in the modern Mayan village of Chinautla where a generalized cultural conservatism led to the abandonment of a new art form. All Chinautla women make ceramic water jars called *tinajas,* which they sell in nearby Guatamala City, but a 12-year-old girl named Delores learned from her grandmother how to make novel clay figurines of animals that sold even better than the jars. Delores' personal life was less successful, however, and after three different marriage proposals fell through she finally quit making the figurines—and promptly found a husband. Reina suggests that Delores' innovative art technique lessened her desirability as a wife because her creativity was taken as a sign of unreliability.

A final cultural pattern should be mentioned with respect to commercialization of traditional arts. Graburn (1969) has noted that a craft that was traditionally somewhat ephemeral to a society often has a better chance of successful commercialization than does one that played a central and fundamental role in traditional culture. Thus, for example, Canadian Eskimos did indeed carve soapstone before 1948, but in this medium they produced only utilitarian items—cooking pots and lamps—with little or no decoration. When James Houston arrived with news of possible markets for soapstone sculpture, carvers were able to explore this new art medium without too many restraints from traditional taboos and hidebound aesthetic predispositions. Similar patterns of change have been noted for Navajo textiles (Kent 1976) and silversmithing (Adair 1944), Beni woodcarvers (P. Ben-Amos 1976a), and Tzintzuntzan weaving and carpentry (Foster 1967:346).

Finally, several factors that influence the likelihood of successful commercialization of art derive from the *art objects themselves*. Obviously, works that are perishable, fragile, or difficult to transport are unlikely candidates for sale to outsiders. Moreover, the makers of a successful handmade art may find their sales ruined if their work can be mass-produced in factories.

An experiment by Graburn (1978) reveals just how capricious market factors can be. Two types of art from Canada were placed on display during successive semesters at the University of California at Berkeley. First, wooden carvings, called Cree Craft, from the Naskapi-Cree of the Canadian sub-Arctic were exhibited, and these were followed by a show of Eskimo soapstone carvings. When questioned about their preferences, people who saw the exhibitions generally preferred the Inuit work because it was less polished and because they thought soapstone was a more "primitive" medium than wood, although, as we know, figurative soapstone carving is a very recent innovation in the Arctic. Also, the apparent "man and nature" theme, suggested by the Inuit portrayals of hunters and fishermen after their prey (another novelty), appealed to viewers. By comparison, some thought that the Cree Craft looked a little too "middle class." Given these reactions among potential buyers, it is not surprising that Cree Craft had become a commercial failure even before Graburn could publish his findings.

Sociocultural Repercussions of Commercialization

The development of an art market brings with it all the problems of commerce. For example, the scarcity of ivory from walrus tusks forces the Alaskan Eskimo carver to decide whether to make "quick money" by carving a cribbage board from a tusk, or to maximize his profits by carving several smaller items that will sell well and that will minimize the amount of wasted ivory (Ray 1961:112). Whatever his decision, he, like artists else-where in Fourth World societies, can hardly expect to get rich. Graburn found (1976b:47) that the majority of Inuit carvers would gladly forsake carving for full-time wage labor, thinking it would provide greater security and higher wages. (One may question whether or not cottage industries such as commercial art are really more desirable than the types of wage labor available in many parts of the world—for example, in South African gold mines or the textile sweatshops of India.)

But if commercialization of art is not altogether an economic boon, it does offer a different sort of benefit to the producing society: It may serve as a focus for an emergent ethnic identity, a symbol of the makers' unique cultural heritage. Modern beadwork made by the Kiowa of the American Great Plains is novelty art, originating in the culture contact situation and now made for tourist consumption, but its importance extends beyond the realm of economics. Mary Jane Schneider notes,

> The people engaged in this tourist production regard their work as tradi-tionally Indian. Most recall mothers or grandmothers who did similar work. . . . Because these items are made specifically by Indians for sale to non-Indians, the production serves to reinforce Indian identity. The colors, de-signs and techniques are aimed at presenting an Indian art to the purchaser. As one woman said, "God gave White people reading and writing, he gave us Indians beadwork to earn our living." In order to continue this tradition, there is a continuing, consistent demand to have beadwork and other skills taught in the schools. With language and history it is part of Kiowa identity (1976:7).

The Effects of Commercialization on Art Works

Can any general statements be made in evaluating the influence of commercialization on the art works themselves? This is a controversial issue, with some of the more intrepid scholars not hesitating to decry all cases of commercialization. For example the British anthropologist William Fagg has remarked that, "tourist art . . . of course, is not art in any proper sense, but more or less mechanically produced Kitsch, or trashy souvenirs, for the less sophisticated traveler" (1969:45). And Abramson (1976) has labeled much of the work currently sold in New Guinea "degenerate, slap-dash junk." Some pieces made for sale, he continues, "are actually ex-tremely well done in terms of pure craftsmanship, but something vital is missing in every one" (p. 259).

The debate, of course, concerns several different aspects of art pro-duction. There is, first, the question of whether or not art made for sale to outsiders appeals to our own aesthetic tastes. Inasmuch as we typically consider the conditions under which a Western art work was produced to be irrelevant to an evaluation of its aesthetic merit, and since in any case we applaud Western artists regardless of whether or not they derive any mon-etary benefit from their work, I feel we are totally unjustified in dogmatically assuming that commercialization inevitably results in the production of art that is poor by our own standards of taste.

There are, however, other aspects of the effects of commercialization that can be noted. For one thing, even art made expressly for sale to outsiders is typically governed by native standards of quality. Predictably, such standards are often an amalgam of traditional and introduced values, but they are nevertheless widely held and have a significant effect on current art production. Contemporary Inuit aesthetic values were described earlier in the present chapter; and Paula Ben-Amos (1976a) has described how Beni carvers in Nigeria, working in the nontraditional medium of ebony, place a high value on craftsmanship as reflected in accuracy of portrayal of naturalistic subjects, shininess of finish, and carefulness of detail.

It is difficult to generalize about the effects of commercialization on quality of workmanship. First, it should be noted that even traditional noncommercial art items vary widely with regard to craftsmanship: Many are carefully made whereas others fall far short of either native or Western standards of excellence. The same situation prevails regarding art produced for sale: Some is well made, and some reflects the maker's carelessness or lack of skill. Cordwell (1959) has gone so far as to suggest with respect to African art that "the same percentage of 'hack' artists has continued to exist with only their subject matter changed as a result of contact with Euroamerican norms" (p. 47).

Besides intrasocietal variation, however, quality of workmanship also can vary from one society to another. Several factors may lead to a lessening of skill or carefulness of production. Among the Bangwa of Cameroon, for example, Western influences were so pervasive that for nearly a generation there was no carving of the once well-made Night masks and ancestral figures. Then, when possibilities of sales to outsiders became apparent in the mid-1960s, the old art forms were reborn. Brain and Pollock (1971) note that "today, spurred on by recent European interest in their work, everyone, trained or not, is chip-chipping away, copying a Night mask, or an ancestral figure. Even the professional works as fast as possible since the prices given cannot compare with those paid by wealthy chiefs in the past" (p. 62). This situation results in carvings made of unseasoned wood, the extremities of which may break off with the slightest mishandling.

The Bangwa case raises a problem of interpretation, however. Brain and Pollock go on to say:

A statue used to take several months to complete. Now a carver spends less than a week. Older men know that these rough and ready methods must detract from the perfection of the work. They say that it used to take twenty years of apprenticeship before a sculptor could or should tackle an ancestral figure, and that a Night society mask should not be attempted with any chance of success until a carver had both a daughter and a son. The total commitment of the old masters included abstinence from sex and certain foods throughout the period of work. Modern carvings, say the elders, cannot compare with the inspired work of the past (1971:62,63).

But the devil's advocate might ask, Are these changes in Bangwa carving methods signs of an inevitable lowering of actual workmanship, or do they merely indicate a *change* from past ways? Did it really take Bangwa novices 20 years to acquire the skills needed to undertake the most elaborate sculptures, or was the long apprenticeship largely a ritualistic requirement, with no more artistic importance than the rule that artists must have had a daughter and a son before undertaking certain pieces? And of the acceleration of carving—from "several months" to "less than a week"—how much is due to the carver's working longer hours each day and using imported tools that permit carving to be done more quickly with no detrimental effect on the end product? Brain and Pollock do not answer these questions, but rather they accept the view of the older generation of carvers that things aren't as well made as in "the good old days." Assuming that quality of workmanship is a cross-culturally identifiable trait, ethnographic descriptions of art in transition would be more valuable if they specified the details of the changes that have actually occurred in specific art traditions, using less subjective criteria than to describe contemporary work as "uninspired."

I am not suggesting that the quality of workmanship is never impaired by the commercialization of an art form. The use of unseasoned wood by contemporary Bangwa sculptors *is* a very unfortunate development. But what of the fact that the same carvers rub their creations with oil and soot and hang them over smokey fires to give them an aged appearance? Certainly this involves a break with tradition, and dishonesty is involved if gullible tourists are told that the works actually are quite old. But these factors, again, are not the same thing as quality of workmanship. Instead, they reflect changes in tastes and shifts in audience.

A final question with respect to the effects of commercialization of art is related to originality and copying. Again, the picture is mixed. On the one hand, there are numerous cases like that of the so-called billikins that are carved in large numbers for sale by Alaskan Eskimos. The original billikin figure was created (and patented!) in 1908 by a Miss Florence Pretz, an art teacher in Kansas City, Missouri (Ray 1961). The rather Buddha-like figure was supposed to represent Pretz's idea of "The God of Things as they Ought to Be." Billikins were soon the rage throughout the United States, and in 1909 an influential Alaskan carver named Happy Jack carved one in ivory, at the insistence of a local shopkeeper. Since then, Ray says, "thousands, if not millions, [of billikins] have been made in all sizes by the Alaskan carvers" (Ray 1961:122).

But although billikins have been copied excessively, the carvers themselves chafe at the mindless job of endless duplication of the original billikin. Given a market for other ivory carvings, they avoid making billikins when possible. And over the years, substantial changes have occurred in the billikin figure: It has been simplified in shape, details have been omitted, and various novelty features, such as movable male genitals, have sometimes been added (Ray 1961:123). Thus, although the pressures of the market may force commercial artists to copy, there is often a countervailing desire on their own part to innovate—contrary, perhaps, to the wishes of outsiders.

The preceding sections have dealt with the sweeping changes that are taking place in the arts of Fourth World societies. Many objective, field-work-based accounts of commercialization of art are only now seeing the light of day. There is no question as to the importance of the phenomenon: It is significantly affecting the lives of an enormous number of people, and for this reason alone it should command our attention. The art itself is highly diverse. Certainly the best of it—best with regard to workmanship and our own aesthetic standards and interests—deserves a place in Western collections of ethnographic art alongside the best traditional art. And, as Third World countries increasingly (and justifiably) restrict the number of older traditional art works that can be exported, commercial Fourth World art will take on an even greater significance in Western collections. We can hope that as our understanding of the processes of change increases we will be able to foster those circumstances that make the best of the inevitable situation, both for the members of societies that produce the art and for the art itself.

PORTFOLIO

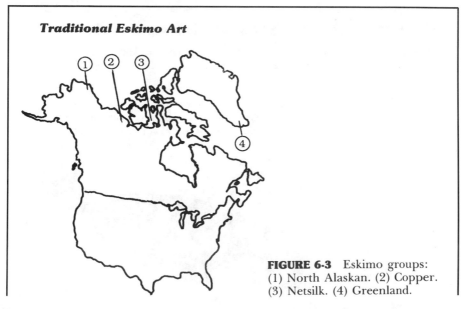

Traditional Eskimo Art

FIGURE 6-3 Eskimo groups: (1) North Alaskan. (2) Copper. (3) Netsilk. (4) Greenland.

Until recently, Eskimos lived as all human beings did before the Neolithic revolution: They were hunters/gatherers/fishers. But like the Australian Aborigines described in the Portfolio of Chapter 3, a close look at Inuit culture reveals that simplicity of means does not imply brutish sensibilities incapable of producing art. In fact, some prehistoric Eskimo sculpture now brings quite high prices from Western art collectors who are attracted by its subtle modeling, patina, and rarity.

Inuits first arrived in North America from northeast Asia between 4,000 and 6,000 years ago. They gradually dispersed across the vast Arctic, traveling both southwestward along the Alaskan coast and eastward across Canada to the shores of Greenland. (Even today, Inuits remain genetically, linguistically, and culturally distinct from the Native American Indians living south of the treeline.) With only minor variations, traditional Eskimos everywhere reside in small, nomadic bands of individuals who are related to each other either by blood or through formalized bonds of reciprocity. They survive by means of a elementary but ingenious technology, imbued with a religion that makes many specific activities taboo and that posits numerous animistic spirits.

Virtually the only durable, rigid material in the Arctic environment is ivory, in addition to limited amounts of wood; and most Inuit art in Western museums is predictably executed in these media. (Figures are also carved in ice and snow.) These are typically small in scale and

FIGURE 6-4   Ivory bucket handle, Port Clarence, Alaska. *(Courtesy Field Museum of Natural History, Chicago.)*

FIGURE 6-5   Eskimo wooden box for storing harpoon blades used in whaling, Port Clarence, Alaska. *(Courtesy Field Museum of Natural History, Chicago.)*

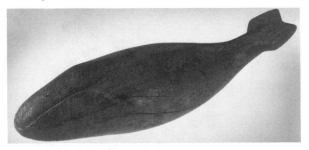

FIGURE 6-6 Eskimo masks, Port Clarence, Alaska. *(Courtesy Field Museum of Natural History, Chicago.)*

modeled in the round, their elongated outlines often determined by the shape of the raw material. The smooth surfaces of ivory carvings may be embellished by incised patterns of lines and dots that are blackened with charcoal. Extrapolating from modern practices, prehistoric ivory carvings of human and animal figures probably served as amulets worn by individuals to bring specific types of good fortune, as shamans' tools, or even as children's toys or utilitarian items such as fishing and hunting implements (Figures 6–4 and 6–5).

Masks are sometimes carved in ivory, but wooden masks are more common. Ranging in size from 2 to 20 inches (2.5 to 50 cm), some are meant to be worn over dancers' faces during various sorts of performances, others held in dancers' hands or used by shamans. Many portray the face through devices that are imaginative to the point of surrealism (Figure 6–6), sometimes adding feathers and other media to enhance the effect.

Whereas carving was a masculine skill, the making of clothing provided Inuit women with an avenue of artistic expression. Among some groups, festive occasions called for special parkas made of contrasting furs and bearing embroidered designs (Figure 6–7). Tattoos and many types of jewelry, including lip- and earplugs, were also worn. Kayaks and mortuary boards were sometimes painted, and some groups produced baskets and pottery. Everywhere the performing arts of dance, music, and song were very important, for both ritual and recreational purposes (Figure 6–8).

Traditional Eskimo art was motivated by a desire to improve life in two ways. First, art in the form of toys for children, gaming devices for adults, and the sensuous decoration of the human body served to enhance day-to-day existence, making life significantly more enjoyable, especially during the winter months with their long hours of darkness. Second, art ensured future well-being by providing a supernatural means to make tomorrow happier, healthier, and more prosperous. For example, although most of a woman's tatoos were made to augment her beauty, some were created to ensure future good fortune—easier childbirth and nursing while she was alive, or else residence in a more desirable region of the underworld after her death. Amulets also brought desirable consequences in the future by ensuring, for example, that a boy would grow up with a strong back or that a hunter would encounter many caribou.

FIGURE 6-7   Eskimo dolls with decorated fur parkas. *(Courtesy Field Museum of Natural History, Chicago.)*

FIGURE 6-8 Dance performed by natives of Dolphin and
Union Strait, given at a farewell celebration for members
of the Fifth Thule Expedition. The dancer, accompanied
by a drum, sings songs he has composed and owns. Others
in the group may join in the refrain. *(Photograph by Leo
Hansen, 1924. Photograph courtesy Nationalmuseet,
Copenhagen.)*

In Eskimo thought, art's ability to accomplish these ends may derive from its transcendent nature. We can distinguish between three
realms of existence—the supernatural world, with its awe-inspiring
power; the social world of day-to-day human actions; and the natural
world of animals, plants, and inanimate objects. But in what way are
these separate worlds related to each other? How, one might ask, can
lifeless chemicals become living human flesh; and how can the spirit
that seems to live within the flesh transcend mortality to confront the
eternal and divine? Some of the Inuit's myths suggest that they tacitly
believe art to be the magic philosopher's stone that makes such transformations possible.

Consider, for instance, an episode in an Eskimo creation story in
which Man, having just emerged from a pea pod, is encountered by
the spirit figure, Raven. Seeing Man, Raven pushed up his beak (as if
it were a mask) to the top his head, and thus changed into a man.
After expressing his surprise at seeing a living creature that looked so
much like himself, Raven set about creating the things of the world,
the last of which was a clay figure that, in fact, resembled Man. As a
last touch, Raven "fastened a lot of fine water grass on the back of the

head for hair, and after the image had dried in his hand, he waved his wings over it . . . and a beautiful young woman arose and stood beside Man" (Nelson 1899:454). Aside from the fact that the tale describes males as coming into existence spontaneously whereas females are created by male artificers, the interesting point in the story is the way transitions occur among the natural, human, and supernatural realms. First, Raven, a being that possesses miraculous abilities, removes an art work—a mask—and is thereby transformed into something just like Man. (Similarly, when an Eskimo shaman dons a mask and goes into a trance, he becomes the spirit he represents.) Then, through another artistic act, the modeling of clay, Raven transforms an inert substance, earth, into living flesh, Woman.

The idea of art as a transcender of realities, although it does appear in other Inuit myths (cf. Anderson, in press), is not overtly voiced by Eskimos. But regardless of its psychological salience, art did help Eskimos transcend their otherwise harsh and barren world by making today more enjoyable and tomorrow more secure. And whatever their rationale, Inuits produced art that has a unique ability to catch the eye and engage the mind of the viewer.

CONCLUSIONS

All cultural phenomena are inherently dynamic rather than static, and art is no exception to this pattern. But the ubiquity of change in art is matched by the difficulty we have in understanding its fundamental causes and processes.

Even in the absence of outside influences, art changes. The concept of "drift," developed by linguists and geneticists, seems also to apply to art. As the case of the north Alaskan prehistoric winged objects illustrates, changes which individually are minor in importance and random in direction add up, with the passage of time, to produce substantial changes in the overall style and appearance of art.

Whereas drift is a slow, evolutionary process, changes that result from culture contact are often quite rapid. The best documented instances of this are the changes that have resulted from the impingement of the First, Second, and Third World nations upon the societies of the Fourth World.

Every instance of culture contact is unique in some ways, but Graburn has brought some order to the rapidly growing study of changes in Fourth World art. He has proposed a typology that distinguishes the major varieties of art now being produced. The typology is based on two significant dimensions of differences, namely (1) the extent to which subject matter, medium, and style are traditional rather than alien, and (2) the intended market for the art work, be it indigenous or foreign. Using this typology as a guide, the arts of the rapidly changing Fourth World societies can be systematically catalogued and studied.

As time passes we can expect the art traditions of small-scale societies to change drastically. In one sense these changes are tragic. Alexander Alland, Jr., has noted: "Most of us see anthropology as a means of documenting the richness of our species' creative capacities. Each time a way of life disappears, the repertoire of human experience is diminished" (1975:viii). Alland's point is well taken, but whether we like it or not such changes are taking place. We cannot make time stand still any more than we can convince Fourth World peoples to forego those alien things that they themselves desire or persuade the First and Second World nations to desist from influencing other peoples.

GUIDE TO ADDITIONAL READINGS

Much writing by archaeologists deals with long-term culture change, and any one of the many texts that survey the field of archaeology can provide numerous descriptions—if not explanations—of autonomous culture change, including stylistic changes in art.

Research on the transformations that art undergoes in culture contact situations has been particularly active ever since the seminal work of Graburn, whose edited volume (1976a,b) contains numerous excellent articles.

For Africa, in addition to the rich material presented by Jules-Rosette (1984), one might consult Cordwell (1959) for a survey of events before the late 1950s, while more specialized topics are discussed in Reinhardt's study of West African textile dyeing (1976) and Biebuyck's account (1970) of the effects on Lega art of the banning of the Bwami association.

The emergence of soapstone carving among Canadian Inuit is discussed in this chapter, but the innovations that occurred in Alaska are equally interesting and have been masterfully reported by Ray (1961, 1967, 1980, 1981).

Similarly, silversmithing is only one of the fascinating stories of change in Southwestern art. Most Pueblo pottery is now made for sale to outsiders, and its dynamic history is the subject of numerous studies (see, for example, Toulouse 1976, 1977; Wade 1985; Tanner 1960). Also commendable for its thoroughness is Parezo's study (1982, 1983) of the emergence of commercial sandpaintings among the Navajos. Regarding changes in Northwest Coast art, Arima and Hunt (1976) and Wyatt (1984) are noteworthy.

This chapter has not discussed three types of changes in art that primarily involve complex societies. The "fine" arts are those created for appreciation by, and sale to, an elite segment of society. But although they have previously been characteristic of complex societies, fine art traditions have begun to appear in several non-Western settings. For Australia, see Tuckson (1964); for the American Southwest, see Dunn (1968) and Brody (1980); and for Africa, see Mount (1973), Wahlman (1974), Beier (1968), and Jules-Rosette (1984).

The changes wrought in the arts of Black Africans during their forced migration to the New World, although not discussed here, is pertinent for its significance to contemporary Black Americans. R. Thompson (1983) has described five tribal vectors of change; and Price and Price (1981) have given an in-depth account of the changes that occurred when Black slaves in northeastern South America escaped coastal plantations and forged a unique identity as the Maroons of the Surinam rain forest.

A third intriguing theme omitted from this chapter is the way in which artists in small-scale societies have portrayed the Westerners who invaded their homelands. The classic study is Lips' *The Savage Hits Back* (1966 [orig. 1937]), now supplemented by Blackburn (1979) and Ewers (1979).

CHAPTER 7

Art:
Cross-Cultural
Perspectives

Two issues remain to be discussed, and dealing with them provides an opportunity to review some of the points made in the preceding chapters. The first question is: What cross-cultural patterns can be discerned in the phenomenon we call art? Specifically, what aspects of art appear to be universal, and what aspects vary from one culture to another in a systematic fashion? The other, and final, question to be asked as we complete this worldwide excursion through other societies' art is this: What are the significant similarities and differences between Western art and the arts we have looked at in other societies?

UNIVERSAL PATTERNS IN ART AND AESTHETICS

Anthropology has a dual goal, first describing the diverse social and cultural systems found throughout the human species, and then attempting to discover regularities of pattern that occur in this bewildering diversity. (Attaining the former, descriptive goal is usually easier than the latter, analytic one.)

In the first chapter of this text, art was defined as having a culturally significant meaning, encoded in a traditional style, executed in a sensuous, affecting medium, by individuals who are locally known for their exceptional skill. Granted, some of the things that we think of as being art lack some of the qualities specified by the definition, and our conception of art will undoubtedly evolve with the passage of time. Nevertheless, the many instances of non-Western art discussed in the preceding chapters illustrate quite well the criteria contained in this definition.

The *culturally significant meaning* conveyed by art differs considerably in content from one society to the next, but nowhere is art a trivial luxury, mere icing on the cake of custom. For the Yoruba, whose art was described in Chapter 1, art embodies fundamental moral and ethical principles. From the stylistic conventions that inform the carved Yoruba statuettes, to the demeanor of a masked performer dancing a tribute to an *orisha* spirit, Yoruba art urges all people to seek the twin goals of energy and harmony. Meanwhile, on the other side of the globe, Australian Aborigines (Chapter 3) make art in an effort to come into intimate contact with the world of the Eternal Dreamtime, thereby sustaining its life-giving fertility. Clearly, this spiritual message is as potent for the Australian Aborigines as the ethical message is for the Yoruba.

As these and other cases reveal, the range of meanings that art can embody is wide indeed. But from the evidence now available, it seems likely that in the majority of societies, much of art's message concerns the realm of the supernatural, providing a sacred means through which mortals attempt to control, or at least to understand, the world around them. For the Navajos (Chapter 5), for example, art both embodies *hozho*, the natural state of balance, harmony, and beauty that the world was created in, and also provides a means of restoring *hozho* when it is jeopardized by human negligence or error.

But if art serves essentially sacred purposes in the majority of cases, ample instances exist of art meeting fundamentally secular needs. In the aforementioned Yoruba case, for example, art is made not only for cult use but also to display the prestige of the powerful. And underlying both sacred and secular Yoruba art, the message of prosperous harmony is ultimately directed at mortals, embodying ideal principles about how people should behave toward one another.

Also, the impulse to body decoration that occurs in virtually every society cannot be overlooked as a largely secular art form. If art can be sacramental, it is also necessarily created in a *sensuous, affecting medium*, and its capacity to bring beauty into day-to-day life is appreciated in the smallest of societies just as much as in complex ones. The San people, nomadic hunter–gatherers living in the Kalahari Desert of southwestern Africa, for example, produce very little in the way of visual art intended for religious purposes.[1] But the San, eking out their subsistence with an extremely limited technology, are themselves virtual walking works of art. Many San trim their hair, paint and tattoo their bodies, wear jewelry of vast numbers

[1]The performing arts of the San do occur in ritual contexts, particularly for curing and fertility. But even song and dance are not used exclusively for religious purposes in that the San often informally sing and dance solely for enjoyment's sake.

FIGURE 7-1 Group of San young women profusely adorned with beads and other decorations. *(Photo courtesy John Marshall, Documentary Education Resources, Watertown, Massachusetts.)*

of tiny beads painstakingly made from ostrich eggshells, scented wood, and other materials, all for the express purpose of enhancing their natural beauty (Figure 7–1).

Information theorists have long known that meaning must be encoded in a medium, and the various dimensions of meaning conveyed by art are *encoded in traditional style.* Every time and place has its distinctive conventions of style; consequently, style serves as a sort of cultural signature for the group that produces the art. Archaeologists constantly utilize this phenomenon to identify and typologize the artifacts they unearth. For example, from about 1000 A.D. to 1200 A.D. a long-forgotten tribe of people lived in what is now southern New Mexico. Tilling their fields and revering their gods, they lived lives full of practical and symbolic meaning. We will never know the name they used to refer to themselves; but the fact that they produced a type of pottery clearly distinguishable from that made by their neighbors to the north and south, and unlike that of either their predecessors or their successors, prompts us to call them "Mimbres people" and their lifeway, "Mimbres culture," all because of the distinctive—indeed, striking—type of ceramics, "Mimbres pottery," that has been discovered at numerous sites along the Mimbres River (Figure 7–2). Thus, style is intentionally or unintentionally a public statement of the maker's identity.

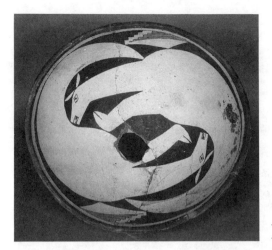

FIGURE 7-2 Mimbres painted pottery bowl. 12 cm. high; top diameter, 29 cm. *(Nelson-Atkins Museum of Art, Kansas City, Missouri, Nelson Fund.)*

Style in art, although universal, should not be taken for granted. What, after all, prevents the artist from breaking free of the constraints of style that characterize the time and place of manufacture by making art works that are unique? In theory, of course, nothing keeps a person from producing idiosyncratic art; but in practice, two factors make this unlikely to happen. First, as discussed in Chapter 5, most societies foster "cautious innovativeness" in art, rather than unbridled creativity. When novelty occurs, it almost always results from artists playing with ideas from the past—developing traditional themes, augmenting long-standing motifs—rather than originating something that is altogether unprecedented. Thus, a given society's art style almost always stylistically reflects its past heritage.

A second restraint on the artist's creativity is this: If art is to communicate culturally significant meaning, then obviously it must speak a language that members of the culture comprehend. The conventions of artistic style make this possible. Recall the discussion in Chapter 3 of the iconography and symbolism of Northwest Coast art. If a Northwest Coast carver makes a totem pole recounting a tale involving a mythic beaver, he can be certain that viewers will recognize the beaver only if his carving depicts an animal with the large front teeth and hatched tail that mean "beaver" in the vernacular of Northwest Coast iconographic style. Likewise, the pole's symbolic message of proclaiming the wealth and power of its owner is apparent only to a person who knows that a pole's size and grandness exhibits the owner's elevated social standing—rather than, say, his religious devotion. Thus, if the conservatism found in most societies leads to historical continuity of art style, the need for communication necessitates a degree of stylistic uniformity within a population of contemporaries.

"Art," as we commonly use the word, implies *exceptional skill*. In fact, it is difficult for most of us to imagine any individual being considered an artist unless an uncommon degree of manual, perceptual, and/or conceptual skill is evident in the person's work. The types of skills emphasized vary from place to place, of course, but exceptional skill is always present in local ideas about who is and who isn't an artist. Certainly this is the case in complex societies, with their characteristically high degree of economic specialization. For example, the precontact Aztecs described the true artist in these words: "Capable, practicing, skillful; maintains dialogue with his heart, meets things with his mind" (quoted in Léon-Portilla 1963:168). By contrast, "The carrion artist works at random; sneers at people; makes things opaque; brushes across the surface of the face of things; works without care; defrauds people; is a thief" (Léon-Portilla 1963:168).

In horticultural societies too, artists are recognized for their special skills. In New Guinea, for example, all Sepik men carve wood with a facility that most Westerners could not match, but only the most accomplished Sepik carver is commissioned to produce the masks and other paraphernalia needed for cult activities; and as a reward for his unique abilities he receives both payment and prestige. Sepik artists themselves are consciously aware of standards of critical perfection. Abelam carvers, we are told, "carefully examine and discuss works by other artists and rate one another as more or less talented" (Forge 1967:82). Even in the relatively homogeneous hunter–gather societies, the artist's abilities exceed those of others. For example, Mountford says that although all Australian Aborigines are potential artists, "some are more skilled than others and take more care" (Mountford 1961:7).

The artist's special skills are usually more mental than manual. In a society where all men daily wield adze and knife for utilitarian purposes, the artist is the person who can concentrate his attention and visualize the end product of his work sufficiently to execute an intricate carving successfully. Or, to cite a specific case, although all Navajo men can sing and most of them write songs during the course of their lifetime, the man who is recognized as a Singer (and who receives payment for his services) is the one who can commit to memory the many details of a Sing (which lasts as many as nine days) and who has the stamina to direct the entire proceeding.

Is There Any Accounting for Taste?

The difference between art and non-art is one thing; between good art and mediocre art, another. Since all societies have standards for evaluating art, it is reasonable to wonder whether or not any cross-cultural patterns can be discerned in such standards.

Clearly, a sizable component of critical judgment is determined by the vicissitudes of cultural circumstance. For example, in a clever, and now classic, paper entitled "The Mona Lisa in the History of Taste" (1963 [orig. 1940]), George Boas traces the changing evaluations of Leonardo da Vinci's portrait of a burgher's young wife. During the painter's lifetime the work was apparently not considered particularly outstanding, but the late Renaissance emphasis on graphic accuracy brought posthumous praise to the painting. Subsequent neoclassical criticism focused on the way the painting's subject embodied the quintessence of proper femininity and decorum, only to have the Romantic critics recast her as a *femme fatale* about whom they could embroider their own fantasies. The rise of formalism in the twentieth century witnessed a still different evaluation of the same painting.

At first glance, cross-cultural standards of taste seem as unpredictable as Western estimates of the *Mona Lisa*. Even something as supposedly free of cultural associations as the golden mean, whose proportions have been considered to be harmoniously beautiful in Western art since the time of classical Greece, may not have universal appeal: A group of Japanese subjects tended to choose rectangles that were nearly square in preference to ones whose length and width reflected the golden mean (Berlyne 1970, 1980:344). And in a different experiment, Francés and Tamba (1973) asked Japanese musicology students to rank 10 excerpts of Japanese music in order of preference. They then compared this ordering to the preferences of three French groups—professional musicians, music students, and nonmusic students. Not only did the researchers find no tendency for Japanese and French subjects to have similar preferences, but the choices of the French professional musicians tended to be just the opposite of the Japanese music students!

Some studies have produced results suggesting that aesthetic standards do, however, transcend cultural boundaries. Child and Siroto (1971) surveyed the opinions of two groups of people with special expertise in art: 13 individuals in New Haven, Connecticut, and 16 elderly BaKwele men living in central Africa. Subjects in both groups were shown 39 photographs of BaKwele masks and asked to rank them in order of aesthetic merit. Child and Siroto found a correlation between the American and BaKwele art experts, and they conclude that individuals with exceptional artistic talent or experience can have similar tastes despite great differences in cultural background.

Unfortunately, Child and Siroto's experiment has serious methodological flaws in that the correlation they found in the responses of American and BaKwele art experts could have resulted from factors other than similarities in aesthetic values. As the researchers concede, they used photographs of uneven quality, and the masks themselves reflected different levels of craftsmanship. So perhaps both American and BaKwele subjects were attracted to well-made photographs of masks carved with technical (as opposed to aesthetic) proficiency. Also, there is no way to be sure that the correlation is not due to some extent to acculturation of the BaKwele subjects, who were interviewed in French, through a French-BaKwele interpreter. (Significantly, the younger BaKwele subjects tended to agree more with the American responses than did the older men.)

All of the experiments just described are based on the assumption that the essential ingredient in an art work is its *form,* as manifest in the visual composition of a BaKwele mask, the tonal qualities and thematic patterns of Japanese music, or even the proportions of a regular polygon's sides. As will be discussed below, the doctrine of formalism has influenced most of the academic thinking about art and aesthetics in the West during the twentieth century, but our survey of non-Western art has revealed that the preeminent artistic concern in most societies is not form but rather subject matter and, to a lesser extent, technique. If similarities of taste are to be found in art cross-culturally, they probably should be sought in these dimensions rather than in the formal one.

Art's subject matter generally reflects human concerns; furthermore, we tend to couch our concerns in thoroughly human terms. Our gods are largely, if not entirely, anthropomorphic; our environment is significant only insofar as it has a bearing on human needs; and perhaps the thing that looms largest in our consciousness is our constant involvement with each other, as kin, friends, or mates, as leaders or enemies. We could well paraphrase the famous aphorism attributed to Protagoras by observing, man (and woman) is the measure of all art.

And when we take the measure of art's subject matter, we often turn to the same standards that we apply to men and women. Obviously, criteria of physical beauty vary from one society to another, but they do so within limits determined by practical considerations. "Beautiful" skin is usually healthy skin, free of the blemishes of disease and the wrinkles of age. Likewise, smoothly carved wood figures are usually preferable to rough-hewn ones. (A small proportion of Yoruba masks are intentionally meant to be ugly, and predictably they portray sick or disfigured individuals.) Where women nurse their children, the female breast is often a symbol of desired fecundity, leading to art that tends toward the ideal of either young, firm breasts that show the promise of nurturing many children (as in Yoruba and north-central Australian cultures) or else pendulous breasts that have already done so (as among the Mountain Arapesh of New Guinea and the Anang of Nigeria). Standards of male beauty tend to be at least as rigorous as those for women, and these standards also usually derive from considerations of health, strength, and vigor.

Skill, also, may be amenable to approximate translation across cultural boundaries. Given two randomly chosen ceramic pots from a particular non-Western people, a nonnative probably stands a better than fifty-fifty chance of guessing which one would be selected by the potters themselves as displaying greater skill on the part of the maker. Such cross-cultural judgments of technical expertise are, obviously, subject to error from several quarters. For one thing, the challenges of a particular medium are not always apparent to one who has not attempted to master it; and the higher the level of craft specialization, the more this is the case. Also, as noted earlier, manual skills are often less important than perceptual and conceptual skills, and these too may prove difficult for the nonnative to appraise.

But although many aspects of taste are determined by cultural context, art probably does not float freely in a sea of total relativism. Art has, as it were, feet of clay: It is inevitably tied to the material world by being executed in a sensible medium, and it is often linked in some way to a subject matter that, again, has a tangible referent, most usually humans themselves. By virtue of its being grounded in the material world, art is often subject to the same judgments that we make about technical skills and human beings in non-artistic contexts. Granting the existence of many exceptions, the indications of health are usually preferable to sickness, and skill of craftsmanship is generally praiseworthy; and these standards typically apply as much to art as they do to life.

WESTERN ART IN PERSPECTIVE

The reasons for studying anthropology differ from one person to another, but many believe that learning about other people's ways can help us see our own society in a new light. If this is true, then an appropriate final question is to ask how our own art, artists, and aesthetics compare to their counterparts in small-scale societies.

To put this matter in its proper perspective, recall that Chapter 1 posited a rough continuum ranging from small-scale to complex societies. Small-scale societies were said to be relatively limited in population, fairly homogeneous socially and culturally, and possessed of a comparatively simple technology. So we now ask: Are there any systematic differences between the art of such societies and that of the complex society of the West—and, for that matter, other complex societies such as the Chinese civilization and its congeners, the traditions that developed in the Indus Valley, and the prehistoric civilizations of the Near East, Mesoamerica, and the Andes?

Media, Functions, and Practitioners

A society's economic foundation predictably affects its art, both directly and indirectly. For example, the vicissitudes of subsistence sources require nomadic hunter–gatherer groups such as the Inuit and Australian Aborigines to periodically gather all their possessions together and move their camps from one location to another. Consequently, any art they produce must be portable; and the most portable of art takes the form of body decoration, decorated utilitarian items, and the performing arts.[2] Nomadic hunter–gatherers probably never produce tangible, three-dimensional items as "art for art's sake." When religious art is produced (and carried from one habitation site to another) it is more because it is religious than because it is art. From the Eskimo perspective, an ivory amulet carved in the form of an animal is as necessary for survival as a harpoon point, which, as a matter of fact, may be carved to resemble a person's head. The aesthetic component may be thought to enhance the practical efficacy of each one, but is not an end in itself.

By contrast, art in sedentary Western society is not made under such a mobiliary imperative. Western artists are free to produce not only small, portable art items but also art that is too heavy, bulky, or fragile to move conveniently. In fact, the durable nature of Western art has prompted the creation of special institutions, namely art museums, whose primary purpose is to house "permanent collections" of art for successive generations of viewers. (As curators know, the challenge of traveling exhibitions is as much logistical as scholarly.)

Also, of course, Western artists can work in media that are unavailable in smaller-scale societies. Ceramics and monumental architecture were developed in the few locations where the Neolithic revolution ran its course; metallurgy came with the Bronze Age; and the Industrial Revolution has provided artists with a vast repertoire of energy-intensive techniques.

In contrast to the relative homogeneity of small-scale cultures, complex socieites that characterize the West are internally diverse. Economic specialization permits some individuals to become full-time specialists in producing art, a fact that will be discussed in a moment. But an equally important consequence of the heterogeneity of complex societies is the presence of social classes, with some groups having much more power and wealth than others. This societal diversity results in artistic diversity, bringing about distinctions between "fine art," "popular art," and "folk art," that have no counterpart in hunter–gatherer groups.

But as we saw in the case of the Northwest Coast, when affluence increases and is differentially distributed within a society, art often starts serving a function that is only little developed in egalitarian societies: Art becomes a symbol of elevated social standing. Western fine art serves many purposes, but there can be no doubt that one of them is as an emblem of membership in the socioeconomic elite. Sponsoring, owning, and appreciating the "best" in art has long been, and remains, a prerogative of the

---

[2]An alternative solution is to make art that can be left behind and then returned to when the cycle of migration brings its makers back to the same site. Painting and engraving on rock shelters and cave walls serve this purpose admirably. And, in fact, such paintings have been made until recent times by several hunter–gatherer groups including the Australian Aborigines and the African San.

privileged class. (This right is not entirely exclusive, of course, in that others in the society are also permitted to experience fine art in some contexts—to visit public art museums and galleries, for example. It is unlikely, however, that a person from the lower socioeconomic stratum would be invited to the opening of an art exhibition: Gallery owners and museum directors usually know who are the buyers and patrons of fine art.)

The virtues and vices of art being used as a status symbol in complex societies could be debated at length, and art in the West clearly has additional functions: It provides psychological gratification for many people, as well as jobs for the cadre of the art world. But one of the most striking differences between art in the West versus art in small-scale societies is that the social pluralism of complex societies spawns an equally pluralistic art. Generally, the greater the discrepancy between the top and bottom levels of society, the more removed fine art is from the lives of the common people.

As noted, the heterogeneity of complex cultures permits specialization of the artist's trade. Most of those who are successful in the fine arts have undergone years of training, and their technical and aesthetic skills set them clearly apart from non-artists. As was mentioned in Chapter 5, the actual mode of learning art in the West is not unique, being confined largely to instruction in practical areas of media use, observation of teachers as they make art, and having one's own art works criticized by teachers and others.[3] But the degree of specialization in the arts *is* unusual, with artists devoting their lives to working in media that non-artists, and indeed many other artists, have no firsthand experience with. Contrast this situation in the West, for example, with the Navajo, about whom Witherspoon reports, "All Navajos are singers, and most Navajos have composed many songs. Traditionally, over ninety percent of all adult women wove rugs" (1977:152). Even initial recruitment into the arts is conditioned in Western society by our specialized institutions. Griff (1968) has found that individuals are often enlisted into the artist's profession by art teachers in the public schools and through classes in art museums.

The specialized training of students of the fine arts in the West gives them an unequalled facility with artistic techniques, and the sheer quantity of work they produce, executed in highly complex media, is remarkable indeed. But there is a price to be paid for this. Artists' special skills take them out of the mainstream of society; consequently, they experience alienation of two sorts. First, they may be scorned by an audience that is unequipped to appreciate their technical virtuosity; and, second, artists' characteristic life-style may remove them from many of the day-to-day

---

[3]This practice may place Western art students in something of a dilemma. Overt copying of another's art style is frowned upon, but guidelines for creating a unique style are seldom explicitly taught.

concerns of the public at large, resulting in their art not meeting the public's needs. The contrast between this situation and that of an artist in a small-scale society is dramatic indeed.

Ever since the Romantic Rebellion, Western artists have been variously stereotyped as "neurotic" individuals and "rebels" (cf. Zucker 1969; Trilling 1945). Such a characterization of artists, although not universal, is not unique. For example, the West African Dahomeans describe the "typical" wood carver in these terms:

> He is, they say, always eager to go off into the bush in search of fine wood, and once gone, he may not return for weeks. Upon his return, he will busy himself making a figure from some piece of rare wood, working long and contentedly, and neglect to make a mortar or stool for which a buyer is waiting. That is why, say the Dahomeans, wood carvers are poor providers for their wives and children. In the days of the kings they were no less dilatory, so that when a monarch wished one of these famous carvers to make certain objects for him, he would send out a detachment of soldiers to bring him to the palace, where he was kept under guard until he finished his task. "The king could have had him killed for not obeying him, but that wouldn't have got him the carvings. . . . And they were all like that, these carvers." (Herskovits and Herskovits (1934:128)

Aesthetic Values

Several of the Portfolios in previous chapters have described the aesthetic assumptions that underlie art production in various non-Western culture areas. But why do *we* make art? In our view of the world, what is the fundamental nature of art, and why is its existence justified? Although many Westerners rarely verbalize answers to these queries, many generations of aestheticians have thought long and hard about these questions. For the most part, their theories fall into four broad categories.[4]

Mimetic theories focus on the relationship between the work of art and something in the sensible world that the art work resembles. The relationship may be quite literal, as in the case of Renaissance, *trompe l'oeil*, and photorealist painters; or else the artist can attempt to capture the idealized essence of the subject, as did ancient Greek sculptors.

Pragmatic theories emphasize the functional capacity of art. They assert that art's ultimate purpose is to make some kind of positive contribution to

---

[4]Three qualifications should be made explicit at this point. First, although specific Western aesthetic theories tend to fall into one or four categories, actual people and art works can't always be so straightforwardly classified. A person often uses different aesthetic criteria to think about varied art works; and a particular work may be responded to from more than one aesthetic perspective.

Second, aesthetic theories during the twentieth century have focused on the fine arts. A rigorous study of the aesthetic bases of contemporary popular art has yet to be undertaken.

Third, Western theories of art criticism, which are meant to evaluate art works differentially, are probably more numerous and varied than are Western art philosophies, which deal with the ultimate nature and purpose of art.

the well-being of individuals or society. Thus, art during the Middle Ages was largely religious and was made expressly for the purpose of increasing the devotion of those who came in contact with it, even if this required some sacrifice of literalism. But religion is not the only patron of pragmatic art. Art created in the interest of political reform or revolution also serves a pragmatic purpose, attempting through propaganda to bring about a different, and better, regime.

Emotionalist theories focus neither on the material world (as do mimetic theories) nor the social world (as do pragmatic theories) but rather on the psychological realm of an individual's inner experience and feelings. Nineteenth-century apostles of Romanticism heralded art's ability to embody the passions of the sensitive artist's soul, but as long ago as Aristotle's time people knew that emotional involvement in an art work can cause audience members to experience a positive purging of pent-up feelings. Emotionalist theories often posit a close relationship between the turbulent forces of nature and the deepest and most personal of feelings experienced by mortals, the suppression of which can be harmful. The mid-nineteenth-century French painter Jean Corot exhorted his students: "Be guided by feeling alone . . . [follow] your own convictions. . . . If you have really been touched, you will convey to others the sincerity of your emotions" (quoted in Stolnitz 1960:158).

Formalist theories do not focus on the material, social, or psychological world, but rather on the stylistic world that is manifest in the art work itself. The painter's use of color and composition, the musical composer's mastery of counterpoint, or the poet's command of the sonnet form—those, in the view of formalist theorists, are the things that separate art from non-art. An abstract painting by Mondrian, for example, may not resemble anything in the sensible world, as called for by mimetic theories; it may not lead to spiritual, social, or political betterment of the community, as pragmatic theories require; and it may not make its viewers laugh or cry, as emotionalist theories might wish. But as a supreme example of "significant form," it can prompt a distinctive aesthetic response in those who understand it, and thus it qualifies (say the formalists) as art of the first magnitude.

How do these four aesthetic theories compare to those in the small-scale societies we have studied? One difference is the explicitness with which these theories are voiced in our culture. Although most of us may not give much thought to the "real" meaning of art, a small but persistent number of thinkers have talked about, indeed often argued about, art's role in the world at large. Intellectuals are found in every culture, but in small-scale societies they must spend much of their time engaged in subsistence activities like everyone else. But in every region where the Neolithic revolution occurred, specialists emerged who devoted themselves to non-manual skills such as governance, record-keeping, and, significantly, speculation about the meaning of art. Classical India had its *rasa*-theorists, the

Aztecs their *tlamatinime,* and since at least the time of classical Greece the West has had its philosophers of art.

The presence of full-time art theoreticians has interesting consequences. For one thing, the theorists are historically linked to the socioeconomic elite. (Given the high degree of specialization in complex societies, one reason for the theoreticians' existence is to mediate between art producers and art consumers, two groups that tend to be mutually exclusive.) Consequently, aestheticians' theories tend to focus on fine art; and their application to the popular arts is inexplicit—a situation similar to that in small-scale societies, where aesthetic principles are seldom overtly stated.

Also, the aestheticians' theories tend to become quite intricate. A special vocabulary is used for discussing art, minor distinctions are examined in great detail, and so on. But "intricate" is not the same as "profound," and we would be mistaken to assume that aesthetics in small-scale societies is generally simpler than that in complex societies. Recall, for example, the Inuit belief that art has the capacity to transmute things between the realms of the natural, the human, and the supernatural. Surely the intellectual sophistication of this theory is as great as any of the four Western traditions of aesthetics.

Nor is there a qualitative difference between Western art and the art of small-scale societies regarding what might be called the "spiritual" dimension of art. As we have seen, art in small-scale societies is often motivated by secular ends, and although religion is not the primary impetus for contemporary Western fine art, it was important in the not-too-distant past and it still remains a serious force in popular art today.

But for all these distinctions, what about the *merit* of Western art and aesthetics? Is there any basis for judging it to be better or worse than art in small-scale societies? In answering such a question, of course, we all have our own ideas of what "better" and "worse" mean, but one reasonable criterion is *comprehensiveness.* Thanks to the efforts of many generations of aestheticians, Western theories of art, taken as a whole, cover a great deal of territory, and they do so in great detail. They take into consideration the relationship of art to its subject matter (mimetic theories), art's contributions to the culture that produces it (pragmatic theories), its role in the feelings of individuals (emotionalist theories), and the dynamics intrinsic to the art work itself (formalist theories). So in terms of comprehensiveness, Western philosophies of art seem unsurpassed. (All of these questions may well have occurred to thinkers in other societies at one time or another, but the Western penchant for writing theories down and for reading the ideas of past generations have had a cumulative effect on our thinking about art.)

Another reasonable criterion for judging art and aesthetics is their *pervasiveness* within the belief system of the society at large. One way of addressing this issue is to ask: Are most members of the society involved in making and experiencing art, or is art the domain of only a small segment of the population? One's first impulse might be to give the West a low rating in this department: After all, full-time artists make up only a very small segment of the population, and visiting art museums is the favorite pastime of only a few more. But this view neglects the great importance of popular art in Western culture. Like all other societies, we indulge in body decoration, we ornament our residences with affecting drawings and designs, and we are exposed to endless amounts of popular performing arts, from the recorded music on the elevator to the popular dramas of commercial television. So the demographic pervasiveness of art in Western culture depends on which "art" one has in mind.

But the pervasiveness of art can be thought of in another way. Instead of asking how many sectors of the population come into close contact with art, we might ask: How many sectors of *life* does art touch? Is the artistic enterprise clearly demarcated from other endeavors such as subsistence activities, social interaction, and political affairs?

As we have seen, for example, aesthetics for the Navajos and the Australian Aborigines is not just a rationale for making works of art; it is, rather, a charter for daily life. Compared to such cultures, art is certainly not very pervasive in Western society. Art has little place in Western technology, commerce, politics, education, or family life. Unlike the Navajos, Westerners are not generally "admonished to walk in beauty, speak in beauty, act in beauty, sing in beauty, and live in beauty" (Witherspoon 1977:153).

Instead, the Western tendency has been to parcel out to other institutions those duties that in some small-scale societies are involved with art. The medical doctor, not the ritual-wise Singer, attends to our health; our ethical behavior is in the hands of legal and religious institutions, and not masked, costumed dancers; and our relationship to the environment is determined by scientists and technocrats, not the carvers of amulets and shrine figures. (Even art's role in religion has been somewhat uneven in the West, proscribed as Judeo-Christians are from making "graven images.")

Other criteria could be used to compare the merits of Western and non-Western art, but these observations show that only a thoroughgoing ethnocentrism can bring one to the conclusion that Western art is altogether better than that from small-scale societies.

The foregoing comparison of Western art with that from small-scale societies is necessarily tentative. Like all natives, we have a somewhat myopic perspective on our own culture; and we desperately need more objective, fieldwork-based studies of Western art, artists, and aesthetics.

Equally necessary are more sound, empirical studies of non-Western art. Although a few scholars have given us exemplary research and analysis, many societies and many arts have been grievously ignored. Each chapter of this book has had to admit, "We don't have the answer to this question—yet." Results to date are intriguing, but much remains to be done. As stated at the outset, the intent of this book has been to report on the state of the anthropological study of art in small-scale societies, the goal being to bring together the fruits of our efforts thus far. But quite literally, this book is a work in progress, reflecting a field that is itself "in progress."

GUIDE TO ADDITIONAL READINGS

Pickford (1972) and Berlyne (1980) survey the literature of experimental studies of cross-cultural differences and similarities in aesthetic values.

Regarding the increasing specialization and diversity of art as one moves from small-scale to complex societies, see Thomas Munro's monumental *Evolution in the Arts and Other Theories of Culture History* (1963). An insightful, and often humorous, account of art's role in contemporary status-conscious America is found in two works by Tom Wolfe, "The Painted Word" (1975) and *From Bauhaus to Our House* (1981).

Overviews of the four major schools of aesthetic thought in the West appear in Abrams (1958), Stolnitz (1960), Pepper (1945), and Anderson (in press: chapter 10). Tatarkiewicz (1970a,b, 1974) is an unrivaled sourcebook of primary writing.

Finally, Anderson (in press: chapters 13 and 14) provides a cross-cultural analysis of aesthetic systems.

Bibliography

ABRAMS, MEYER HOWARD   1958   *The Mirror and the Lamp.* New York: W.W. Norton.

ABRAMSON, J.A.   1976   "Style Change in an Upper Sepik Contact Situation," in *Ethnic and Tourist Arts* ed. Nelson H.H. Graburn, pp. 249–265. Berkeley: University of California Press.

ADAIR, JOHN   1944   [reprinted 1970] *Navajo and Pueblo Silversmiths.* Norman: University of Oklahoma Press.

ADAMS, MARIE JEANNE   1973   "Structural Aspects of Village Art." *American Anthropologist* 75:265–279.

ADAMS, FRANCIS L., and CHARLES E. OSGOOD   1973   "A Cross-Cultural Study of the Affective Meanings of Color." *Journal of Cross-cultural Psychology* 4(2):135–157.

ALLAND, ALEXANDER, JR.   1975   *When the Spider Danced.* Garden City, N.Y.: Anchor Press.

———   1977   *The Artistic Animal.* Garden City, N.Y.: Doubleday.

———   1983   *Playing with Form: Children Draw in Six Cultures.* New York: Columbia University Press.

ANDERSON, RICHARD L.   (In press)   *Calliope's Sisters: The Role of Art in Human Thought.* Englewood Cliffs, N.J.: Prentice Hall.

ARIETI, SILVANO   1976   *Creativity: The Magic Synthesis.* New York: Basic Books.

ARIMA, EUGENE Y., and E.C. HUNT   1976   "Notes on Kwakiutl 'Tourist Mask' Carving," in *Contributions to Canadian Ethnology,* 1975, ed. David Brez Carlisle. National Museum of Man, Mercury Series, Canadian Ethnology Service, Paper 31.

BALIKCI, ASEN   1970   *The Netsilik Eskimo.* Garden City, N.Y.: Natural History Press.

BARNETT, H.G.   1953   *Innovation: The Basis of Cultural Change.* New York: McGraw-Hill.

BARRY, HERBERT, III   1957   "Relationships between Child Training and the Pictorial Arts." *Journal of Abnormal and Social Psychology* 54:380–383.

BASCOM, WILLIAM RUSSELL   1969   *The Yoruba of Southwestern Nigeria.* New York: Holt, Rinehart and Winston.

———   1973   "A Yoruba Master Carver: Duga of Mękǫ," in *The Traditional Artist in African Societies,* Warren L. d'Azevedo, pp. 62–78. Bloomington: Indiana University Press.

BATESON, GREGORY   1958   [orig. 1936] *Naven.* Second edition. Stanford, Calif.: Stanford University Press.

——— 1972a "Metalogue: What Is an Instinct?" in Bateson. *Steps to an Ecology of the Mind,* pp. 38–58. New York: Ballantine.

——— 1972b "Style, Grace, and Information in Primitive Art," in Bateson, *Steps to an Ecology of the Mind,* pp. 128–152. New York: Ballantine.

——— 1972c "Metalogue: Why a Swan?" in Bateson, *Steps to an Ecology of the Mind,* pp. 33–37. New York: Ballantine.

BAUMAN, RICHARD   1984   *Verbal Art as Performance.* Boulder, Colo.: Waveland Press.

BEIER, ULLI   1960   *Art in Nigeria, 1960.* Cambridge, England: Cambridge University Press.

——— 1968   *Contemporary Art in Africa.* New York: Praeger.

BELLAH, ROBERT N., ed.   1965   *Religion and Progress in Modern Asia.* New York: Free Press.

BEN-AMOS, DANIEL   1975   *Sweet Words: Storytelling Events in Benin.* Philadelphia: Institute for the Study of Human Issues.

BEN-AMOS, PAULA   1976a   " 'A la Recherche du Temps Perdu': On Being an Ebony-Carver in Benin," in *Ethnic and Tourist Arts,* ed. Nelson H.H. Graburn, pp. 320–333. Berkeley: University of California Press.

——— 1976b   "Men and Animals in Benin Art." *Man* 11 (2):243–252.

BENEDICT, RUTH   1934   *Patterns of Culture.* Boston: Houghton Mifflin.

BENSON, ELIZABETH P., ed.   1972   *The Cult of the Feline.* Washington, D.C.: Dumbarton Oaks Research Library.

BERLYNE, DAVID E.   1970   "The Golden Section and Hedonic Judgments of Rectangles." *Sciences de l'Art/Scientific Aesthetics* 7:1–6.

——— 1971   *Aesthetics and Psychobiology.* New York: Appleton-Century-Crofts.

——— 1980   "Psychological Aesthetics," in Harry C. Triandis and Walter Lonner, eds., *Handbook of Cross-Cultural Psychology,* pp. 323–361. Boston: Allyn & Bacon.

BERNDT, RONALD M.   1958   "A Comment on Dr. Leach's 'Trobriand Medusa.' " *Man* 58(65):65–66.

———, ed.   1964   *Australian Aboriginal Art.* New York: Macmillan.

——— 1976   *Love Songs of Arnhem Land.* Chicago: University of Chicago Press.

BERRY, HERBERT, III   1957   "Relationships Between Child Training and the Pictorial Arts." *Journal of Abnormal and Social Psychology* 54(3):380–383.

BIEBUYCK, DANIEL P.   1968   "Art as a Didactic Device in African Initiation Systems." *African Art Forum* 3(4)/4(1):35–43.

——— 1969   "Introduction," in *Tradition and Creativity in Tribal Art,* ed. Daniel P. Biebuyck, pp. 1–23. Berkeley: University of California Press.

——— 1970   "Effects on Lega Art of the Outlawing of the Bwami Association," in *New African Literature and the Arts,* Vol. 1, ed. Joseph Okpaku, pp. 340–352. New York: Crowell.

——— 1972   "The *Kindi Aristocrats and Their Art among the Lega,"* in *African Art and Leadership,* ed. Douglas Fraser and Herbert M. Cole, pp. 7–20. Madison: University of Wisconsin Press.

——— 1973   *Lega Culture.* Berkeley: University of California Press.

BLACKBURN, JULIA   1979   *The White Men: The First Response of Aboriginal Peoples to the White Man.* New York: Time Books.

BLACKING, JOHN 1973   *How Musical Is Man?* Seattle: University of Washington Press.

——— and Joann Keali'inohomoku, eds.   1979   *The Performing Arts.* The Hague: Mouton.

BLACKWOOD, BEATRICE   1961   "Comment on Herta Haselberger's 'Method of Studying Ethnological Art.' " *Current Anthropology* 2:360.

BOAS, FRANZ   1897   "The Decorative Art of the Indians of the North Pacific Coast." *Bulletin of the American Museum of Natural History* 9(9):123–176.

——— 1908   "Decorative Designs of Alaskan Needlecases." *Preceedings of the U.S. National Museum* 34:321–344. (Reprinted in Boas, 1940, *Race, Language and Culture,* pp. 564–592. New York: Free Press.

——— 1940   "Representative Art of Primitive People," in Boas, *Race, Language and Culture,* pp. 535–540. New York: Free Press.

——— 1955   [orig. 1927] *Primitive Art.* New York: Dover.

BOAS, GEORGE   1963   [orig. 1940] "The Mona Lisa in the History of Taste," in Marvin Levich, ed., *Aesthetics and the Philosophy of Criticism,* pp. 576–594. New York: Random House.

BOHANNAN, PAUL 1971 "Artist and Critic in an African Society," in *Anthropology and Art,* ed. Charlotte M. Otten, pp. 172–181. [Orig. in *The Artist in Tribal Society,* ed. Marian W. Smith, 1961:85–94. London: Routledge and Kegan Paul.]

BRAIN, ROBERT, and ADAM POLLOCK 1971 *Bangwa Funerary Sculpture.* Toronto: University of Toronto Press.

BRODY, J.J. 1980 "Modern Hopi Painting," in Dorothy K. Washburn, ed., *Hopi Kachina: Spirit of Life.* Seattle: University of Washington Press.

BRUNER, JEROME 1963 "The Conditions of Creativity," in *Contemporary Approaches to Creative Thinking,* ed. H.E. Gruber, G. Terrell and M. Wertheimer, pp. 1–30. New York: Atherton Press.

BUNZEL, RUTH 1972 [Orig. 1929] *The Pueblo Potter: A Study of Creative Imagination in Primitive Art.* New York: Dover.

BURTON, MICHAEL L., LILYAN A. BRUDNER, and DOUGLAS R. WHITE 1977 "A Model of the Sexual Division of Labor." *American Ethnologist* 4(2):227–272.

BYERS, PAUL 1964 "Still Photography in the Systematic Recording and Analysis of Behavior." *Human Organization* 23(1):78–84.

CAMERON, CATHERINE M. 1983 "Patronage and Artistic Change." Paper read at the 82nd annual meeting of the American Anthropological Association, Chicago, Illinois.

CARPENTER, EDMUND 1966 "Image Making in Arctic Art," in *Sign, Image, Symbol,* ed. Gyorgy Kepes, pp. 206–225. New York: George Braziller.

——— 1973 "Some Notes on the Separate Realities of Eskimo and Indian Art," in *The Far North: 2000 Years of American Eskimo and Indian Art,* pp. 281–289. Washington, D.C.: United States National Gallery of Art.

——— 1971 [orig. 1961] "The Eskimo Artist," in *Anthropology and Art,* ed. Charlotte M. Otten. Garden City, N.Y.: Natural History Press. [Orig. in *Current Anthropology* 2(4):361–63.]

CARROLL, KEVIN 1967 *Yoruba Religious Carving.* Dublin: Geoffrey Chapman.

CHAPPEL, T.J.H. 1972 "Critical Carvers: A Case Study." *Man,* n.s. 7(2):296–307.

CHERNOFF, JOHN MILLER 1979 *African Rhythm and African Sensibility: Aesthetics and African Musical Idioms.* Chicago: University of Chicago Press.

CHILD, IIRVIN L., and LEON SIROTO 1971 "BaKwele and American Aesthetic Evaluations Compared," in *Art and Aesthetics in Primitive Societies,* ed. Carol F. Jopling, pp. 271–289. [Orig. in *Ethnology* 4(4):349–360, 1965.]

COLE, HERBERT M. 1972 "Ibo Art and Authority," in *African Art and Leadership,* ed. Douglas Fraser and Herbert M. Cole, pp. 79–97. Madison: University of Wisconsin Press.

COLLINS, HENRY B. 1962 "Eskimo Culture," in *The Encyclopedia of World Art,* Vol. 5, pp. 4–28. New York: McGraw-Hill.

——— 1964 "The Arctic and Subarctic," in *Prehistoric Man in the New World,* ed. Jesse D. Jennings and Edward Norbeck, pp. 85–114. Chicago: Chicago University Press, for William Marsh Rice University.

COOMARASWAMY, ANANDA 1924 *The Dance of Siva.* New York: The Sunwise Turn.

CORDWELL, JUSTINE M. 1959 "African Art," in *Continuity and Change in African Cultures,* ed. William R. Bascom and Melville J. Herskovits, pp. 28–48. Chicago: University of Chicago Press.

CROWLEY, DANIEL J. 1968 "Crafts," in *International Encyclopedia of the Social Sciences,* ed. Edward L. Sils, Vol. 3, pp. 430–434. New York: Macmillan.

——— 1971 "An African Aesthetic," in *Art and Aesthetics in Primitive Societies,* ed. Carol F. Jopling, pp. 315–327. New York: Dutton. [Orig. in *The Journal of Aesthetics and Art Criticism* 24(4):519–524, 1966.]

——— 1972 "Chokwe: Political Art in a Plebian Society," in *African Art and Leadership,* ed. Douglas Fraser and Herbert M. Cole, pp. 21–39. Madison: University of Wisconsin Press.

——— 1973 "Aesthetic Value and Professionalism in African Art: Three Cases from the Katanga Chokwe," in *The Traditional Artist in African Societies,* ed. Warren L. d'Azevedo, pp. 221–249. Bloomington: Indiana University Press.

DARK, PHILIP J.C. 1978 "What Is Art for Anthropologists?," in Michael Greenhalgh and Vincent Megaw, eds., *Art in Society,* pp. 31–50. New York: St. Martins Press.

DAVENPORT, WILLIAM H. 1971 "Sculpture of the Eastern Solomons," in *Art and Aesthetics in Primitive Societies,* ed. Carol F. Jopling, pp. 382–423. New York: Dutton. [Orig. in *Expedition* 10(2):4–25, 1968.]

D'AZEVEDO WARREN L. 1958 "A Structural Approach to Esthetics: Toward a Definition of Art in Anthropology." *American Anthropologist* 60(4):702–14.

——— 1966 *The Artist Archetype in Gola Culture.* Desert Research Institute Preprint No. 14, University of Nevada. (Revised and reissued, 1970.)

———, ed., 1973a *The Traditional Artist in African Societies.* Bloomington: Indiana University Press.

——— 1973b "Sources of Gola Artistry," in *The Traditional Artist in African Societies,* ed. Warren L. d'Azevedo, pp. 282–340. Bloomington: Indiana University Press.

DEJAGER, E.J. 1973 *Contemporary African Art in South Africa.* Cape Town, South Africa: C. Strunk (PTY) Ltd.

DIAMOND, STANLEY 1974 *In Search of the Primitive: A Critique of Civilization.* New Brunswick, N.J.: Trans-Action Books.

DOUGLAS, FREDERIC H., and RENE D'HARNONCOURT 1941 *Indian Art of the United States.* New York: Museum of Modern Art.

DOUGLAS, MARY 1970 *Natural Symbols.* London: Cresset.

DRESSLER, WILLIAM W., and MICHAEL C. ROBBINS 1975 "Art Styles, Social Stratification, and Cognition: An Analysis of Greek Vase Painting." *American Ethnologist* 2:427–434.

DUNN, DOROTHY 1968 *American Indian Painting of the Southwest and Plains Areas.* Albuquerque: University of New Mexico.

DUNN-RANKIN, PETER 1978 "The Visual Characteristics of Words." *Scientific American* 238(1):122–130.

DUTTON, BERTHA P. 1974 *Indians of the American Southwest.* Englewood Cliffs, N.J.: Prentice-Hall.

EHRESMANN, DONALD L. 1975 *Fine Arts: A Bibliographic Guide to Basic Reference Works, Histories, and Handbooks.* Littleton, Colo.: Libraries Unlimited.

ELKIN, A.P., RONALD M. BERNDT, and CATHERINE H. BERNDT 1950 *Art in Arnhem Land.* Chicago: University of Chicago Press.

EWERS, JOHN C. 1979 "Images of the White Man in Nineteenth-Century Plains Indian Art," in Justine M. Cordwell, ed., *The Visual Arts: Plastic and Graphic,* pp. 411–438. The Hague: Mouton.

FAGG, WILLIAM 1969 "The African Artist," in *Tradition and Creativity in Tribal Art,* ed. Daniel Biebuyck, pp. 42–57. Berkeley: University of California Press.

FARELLA, JOHN R. 1984 *The Main Stalk: A Synthesis of Navajo Philosophy.* Phoenix: University of Arizona Press.

FARIS, JAMES C. 1972 *Nuba Personal Art.* Toronto: University of Toronto Press.

FERNANDEZ, JAMES W. 1971 "Principles of Opposition and Vitality in Fang Aesthetics," in *Art and Aesthetics in Primitive Societies,* ed. Carol F. Jopling, pp. 356–373. New York: Dutton. [Orig. *Journal of Aesthetics and Art Criticism* 25(1):53–64, 1966.]

——— 1973 "The Exposition and Imposition of Order: Artistic Expression in Fang Culture," in *The Traditional Artist in African Societies,* ed. Warren L. d'Azevedo, pp. 194–220. Bloomington: Indiana University Press.

FIELD, KAREN L. 1982 "Artists in Liberia and the United States—A Comparative View." *Journal of Modern African Studies* 20(4):713–730.

FIRTH, RAYMOND 1925 "The Maori Carver." *Journal of the Polynesian Society* 34:277–291.

——— 1951 *The Elements of Social Organization.* London: Watts and Company.

——— 1973 *Symbols: Public and Private.* Ithaca, N.Y.: Cornell University Press.

——— 1974 "Tikopia Art and Society," in *Primitive Art and Society,* ed. Anthony Forge, pp. 25–48. New York: Oxford University Press.

FISCHER, JOHN L. 1971 "Art Styles as Cultural Cognitive Maps," in *Anthropology and Art,* ed. Charlotte M. Otten, pp. 141–161. Garden City, N.Y.: Natural History Press. [Orig. *American Anthropologist* 63(1):79–93, 1961.]

FLAM, J.D. 1970 "Some Aspects of Style Symbolism in Sudanese Sculpture." *Journal de la Société des Africanistes* 40(2):137–150.

FORBES, FRED R., JR. 1986 *Dance: An Annotated Bibliography 1965–1982. Garland Reference Library of the Humanities, Vol. 606.* New York: Garland Press.

FORD, C.S., E. TERRY PROTHRO, and IRVIN L. CHILD 1966 "Some Transcultural Comparisons of Esthetic Judgment." *Journal of Social Psychology* 68:19–26.

Forde, Cyril Daryll 1951 *The Yoruba-Speaking Peoples of Southwestern Nigeria.* London: International African Institute.

Forge, J. Anthony 1967 "The Abelam Artist," in *Social Organization: Essays Presented to Raymond Firth,* ed. Maurice Freedman, pp. 65–84. London: Cass.

——— 1970 "Learning to See in New Guinea," in *Socialization: The Approach from Social Anthropology, ASA 8,* ed. Philip Mayer, pp. 269–291. London: Tavistock.

——— 1971 "Art and Environment in the Sepik," in *Art and Aesthetics in Primitive Societies,* ed. Carol F. Jopling, pp. 290–314. New York: Dutton. [Orig. *Proceedings of the Royal Anthropological Institute of Great Britain and Ireland* 1965, pp. 23–31.]

———, ed. 1974 *Primitive Art and Society.* New York: Oxford University Press.

Foster, George M. 1967 *Tzintzuntzan.* Boston: Little, Brown.

Francés, R., and A. Tamba 1973 "Étude interculturelle des préférence et musicales." *International Journal of Psychology* 8:95–108.

Fraser, Douglas 1955 "Mundugamor Sculpture: Comments on the Art of a New Guinea Tribe." *Man* 55:17–20.

——— 1966 "The Heraldic Woman: A Study in Diffusion," in *The Many Faces of Primitive Art,* ed. Douglas Fraser, pp. 36–99. Englewood Cliffs, N.J.: Prentice-Hall.

——— 1971 "The Discovery of Primitive Art," in *Anthropology and Art,* ed. Charlotte M. Otten, pp. 20–36. Garden City, N.Y.: Natural History Press. [Orig. in *Arts Yearbook I: The Turn of the Century,* ed. Hilton Kramer, pp. 119–133, 1957.]

——— 1972a "The Symbols of Ashanti Kingship," in *African Art and Leadership,* ed. Douglas Fraser and Herbert M. Cole, pp. 137–152. Madison: University of Wisconsin Press.

——— 1972b "The Fish-legged Figure in Benin and Yoruba Art," in *African Art and Leadership,* ed. Douglas Fraser and Herbert M. Cole, pp. 261–293. Madison: University of Wisconsin Press.

Fraser, Douglas, and Herbert M. Cole, eds. 1972a *African Art and Leadership.* Madison: University of Wisconsin Press.

——— 1972b "Art and Leadership: an Overview," in *African Art and Leadership,* ed. Douglas Fraser and Herbert M. Cole, pp. 295–328. Madison: University of Wisconsin Press.

Gardner, Howard 1973 *The Arts and Human Development.* New York: John Wiley.

——— 1980 *Artful Scribbles: The Significance of Children's Drawings.* New York: Basic Books.

——— 1981 "Children's Perceptions of Works of Art: A Developmental Portrait," in David O'Hare, ed., *Psychology of the Arts,* pp. 123–148. Atlantic Highlands, N.J.: Humanities Press.

Geertz, Clifford 1973 *The Interpretation of Cultures.* New York: Basic Books.

Gerbrands, Adrian A. 1957 *Art as an Element of Culture, Especially in Negro-Africa.* Mededlingen van het Rijksmuseum voor Volkenkunde, Leiden, Number 12. Leiden, Holland: E.E. Brill.

——— 1967 *Wow-Ipits: Eight Asmat Woodcarvers in New Guinea,* trans. Inez Seeger. The Hague: Mouton.

——— 1978 "Talania and Nake, Master Carver and Apprentice: Two Woodcarvers from the Kilenge (Western New Britain)," in Michael Greenhalgh and Vincent Megew, eds., *Art in Society,* pp. 193–206. New York: St. Martins Press.

Getzels, Jacob W., and Mihaly Csikszentmihalyi 1976 *The Creative Vision: A Longitudinal Study of Problem Finding in Art.* Somerset, N.J.: John Wiley.

Goldberg, Lenore 1978 "The Chilkat." *Heresies* 4:32–33.

Goldwater, Robert 1967 *Primitivism in Modern Art.* New York: Vintage Books.

——— 1969 "Judgments of Primitive Art, 1905–1965," in *Tradition and Creativity in Tribal Art,* ed. Daniel Biebuyck, pp. 24–41. Berkeley: University of California Press.

Gombrich, Ernst H. 1972a "The Visual Image," in *Communication,* the editors of *Scientific American,* pp. 46–60. San Francisco: W.H. Freeman.

——— 1972b *Art and Illusion.* Fourth edition. London: Phaidon Press.

Goodale, Jane C., and Joan D. Koss 1971 "The Cultural Context of Creativity among Tiwi," in *Anthropology and Art,* ed. Charlotte M. Otten, pp. 182–200. Garden City, N.Y.: Natural History Press. [Orig. in *Essays on the Verbal and Visual Arts,* ed. June Helm McNeish, pp. 175–191. Seattle: University of Washington Press, 1967.]

Goodnow, Jacqueline 1979 *Children Drawing.* Cambridge, Mass.: Harvard University Press.

Graburn, Nelson H.H. 1967 "The Eskimo and 'Airport Art.'" *Trans-Action* 4(10):28–33.

———— 1969 "Art and Acculturative Processes." *International Social Sciences Journal* 21(3):457–468.

———— 1971 "Traditional Economic Institutions and the Acculturation of the Canadian Eskimos," in *Studies in Economic Anthropology*, ed. George Dalton, pp. 107–121. Washington, D.C.: American Anthropological Association.

———— 1972 "A Preliminary Analysis of Symbolism in Eskimo Art and Culture," in *Proceedings of the XL International Congress of Americanists*, Rome, 2:165–170. Genoa: Tilgher, December.

———— 1976a "Introduction: Arts of the Fourth World," in *Ethnic and Tourist Arts*, ed. Nelson H.H. Graburn, pp. 1–32. Berkeley: University of California Press.

———— 1976b "Eskimo Art: The Eastern Canadian Arctic," in *Ethnic and Tourist Arts*, ed. Nelson H.H. Graburn, pp. 39–55. Berkeley: University of California Press.

————, ed. 1976c *Ethnic and Tourist Arts*. Berkeley: University of California Press.

———— 1978 "I Like Things to Look More Different Than That Stuff Did: An Experiment in Cross-Cultural Art Appreciation," in Michael Greenhalgh and Vincent Megaw, eds., *Art in Society*, pp. 51–70. New York: St. Martins Press.

GREENHALGH, MICHAEL, and VINCENT MEGAW, eds. 1978 *Art in Society*. New York: St. Martins Press.

GRIFF, MASON 1968 "The Recruitment and Socialization of Artists," in *International Encyclopedia of the Social Sciences*, ed. David L. Sils, Vol. 5 pp. 447–455.

GUIART, JEAN 1963 *Arts of the South Pacific*. London: Thames and Hudson.

GUNTHER, ERNA 1962 *Northwest Coast Indian Art*. Seattle: University of Washington Press.

———— 1966 *Art in the Life of Northwest Coast Indians*. Portland, Oregon: Portland Art Museum.

HANNA, JUDITH LYNN 1979 *To Dance Is Human: A Study of Nonverbal Communication*. Austin: University of Texas Press.

HANSON, F. ALLAN 1983A "Art and the Maori Construction of Reality," in Sidney M. Mead, ed., *Art and Artists of Oceanea*, pp. 210–225. Mill Valley, Calif.: Ethnographic Arts Publishers.

———— 1983b "When the Map Is the Territory: Art in Maori Culture," in Dorothy K. Washburn, ed., *Structure and Cognition in Art*, pp. 74–89. Cambridge, England: Cambridge University Press.

———— 1985 "From Symmetry to Anthropophagy: The Cultural Context of Maori Art." *Empirical Studies of the Arts* 3(1):47–62.

HARLEY, GEORGE W. 1950 *Masks as Agents of Social Control in Northeast Liberia*. (*Papers of the Peabody Museum of Archaeology and Ethnography, Harvard University*, Vol. 32, no. 2.) Cambridge, Mass.: Peabody Museum.

HARNER, MICHAEL J. 1972 *The Jívaro*. Garden City, N.Y.: Anchor Press-Doubleday Books.

HARRIS, MARVIN 1975 *Culture, People, Nature*. Second edition. New York: Thomas Y. Crowell.

HASELBERGER, HERTA 1961 "Method of Studying Ethnological Art." *Current Anthropology* 2:341–355.

HATCHER, EVELYN PAYNE 1974 *Visual Metaphors: A Formal Analysis of Navajo Art*. American Ethnological Society, Monograph No. 58. St. Paul, Minn.: West Publishing Company.

HATTERER, LAWRENCE J. 1965 *The Artist in Society: Problems and Treatment of the Creative Individual*. New York: Grove Press.

HAWTHORN, HARRY B. 1961 "The Artist in Tribal Society: The Northwest Coast," in *The Artist in Tribal Society*, ed. Marian W. Smith, pp. 58–70. New York: Free Press.

HEMPEL, CARL 1959 "The Logic of Functionalist Analysis," in *Symposium on Sociological Theory*, ed. L. Gross, pp. 271–307. Evanston, Ill.: Row Peterson.

HERSKOVITS, MELVILLE J. 1959 "Art and Value," in *Aspects of Primitive Art*, eds. Robert Redfield, Melville J. Herskovits, and George F. Ekholn, pp. 43–60. New York: Museum of Modern Art.

HERSKOVITS, MELVILLE J., and F.S. HERSKOVITS 1934 "The Art of Dahomey II: Wood Carving." *American Magazine of Art* 27:124–131.

HESS, ECKHARD H. 1975 "The Role of Pupil Size in Communication." *Scientific American* 233(5):110–119.

HIMMELHEBER, HANS 1960 *Negerkunst und Negerkünstler*. Braunschweig: Klinkgardt and Bierman.

—— 1963 "Personality and Technique of African Sculptors," in *Technique and Personality*, by Margaret Mead, et al., pp. 80–110. New York: Museum of Modern Art.

HIRSHFIELD, LAWRENCE A. 1977 "Cuna Aesthetics: A Quantitative Analysis." *Ethnology* 16:147–166.

HOLM, OSCAR WILLIAM (BILL) 1965 *Northwest Coast Indian Art: An Analysis of Form.* Seattle: University of Washington Press.

—— 1972 *Crooked Beak of Heaven: Masks and Other Ceremonial Art of the Northwest Coast.* Seattle: University of Washington Press.

—— 1974 *The Art of Willie Seaweed.* Baton Rouge: Louisiana State University.

—— 1983 *Smokey Top: The Art and Times of Willie Seaweed.* Seattle: University of Washington Press.

—— and WILLIAM REID 1975 *Form and Freedom.* Houston: Rice University, Institute of the Arts.

HOULIHAN, PATRICK THOMAS 1972 *Art and Social Structure on the Northwest Coast.* Unpublished Ph.D. dissertation, University of Wisconsin, Milwaukee.

HOUSTON, JAMES 1951 "Eskimo Sculptors." *The Beaver,* June issue, pp. 34–39.

—— 1952 "In Search of Contemporary Eskimo Art." *Canadian Art* 9(3):99–104.

—— 1954 *Canadian Eskimo Art.* Ottowa: Queen's Printer, Department of Northern Affairs.

IWAO, SUMIKO, and IRWIN L. CHILD 1966 "Comparisons of Esthetic Judgments by American Experts and Japanese Potters." *Journal of Social Psychology* 68:27–34.

IWAO, SUMIKO, and MIGUEL GARCIA 1969 "Further Evidence of Agreement between Japanese and American Esthetic Evaluations." *Journal of Social Psychology* 75(1):11–15.

JAFFÉ, ANIELA 1964 "Symbolism in the Visual Arts," in *Man and His Symbols,* ed. Carl G. Jung, pp. 230–271. Garden City, N.Y.: Doubleday.

JONES, W.T. 1974 "Talking about Art and Primitive Society," in *Primitive Art and Society,* ed. Anthony Forge, pp. 256–277. New York: Oxford University Press.

JOPLING, CAROL F., ed. 1971 *Art and Aesthetics in Primitive Societies: A Critical Anthology.* New York: Dutton.

JULES-ROSETTE, BENNETTA 1984 *The Messages of Tourist Art: An African Semiotic System in Comparative Perspective.* New York: Plenum.

JUNG, CARL G. 1964 "Approaching the Unconscious," in *Man and His Symbols,* ed. Carl G. Jung, pp. 18–103. Garden City, N.Y.: Doubleday.

KAEPPLER, ADRIENNE L., JUDY VANZILE, and CARL WOLZ, eds. 1977 "Asian and Pacific Dance: Selected Papers from the 1974 CORD-SEM Conference. Committee on Dance Research." *Dance Research Annual,* Vol. 8.

KAPLAN, FLORA S. 1977 "Structuralism and the Analysis of Folk Art." Paper read at the 76th Annual Meeting of the American Anthropological Association, Houston, Texas.

KAUFMANN, CAROLE N. 1976 "Functional Aspects of Haida Argilite Carvings," in *Ethnic and Tourist Arts,* ed. Nelson H.H. Graburn, pp. 56–69. Berkeley: University of California Press.

KAVOLIS, V.M. 1972 *History on Art's Side: Social Dynamics of Artistic Efflorescences.* Ithaca, N.Y.: Cornell University Press.

KENT, KATE PECK 1976 "Pueblo and Navajo Weaving Traditions and the Western World," in *Ethnic and Tourist Arts,* ed. Nelson H.H. Graburn, pp. 85–101. Berkeley: University of California Press.

KIELL, NORMAN 1965 *Psychiatry and Psychology in the Visual Arts and Aesthetics: A Bibliography.* Madison: University of Wisconsin Press.

KISTE, ROBERT C. 1974 *The Bikinians: A Study in Forced Migration.* The Kiste-Ogan Social Change Series in Anthropology. Menlo Park, Calif.: Cummins.

KURATH, GERTRUDE P. 1960 "Panorama of Dance Ethnology." *Current Anthropology* 1:233–254.

LACKEY, LOUANA M. 1981 *The Pottery of Acatlán: A Changing Mexican Tradition.* Norman: University of Oklahoma Press.

LANGER, SUSANNE K. 1951 *Philosophy in a New Key.* Third edition. Cambridge, Mass.: Harvard University Press.

LAWLOR, M. 1955 "Cultural Influences on Preferences for Designs," *Journal of Abnormal and Social Psychology* 61:690–692.

LEACH, EDMUND R. 1961 "Aesthetics," in *The Institutions of Primitive Society*, by E.E. Evans-Pritchard et al., pp. 25–38. N.Y.: Free Press.
————— 1971 "A Trobriand Medusa?" in *Art and Aesthetics in Primitive Societies*, ed. Carol F. Jopling, pp. 45–63. New York: Dutton. [Orig. in *Man* 54(158):103–105, 1954.]
————— 1974 "Levels of Communication and Problems of Taboo in the Appreciation of Primitive Art," in *Primitive Art and Society*, ed. Anthony Forge. New York: Oxford University Press, pp. 221–234.
LEIRIS, MICHEL, and JACQUELINE DELANGE 1968 *African Art*, trans. Michael Ross. New York: Golden Press.
LÉON-PORTILLA, MIGUEL 1963 *Aztec Thought and Culture: A Study of the Ancient Nahuatl Mind*. Third edition, trans. Jack Emory Davis. Norman: University of Oklahoma Press.
LÉVI-STRAUSS, CLAUDE 1963 *Structural Anthropology*, trans. C. Jacobson and B.G. Schoepf. New York: Doubleday.
————— 1966 *The Savage Mind*, trans. George Weidenfeld. Chicago: Chicago University Press.
————— 1970 *Triste Tropiques*, trans. John Russell. New York: Atheneum.
LEWIS, PHILIP H. 1961 "The Artist in New Ireland Society," in *The Artist in Tribal Society*, ed. Marian W. Smith, pp. 71–79. New York: The Free Press.
LINTON, RALPH 1941 "Primitive Art." *Kenyon Review* 3(1):34–51.
————— and PAUL S. WINGERT 1946 *Arts of the South Seas*. New York: Museum of Modern Art.
LIPS, JULIUS E. 1966 [orig. 1937] *The Savage Hits Back*, trans. V. Benson. New York: Yale University Press.
LLOYD, PETER C. 1966 "The Yoruba of Nigeria," in *Peoples of Africa*, ed. James L. Gibbs, Jr., pp. 549–582. New York: Holt, Rinehart & Winston.
McALLESTER, DAVID P. 1971 *Readings in Ethnomusicology*. New York: Johnson Reprint Corp.
————— 1980 "Shootingway, an Epic Drama of the Navajos," in Charlotte Frisbee, ed., *Southwestern Indian Ritual Drama*, pp. 199–237. Albuquerque: University of New Mexico Press.
McCARTHY, F.D. 1938 *Australian Aboriginal Decorative Art*. Sydney: Australian Museum.
McELROY, W.A. 1955 "Abstract: Aesthetic Ranking Tests with Arnheim Land Aborigines." *British Psychological Society, Bulletin* 25:44.
McGHEE, ROBERT 1976 "Differential Artistic Productivity in the Eskimo Cultural Tradition." *Current Anthropology* 17:203–212.
MacKINNON, DONALD W. 1968 "Creativity: Psychological Aspects," in *International Encyclopedia of the Social Sciences*, ed. David Sils, Vol. 3, pp. 434–442.
McLEOD, M.D. 1975 "Traders and Fakers in African Art." *New Society* 31(641):122–125.
McLEOD, NORMA 1974 "Ethnomusicological Research and Anthropology," in *Annual Reviews of Anthropology*, Vol. 3, pp. 99–115, ed. Bernard J. Siegel, et al. Palo Alto, Calif.: Annual Reviews, Inc.
MALINOWSKI, BRONISLAW 1922 *Argonauts of the Western Pacific*. London: Routledge and Kegan Paul.
MANSFIELD, VICTOR N. 1981 "Mandalas and Mesoamerican Pecked Circles." *Current Anthropology* 22(3):269–284.
MAQUET, JACQUES 1971 *Introduction to Aesthetic Anthropology*. Addison-Wesley Module in Anthropology. Reading, Mass.: Addison-Wesley.
————— 1986 *The Aesthetic Experience*. New Haven: Yale University Press.
MARTIJN, CHARLES A. 1964 "Canadian Eskimo Carving in Historical Perspective," *Anthropos* 59:546–596.
MAY, ELIZABETH, ed. 1980 *Music of Many Cultures*. Berkeley: University of California Press.
MEAD, MARGARET 1971 [orig. 1960] "Work, Leisure, and Creativity," in *Art and Aesthetics in Primitive Societies*, ed. Carol F. Jopling. New York: Dutton, pp. 132–145. [Orig. in *Daedalus*, Winter 1960, pp. 12–23.]
MEMEL-FOTÊ, HARRIS 1968 "The Perception of Beauty in Negro-African Culture," in *UNESCO: Colloquium on Negro Art, Dakar 1966*, pp. 45–65. Editions Présence Africaine.
MERRIAM, ALAN P. 1964 *Anthropology of Music*. Evanston, Ill.: Northwestern University Press.

MESSENGER, JOHN C.   1958   "Reflections on Aesthetic Talent." *Basic College Quarterly* 4:20–24.

———   1962   "Anang Art, Drama, and Social Control." *African Studies Bulletin* 5(2):29–35.

———   1973   "The Role of the Carver in Anang Society," in *The Traditional Artist in African Societies,* ed. Warren L. d'Azevedo, pp. 101–127. Bloomington: Indiana University Press.

MEYER, KARL E.   1973   *The Plundered Past.* New York: Atheneum.

MILLS, GEORGE   1971   [orig. 1957] "Art: An Introduction to Qualitative Anthropology," in *Art and Aesthetics in Primitive Societies,* ed. Carol F. Jopling, pp. 66–92. New York: Dutton. [Orig. in *Journal of Aesthetics and Art Criticism* 1957 16(1):1–17.]

MOORE, HENRY 1952   "Notes on Sculpture," in *The Creative Process,* ed. Brewster Ghiselin, pp. 73–78. New York: New American Library.

MORRIS, DESMOND   1962   *The Biology of Art.* New York: Knopf.

MOUNT, MARSHALL W.   1973   *African Art: The Years Since 1920.* Bloomington: Indiana University Press.

MOUNTFORD, CHARLES P.   1960   "Phallic Objects of the Australian Aborigines." *Man* 60(118):81.

———   1961   "The Artist and His Art in an Australian Aboriginal Society," in *The Artist in Tribal Society,* ed. Marian W. Smith, pp. 1–13. New York: Free Press.

MUENSTERBERGER, WARNER   1971   "Roots of Primitive Art," in *Anthropology and Art,* ed. Charlotte M. Otten, pp. 106–128. Garden City, New York: Natural History Press. [Orig. in *Psychoanalysis and Culture,* eds. G.B. Wilbert and Warner Muensterberger, pp. 371–389, 1951.]

MULLER, JON D.   1979   "Structural Studies of Art Styles," in Justine M. Cordwell, ed., *The Visual Arts: Plastic and Graphic,* pp. 139–211. The Hague: Mouton.

MUNDKUR, BALAJI   1976   "The Cult of the Serpent in the Americas: Its Asian Background." *Current Anthropology* 17(3):429–455.

MUNN, NANCY   1962   "Walbiri Graphic Signs: An Analysis." *American Anthropologist* 64:972–984.

———   1964   "Totemic Designs and Group Continuity in Walbiri Cosmology," in *Aborigines Now,* ed. M. Ready. Sydney, Australia: Angus and Robertson.

———   1970   "The Transformation of Subjects into Objects in Walbiri and Pitjantjatjara Myth," in *Australian Aboriginal Anthropology,* ed. Ronald Berndt, pp. 141–163. Nedlands: University of Western Australia Press.

———   1971   "Visual Categories: An Approach to the Study of Representational Systems," in *Art and Aesthetics in Primitive Societies,* ed. Carol F. Jopling, pp. 335–355. New York: Dutton. [Orig. in *American Anthropologist* 68(4):936–950.]

———   1973   *Walbiri Iconography: Graphic Representation and Cultural Symbolism in a Central Australian Society.* Ithaca, N.Y.: Cornell University Press.

———   1974   "The Spatial Presentation of Cosmic Order in Walbiri Iconography," in *Primitive Art and Society,* ed. Anthony Forge, pp. 193–220. New York: Oxford University Press.

MUNRO, THOMAS   1963   *Evolution in the Arts and Other Theories of Culture History.* New York: Abrams.

MURDOCK, GEORGE PETER   1957   "World Ethnographic Sample." *American Anthropologist* 59:664–687.

MURDOCK, GEORGE PETER, and CATHERINA PROVOST   1973   "Factors in the Division of Labor by Sex: A Cross-Cultural Analysis." *Ethnology* 12:203–205.

MURPHY, YOLANDA, and ROBERT F. MURPHY   1974   *Women of the Forest.* New York: Columbia University Press.

MURRAY, K.C.   1961   "The Artist in Nigerian Tribal Society: A Comment," in *The Artist in Tribal Society,* ed. Marian W. Smith, pp. 95–101. New York: Free Press.

NELSON, EDWARD   1899   *The Eskimo About Bering Strait. 18th Annual Report—Bureau of American Ethnology.* Washington, D.C.: Bureau of American Ethnology.

NETTL, BRUNO   1956   *Music in Primitive Culture.* Cambridge, Mass.: Harvard University Press.

———   1983   *The Study of Ethnomusicology: Twenty-nine Issues and Concepts.* Champaign: University of Illinois Press.

NOTON, DAVID, and LAWRENCE STARK   1971   "Eye Movements and Visual Perception."
Scientific American 224(6):34–43.
NUNNALLY, JUM C.   1977   "Meaning-Processing and Rated Pleasantness." *Scientific Aesthetics*
1(3):161:181.
————, T.T. FAW, and M.B. BASHFORD   1969   "Effects of Degrees of Incongruity on Visual
Fixations in Children and Adults." *Journal of Experimental Psychology* 81:360–364.
O'HARE, DAVID, ed.   1981   *Psychology and the Arts.* Atlantic Highlands, N.J.: Humanities
Press.
O'NEALE, LILA M.   1932   "Yorok-Karok Basket Weavers," *University of California Publica-
tions in American Archaeology and Ethnology* 32(1):1–184.
OSBORNE, HAROLD, ed.   1972   *Aesthetics.* New York: Oxford University Press.
OTTEN, CHARLOTTE M., ed.   1971   *Anthropology and Art: Readings in Cross-Cultural Aesthetics.*
Garden City, N.Y.: Natural History Press.
OTTENBERG, SIMON   1975   *Masked Rituals of the Afikpo: The Context of an African Art.* Seattle:
University of Washington Press.
PAREZO, NANCY   1982   "Navajo Sandpaintings: The Importance of Sex Roles in Craft Pro-
duction." *American Indian Quarterly* 6(1–2):125–148.
————   1983   *Navajo Sandpainting: From Religious Act to Commercial Art.* Tucson: University
of Arizona Press.
PAUL, ROBERT A.   1976   "The Sherpa Temple as a Model of the Psyche." *American Eth-
nologist* 3(1):131–146.
PEPPER, STEVEN C.   1945   *The Basis of Criticism in the Arts.* Cambridge, Mass.: Harvard Uni-
versity Press.
PICKFORD, R.W.   1972   *Psychology and Visual Aesthetics.* London: Hutchenson Educational.
POWDERMAKER, HORTENSE   1933   *Life in Lesu: The Study of a Melanesian Society in New
Ireland.* New York: W.W. Norton.
PRICE, RICHARD, and SALLY PRICE   1981   *Afro-American Arts of the Suriname Rain Forest.*
Berkeley: University of California Press.
PRICE-WILLIAMS, D.R., W. GORDON, and M. RAMIREZ   1969   "Skill and Conservation: A
Study of Pottery-making Children." *Developmental Psychology* 1(6):769.
RADCLIFFE-BROWN, A.R.   1935   "On the Concept of Function in Social Science." *American
Anthropologist* 37:394–402.
————   1964   [orig. 1922] *The Andaman Islanders.* New York: Free Press.
RAINEY, FROELICH   1971   "The Vanishing Art of the Arctic," in *Anthropology and Art,* ed.
Charlotte M. Otten, pp. 341–353. [Orig. in *Expedition* 1(2):3–13, 1959.]
RANK, OTTO   1943   *Art and Artist, Creative Urge and Personality Development,* trans. Charles F.
Atkinson. New York: Knopf.
————   1959   *Otto Rank: The Myth of the Birth of the Hero, and Other Writings,* ed. Philip Fred.
New York: Knopf.
RAPPAPORT, ROY A.   1968   *Pigs for the Ancestors.* Second edition, 1984. New Haven, Conn.:
Yale University Press.
RAVICZ, MARILYN EKDAHL   1976   "Ephemeral Art: A Case for the Functions of Aesthetic
Stimuli." Unpublished paper, read at the Annual Meetings of the American An-
thropological Association, November 19, 1976, New York, N.Y.
RAWSON, PHILIP S., ed.   1973   *Primitive Erotic Art.* New York: G.P. Putnam.
RAY, DOROTHY JEAN   1967   *Eskimo Masks: Art and Ceremony.* Seattle: University of Wash-
ington Press.
————   1980 [orig. 1961]   *Artists of the Tundra and Sea.* Seattle: University of Washington
Press.
————   1981   *Aleut and Eskimo Art: Tradition and Innovation in South Alaska.* Seattle: Univer-
sity of Washington Press.
REDFIELD, ROBERT   1971   [orig. 1959] "Art and Icon," in *Anthropology and Art,* ed. Charlotte
M. Otten, pp. 39–65. Garden City, N.Y.: Natural History Press. [Orig. in *Aspects of
Primitive Art,* pp. 12–40. New York: Museum of Primitive Art.]
REICHEL-DOLMATOFF, GERARDO   1972   "The Cultural Context of an Aboriginal Halluci-
nogen: Banisteriopsis Caapi," in *Flesh of the Gods: The Ritual Use of Hallucinogens,* ed.
Peter T. Furst, pp. 84–113. New York: Praeger.
————   1975   *The Shaman and the Jaguar: A Study of Narcotic Drugs among the Indians of
Colombia.* Philadelphia: Temple University Press.

REINA, R.A.   1963   "The Potter and the Farmer: The Fate of Two Innovators in a Maya Village." *Expedition* 5(4):18–30.

REINHARDT, LORETTA   1976   "Mrs. Kadiato Kamara: An Expert Dyer in Sierra Leone." *Fieldiana: Anthropology* 66(2):11–33.

ROBBINS, MICHAEL C.   1966   "Material Culture and Cognition." *American Anthropologist* 68:745–748.

ROBERTSON, R. GORDON   1960   "The Carving Industry of Arctic Canada." *The Commerce Journal, University of Toronto,* spring issue.

ROE, PETER G.   1979   "Marginal Men: Male Artists among the Shipibo Indians of Peru." *Anthropologica* n.s. 21(2):189–221.

ROHEIM, GÉZA   1945   *Eternal Ones of the Dream.* New York: International Universities Press.

ROHNER, RONALD P., and EVELYN C. ROHNER   1970   *The Kwakiutl: Indians of British Columbia.* New York: Holt, Rinehart & Winston.

ROTHENBERG, JEROME, and DIANE ROTHENBERG, eds.   1983   *Symposium of the Whole: A Range of Discourse Toward Ethnopoetics.* Berkeley: University of California Press.

ROYCE, ANYA P.   1977   *The Anthropology of Dance.* Bloomington: University of Indiana Press.

RUBIN, ARNOLD   1976   *The Sculptor's Eye.* Washington, D.C.: Museum of African Arts.

SACHS, CURT   1937   *World History of the Dance.* New York: W.W. Norton.

SALISBURY, RICHARD P.   1959   "A Trobriand Medusa?" *Man* 59(67):50–51.

SALVADOR, MARI LYNN   1976a   "The Clothing Arts of the Cuna of San Blas, Panama," in *Ethnic and Tourist Arts,* ed. Nelson H.H. Graburn, pp. 165–182. Berkeley: University of California Press.

———   1976b   *Molas of the Cuna Indians: A Case Study of Artistic Criticism and Ethno-aesthetics.* Unpublished Ph.D. dissertation, University of California, Berkeley.

SANDELOWSKY, B.H.   1976   "Functional and Tourist Art Along the Okavango River," in *Ethnic and Tourist Arts,* ed. Nelson H.H. Graburn, pp. 350–365. Berkeley: University of California Press.

SARLES, HARVEY B.   1972   "The Dynamics of Facial Expression." Paper read at the Annual Meeting, International Association of Dental Research, March 1972, Las Vegas, Nevada.

SCHECHNER, RICHARD   1985   *Between Theater and Anthropology.* Philadelphia: University of Pennsylvania Press.

SCHILLER, PAUL H.   1971   "Figural Preferences in the Drawings of a Chimpanzee," in *Anthropology and Art,* ed. Charlotte M. Otten, pp. 3–19. Garden City, N.Y.: Natural History Press. [Orig. in *The Journal of Comparative and Physiological Psychology* 44(2):101–111, 1959.]

SCHMITZ, CARL   1962   *Ozeanische Kunst: Sculpture aus Melanesien.* München: F. Bruckmann.

SCHNEIDER, HAROLD K.   1956   "The Interpretation of Pakot Visual Art." *Man* 56:103–106.

———   1966   "Turu Esthetic Concepts." *American Anthropologist* 68:156–160.

SCHNEIDER, MARY JANE   1976   "But, Is it Art?: A Critical Look at Anthropological Studies of Non-European Art." Paper read at the annual meetings of the Central States Anthropological Association, March 1976, St. Louis, Missouri.

SIEBER, ROY A.   1962   "Masks as Agents of Social Control." *African Studies Bulletin* 5(11):8–13.

———   1976   "Art in Traditional Societies," unpublished lecture, Walker Art Center, Minneapolis, Minnesota, June 30, 1976.

SIEBERT, ERNA   1967   *North American Indian Art.* London: Paul Hamlyn.

SILVER, HARRY R.   1980   "The Culture of Carving and the Carving of Culture: Content and Context in Artisan Status among the Ashanti." *American Ethnologist* 7(3):432–446.

SMITH, D.A.   1973   "Systematic Study of Chimpanzee Drawing." *Journal of Comparative and Physiological Psychology* 82:406–414.

SMITH, MARION W., ed.   1961   *The Artist in Primitive Society.* New York: Free Press.

SONTAG, SUSAN   1977   "Photography in Search of Itself." *New York Review of Books* 23(21–22):53–59.

SPECTOR, JACK J.   1972   *The Aesthetics of Freud.* New York: McGraw-Hill.

SPENCER, HAROLD   1975   *The Image Makers: Man and His Art.* New York: Scribner's Sons.

SPENCER, PAUL, ed.   1985   *Society and the Dance: The Social Anthropology of Process and Performance.* New York: Cambridge University Press.

STOLNITZ, JEROME   1960   *Aesthetics and Philosophy of Art Criticism: A Critical Introduction.* Boston: Houghton Mifflin.

STOUT, DAVID B.   1947   *San Blas Cuna Acculturation: An Introduction.* New York: Viking Fund.

STOUT, DAVID B.   1971   [orig. 1960] "Aesthetics in 'Primitive Societies,'" in *Art and Aesthetics in Primitive Societies,* ed. Carol F. Jopling, pp. 30–34. New York: Dutton. [Orig. in *Men and Cultures: Selected Papers of the Fifth International Congress of Anthropological and Ethnological Sciences, Philadelphia, September 1–9, 1956.*]

STUBBS, DACRE   1974   *Historic Art of Australia.* New York: Scribner.

STURTEVANT, WILLIAM C.   1967   "Seminole Men's Clothing," in *Essays on the Verbal and Visual Arts,* ed. June Helm MacNeish pp. 160–174. Seattle: University of Washington Press.

———, ed.   1978, 1979   *Handbook of North American Indians, Volumes 9 and 10.* Washington, D.C.: Smithsonian Institution.

SWINTON, GEORGE   1958   "Eskimo Carving Today." *Beaver,* spring issue, pp. 40–44.

———   1972   *Sculpture of the Eskimo.* Greenwich, Conn.: New York Graphic Society.

SWANN, BRIAN, ed.   1983   *Smoothing the Ground: Essays on Native American Oral Literature.* Berkeley: University of California Press.

——— and ARNOLD KRUPAT, eds.   1987   *Recovering the Word: Essays on Native American Literature.* Berkeley: University of California Press.

TANNER, CLARA LEE   1960   "The Influence of the White Man on Southwest Indian Art." *Ethnohistory* 7:137–150.

TATARKIEWICZ, WLADYSLAW   1970a   *History of Aesthetics. Vol. I: Ancient Aesthetics.* Ed. J. Harrell; trans. Adam and Ann Czerniawski. Warsaw: Polish Scientific Publishers.

———   1970b   *History of Aesthetics. Vol. II: Medieval Aesthetics.* Ed. C. Barrett; trans. R.M. Montgomery. Warsaw: Polish Scientific Publishers.

———   1974   *History of Aesthetics. Vol. III: Modern Aesthetics.* The Hague: Mouton.

TEDLOCK, DENNIS   1972   "Pueblo Literature: Style and Verisimilitude," in Alfonso Ortiz, ed., *New Perspectives on the Pueblos,* pp. 219–242. Albuquerque: University of New Mexico Press.

———   1985   *Popol Vuh.* New York: Simon & Schuster.

TEILHET, JEHANNE H.   1978   "The Equivocal Role of Woman Artists in Non-Literate Cultures." *Heresies* 4:96–102.

THOMPSON, LAURA   1945   "The Logico-Aesthetic Integration in Hopi Culture." *American Anthropologist* 47:540–553.

THOMPSON, ROBERT FARRIS   1969   "Àbátàn: A Master Potter of the Ègbádò Yorùbá," in *Tradition and Creativity in Tribal Arts,* ed. Daniel Biebuyck, pp. 120–181. Berkeley: University of California Press.

———   1971   [orig. 1968] "Aesthetics in Traditional Africa," in *Art and Aesthetics in Primitive Societies,* Carol F. Jopling, ed., pp. 374–381. New York: Dutton. [Orig. in *Art News* 66(9):44–45, 63–66, 1968.]

———   1973   "Yoruba Artistic Criticism," in *The Traditional Artist in African Societies,* ed. Warren L. d'Azevedo, pp. 19–61. Bloomington: Indiana University Press.

———   1974   *African Art in Motion: Icon and Art.* Berkeley: University of California Press.

———   1976   *Black Gods and Kings.* Bloomington: Indiana University Press.

———   1983   *Flash of the Spirit: African and Afro-American Art and Philosophy.* New York: Random House.

TOULOUSE, BETTY   1976   "Pueblo Pottery Traditions: Ever Constant, Ever Changing." *El Palacia* 82(3):14–47.

———   1977   *Pueblo Pottery of the New Mexican Indians.* Albuquerque: University of New Mexico Press.

TRILLING, LIONEL   1945   "Art and Neurosis," in Trilling, *The Liberal Imagination,* by Lionel Trilling, pp. 160–180. New York: Viking Press.

TUCKSON, J.A.   1964   "Aboriginal Art and the Western World," in *Australian Aboriginal Art,* ed. Ronald M. Berndt, pp. 60–68. New York: Macmillan.

TURNER, VICTOR   1966   "Colour Classification in Ndembu Ritual: A Problem in Primitive Classification," in Michael Banton, ed., *Anthropological Approaches to the Study of Religion* (ASA Monographs, No. 3), pp. 47–84. London: Tavistock.

———   1967   *The Forest of Symbols.* Ithaca, N.Y.: Cornell University Press.

—— 1969 *The Ritual Process: Structure and Anti-Structure*. Chicago: Aldine.
—— 1986 *The Anthropology of Performance*. New York: PAJ Publications.
UCKO, PETER J., and ANDRÉE ROSENFELD 1967 *Paleolithic Cave Art*. New York: McGraw-Hill.
VAUGHAN, JAMES H., Jr. 1973 "əŋkyangu as Artists in Margi Society," in *The Traditional Artist in African Societies*, ed. Warren L. d'Azevedo, pp. 162–193. Bloomington: Indiana University Press.
WADE, EDWIN L. 1985 "The Ethnic Art Market in the American Southwest, 1880–1980," in George W. Stocking, ed., *Objects and Others: Essays on Museums and Material Culture. History of Anthropology, Vol. 1*, pp. 167–191. Madison: University of Wisconsin Press.
WAHLMAN MAUDE 1974 *Contemporary African Arts*. Chicago: Field Museum of Natural History.
WAITE, DEBORAH 1966 "Kwakiutl Transformation Masks," in *The Many Faces of Primitive Art*," ed. Douglas Fraser, pp. 265–299. Englewood Cliffs, N.J.: Prentice-Hall.
WARREN, D.M., and J. KWEKU ANDREWS 1977 *An Ethnoscientific Approach to Akan Arts and Aesthetics; Working Papers in the Traditional Arts Number 3*. Philadelphia: Institute for the Study of Human Issues.
WASHBURN, DOROTHY K., ed. 1980 *Structure and Cognition in Art*. Cambridge, England: Cambridge University Press.
—— 1983 *Hopi Kachina: Spirit of Life*. Seattle: University of Washington Press.
WEITZ, MORRIS 1967 [orig. 1957] "The Role of Theory in Aesthetics," in Monroe C. Beardsley and Herbert M. Schueller, eds., *Aesthetic Inquiry*, pp. 3–11. Belmont, Calif.: Dickenson Publishers. (Orig. in *Journal of Aesthetics and Art Criticism*.)
WHITE, LESLIE A. 1959 *The Evolution of Culture*. New York: McGraw-Hill.
WILHITE, MARGARET 1977 "Marketing and Bilingualism: Patterns of Accommodation in Highland Guatemala." Paper presented at the 76th Annual Meeting, American Anthropological Association, Houston, Texas, November 29–December 3, 1977.
WILLETT, FRANK 1971 *African Art*. New York: Praeger.
—— 1972 "The Art of an Ancient Nigerian Aristocracy," in *African Art and Leadership*, eds. Douglas Fraser and Herbert M. Cole, pp. 209–225. Madison: University of Wisconsin Press.
WILLIAMS, NANCY 1976 "Australian Aboriginal Art at Yirrakala: Introduction and Development of Marketing," in *Ethnic and Tourist Arts*, ed. Nelson H.H. Graburn, pp. 266–284. Berkeley: University of California Press.
WINGERT, PAUL 1951 "Tsimshian Sculpture." *Publications of the American Ethnological Society*, ed. Marian W. Smith. 13:73–96.
—— 1962 *Primitive Art: Its Traditions and Styles*. New York: New American Library.
WINNER, ELLEN 1982 *Invented Worlds: The Psychology of the Arts*. Cambridge, Mass.: Harvard University Press.
WITHERSPOON, GARY 1977 *Language and Art in the Navajo Universe*. Ann Arbor: University of Michigan Press.
WOLFE, ALVIN W. 1955 "Art and The Supernatural in the Ubangi District." *Man* 55(article 76):65–67.
—— 1969 "Social Structural Bases of Art." *Current Anthropology* 10:3–28.
—— 1976 "Comment on Robert McGhee's 'Differential Artistic Productivity in the Eskimo Cultural Tradition.'" *Current Anthropology* 17:217–218.
WOLFE, TOM 1975 "The Painted Word." *Harpers*, April issue, pp. 57–92.
—— 1981 *From Bauhaus to Our House*. New York: Farrar, Straus & Giroux.
WYATT, V. 1984 *Shapes of Their Thoughts: Reflections of Culture Contact in Northwest Coast Indian Art*. Norman: University of Oklahoma Press.
ZUCKER, WOLFGANG M. 1969 "The Artist as a Rebel." *Journal of Aesthetics* 23:389–397.

Index

Note: Italicized page numbers indicate illustrations; "fn" indicates footnote.

Duga of Meko, 127–28, *128*
Dunn, Dorothy, 186
Durkheim, Émile, 29, 33
Dutton, Bertha, 155

E

Economic functions of art, 30–33
Egypt, 129
Ehresmann, Donald, 26
Elkin, A. P., 83
Emotionalist aesthetic theories, 198
Ephemeral art, 162
Equatorial Africa, sculpture of, 24
Eskimo art and culture, 5, 13, 89,
    157–61, 157fn, 165, 170–72, port-
    folio 179–84
Eternal Dreamtime, 81, 188
Ethnocentrism, defined, 2
Ethnographic present, defined, 17fn
Evolution of art, 3–5
Evolution of culture, 3–6
Ewers, John, 186

F

Fagg, William, 176
Fang, *24,* 42, 98, 107, 193
Farella, John, 155
Faris, James, 83, 141–47, 155
Feline figure, 83
Female artists, 85
Fernandez, James, 42, 98, 107, 193
Field, Karen, 99
Fieldwork, anthropological, 5
Firth, Raymond, 51, 72, 83, 119, 162
Fischer, John L., 42–43, 43fn
Flam, J. D., 83
Forbes, Fred, 27
Forde, Daryll, 17
Forge, Anthony, 46, 83, 93, 97, 109,
    155, 191
Formalism, 198
Foster, George, 175
Fourth World, defined, 164fn
Francés, C., 192
Fraser, Douglas, 42, 52, 72–76
Freudian iconography, 69
Functions of art, 28–45

G

Gardner, Howard, 127, 154
Geelvinck Bay, 47
Geertz, Clifford, 83
Generative approach to aesthetics,
    141–47
Gerbrands, A., 119, 93, 96
Getzels, Jacob, 154
Ghanaian drumming, 52
Gio, 34
Gola, 90, 93, 118
Goldberg, Lenore, 86
Golden Stool of the Ashanti, 39–40
Gombrich, Ernst, 135fn, 155
Goodale, Jane, 133, 161
Godonow, Jacqueline, 127
Graburn, Nelson, 163–64, 168, 171,
    175–76, 185, 193
Great Basin, 87
Greenhalgh, Michael, 155
Griff, Mason, 196
Guinea Coast of Africa, sculpture of,
    22
Gulf of Papua, *50*
Gunther, Erna, 83, 116, 119
Guro, 163

H

Haida, 55, *58, 60,* 110, *110, 111, 114,*
    116
Hallucinogens, 125–26
Hanna, Judith, 27
Hanson, F. Allan, 83
Harley, George, 34
Harner, Michael, 32fn
Harris, Marvin, 45
Harvard Project Zero, 127
Hatcher, Evelyn, 42
Hatterer, Lawrence, 131
Hawthron, Harry, 96, 119
Hempel, Carl, 52
Heraldic Woman motif, 72–76
Heresies, 119
Herskivits, Melville, 97–98
Himmelheber, Hans, 93, 100, 124,
    129, 132, 163
Holm, Bill, 83, 119
Holmes, W. H., 3
Homeostasis in art, 33–44